KT-508-617

6/71

second edition

the hospitality industry

the world of food service

Joseph A. Villella

McGraw-Hill Book Company

New York   Johannesburg   Paris
St. Louis   Kuala Lumpur   São Paulo
Dallas   London   Singapore
San Francisco Mexico   Sydney
Auckland   Montreal   Tokyo
Düsseldorf   New Delhi   Toronto
               Panama

Library of Congress Cataloging in Publication Data

Villella, Joseph A
    The hospitality industry.
    First ed. published under title: Introduction to hos-
pitality industry of culinary arts and service.
    Includes index.
    1.   Food service—Vocational guidance.   I.   Title.
TX911.2.V54 1975   642'.5'023   74-31467
ISBN 0-07-067450-7

NAPIER COLLEGE OF COMMERCE & TECHNOLOGY

AC. 48573

CL. 640.3

MERCHISTON

PR.   CAT.   S.J.

NAPIER COLLEGE OF COMMERCE AND TECHNOLOGY

RC

AC. 81/048455/01

MERCHISTON

642.5

VIL

CON

**The Hospitality Industry—The World of
Food Service**

Copyright © 1975 by McGraw-Hill, Inc. All rights reserved.
Printed in the United States of America. No part of this
publication may be reproduced, stored in a retrieval
system, or transmitted, in any form or by any means,
electronic, mechanical, photocopying, recording, or otherwise, without the prior written permission of the pub-
lisher.

First Edition published under title *Introduction to Hospitality Industry of Culinary Arts and Service* by Joseph A.
Villella. Copyright © 1968 by Joseph A. Villella.

1 2 3 4 5 6 7 8 9 0   VHVH   7 8 3 2 1 0 9 8 7 6 5

*The editors for this book were Carole O'Keefe
and Myrna Breskin, the designer was Marsha
Cohen, and the production supervisor was
Phyllis D. Lemkowitz. It was set in Optima
Medium by Progressive Typographers, Incor-
porated.
Printed and bound by Von Hoffmann Press,
Incorporated.*

contents

preface

The hospitality industry, and, in particular, the area of food service, is one of the most dynamic and fastest-growing industries in the world. The amazing variety and number of food services are apparent to everyone who has ever eaten a meal away from home—in a restaurant, at a summer camp, on an airplane, in a school cafeteria, in a hospital, or in a coffee shop.

PURPOSE OF THE TEXT

The Hospitality Industry—The World of Food Service is an introductory survey of the kinds and quality of service provided by the industry. It is intended for all those interested in an overview of the industry—those enrolled in high school, two-year college, or short-term programs. The concept of service, which is essential to the food service industry, is also essential to the text. Underlying the descriptions, explanations, and analyses of aspects of the food service industry is the principle of careful attention to the customer or guest. This principle is presented as an integral part of the performance of every task. Such a survey introduces students to career opportunities and concepts of organization and management in food service.

CAREER OPPORTUNITIES

This rapidly expanding industry has a wide range of employment opportunities on many levels: production, service, sales jobs; positions in engineering, maintenance, housekeeping, public relations; and jobs in supervision and management. This range of employment needs has attracted workers who have many different interests and talents. For example, someone who has worked as a cafeteria helper may develop an interest in food preparation and go on to become a cook; the manager of a restaurant or hotel dining room staff may have begun as a waiter. On-the-job training, industry-sponsored programs, and continued education in two- or four-year college programs are necessary to successful food service careers.

FOOD SERVICE EDUCATION

High school programs and both two- and four-year college programs have experienced large enrollments in the areas of food service and hospitality education during the last several years, and these enrollments continue to grow. The Department of Health, Education and Welfare foresees a student population of 120,000 by 1977 in food service programs alone.

For young people who are interested in a food service career while they are still in high school, there are excellent programs providing training in skills suitable for entry-level positions in food service and offering courses which survey the entire hospitality industry and help students make well-informed decisions about their further training.

INTRODUCTION TO THE TEXT

The Hospitality Industry—The World of Food Service was originally published at Boys Town, Nebraska, under the title *Introduction to the Hospitality Industry of Culinary Arts and Service*. In its first edition the text was used successfully in food service courses at Boys Town and in many other high school food service programs. In its present edition, the text has benefited from its several years of use in classrooms. This new edition is expanded to include a more current picture of the industry.

SCOPE OF THE TEXT

Following a history of the growth of the hospitality industry from the first travelers' inns to the present luxury services, the text goes on to describe various types of food service operations and specific tasks involved in the preparation and serving of food. It discusses the importance of sanitation and hygienic practices and includes nine chapters on basic guidelines for the preparation of all kinds of foods. Specific sections devote particular attention to the marketing, distribution, and proper storage of food. There is an additional section on the proper use of convenience foods and on automatic food service. Finally, the text gives students an assessment of the personal qualities needed for a successful career in the hospitality industry and discusses typical "rules of the house" to which employees are expected to conform. There is a chapter carefully illustrating the designs and layouts of several typical food service facilities so that students can see for themselves the many ways in which tasks are interrelated and, further, the way in which a particular environment is organized for efficient service.

FEATURES OF THE TEXT

This text is unique in its comprehensive coverage. Students familiar only with their own kitchens at home or at work can easily come to understand

and appreciate the organization and functioning of various kinds of food service facilities. Since there are many talents and skills required for a career in food service, the book has been organized so that skills are discussed in related clusters—those skills which will best prepare the student for an entry-level position are grouped together. The students may then seek a particular position or use the skills they have acquired to get further specialized training. For example, in Part III I have identified the skills necessary to perform back-of-the-house tasks, with accompanying job descriptions. There are also definitions and illustrations of necessary pieces of equipment which the employee is expected to use. I have also given a clear description of back-of-the-house stations and departments. In this way, the text helps students to approach a food service career with a distinct sense of a particular job and the responsibilities and rewards associated with that job. In all, there are descriptions of some 70 jobs.

AIDS TO LEARNING

Because this book is intended as an introductory text in food service programs, a special effort has been made to define unfamiliar or specialized words and phrases. There is a glossary of culinary terms. The language throughout the book is that used by professionals in the industry. Thus, students may become familiar with the professional vocabulary they will be expected to use with ease once they are employed in some area of food service.

The precise definitions and illustrations of kitchen facilities, various types of food service operations, and equipment are invaluable aids to learning. Ideally, the instructor might provide work and/or laboratory experiences to supplement and enrich the study of this text. In many cases this will be impossible, and the text is structured so as to come as close as possible to real-life professional situations. An Instructor's Manual which accompanies the book contains many teaching suggestions including quizzes and the lab assignments. The manual also offers illustrations (from which transparencies may be made) to highlight aspects of the course.

I hope that the students who use *The Hospitality Industry—The World of Food Service* will be encouraged by the information and insight they have gained to make a well-informed commitment to a successful career in the food service industry.

Joseph A. Villella

To Vera, Charise, and Lisa
who traveled this way with me

acknowledgments

In the preparation of this material many people: restaurateurs, teachers, school administrators, typists, hotel managers, club managers, dietitians, students, designers, associations, and related industries have cooperated in providing information or making available to me photographs and other materials.

I would like to acknowledge their warm and enthusiastic help, in particular the help of the late Mr. Harry J. Fawcett, author in his own right and past president of the Club Manager's Association of America. Mr. Fawcett studied my work page by page and offered valued assistance. I also wish to acknowledge the invaluable experience gained while inaugurating and teaching the Hospitality Industry Program at Boys Town, during which time this material was developed and ultimately summarized in this book.

The kind and willing efforts of the following have helped in great measure to make possible the first and second editions. They have helped make this book one that will, I hope, intensify the knowledge, interest, and enthusiasm of people engaged in the noble art of commercial cookery and service.

Monsignor Nicholas H. Wegner, formerly, Director, Boys Town, Boys Town, Nebraska

Reverend John Farrald, Director of Counseling, Boys Town, Boys Town, Nebraska

The late Dr. Edwin Parrish, formerly, Assistant Superintendent of Schools, Omaha Public Schools System, Omaha, Nebraska

Mr. Harold Crawford, formerly, Superintendent of Schools, Boys Town,, Boys Town, Nebraska

Mr. Clarence Stoffel, formerly, Principal, Boys Town High School, Boys Town, Nebraska

Mr. Edwin Novotny, Director, Career Center, Boys Town, Boys Town, Nebraska

Dr. Marie E. Knickrehm, Professor, Department of Food and Nutrition, University of Nebraska, Lincoln, Nebraska

Dr. Louis F. Batmale, City College of San Francisco, San Francisco, California

Mr. Lawrence B. Wong, Chairman, Hotel and Restaurant Department, City College of San Francisco, San Francisco, California

Mr. Roy Hammerich, Chef Instructor, Hotel and Restaurant Department, City College of San Francisco, San Francisco, California

Mr. John Scopazzi, Chef Instructor, Hotel and Restaurant Department, City College of San Francisco, San Francisco, California

Mr. Tony Achermann, Chef Instructor, Hotel and Restaurant Department, City College of San Francisco, San Francisco, California

Miss Margaret Patricia Killian, Professor Emeritus, former Director, Department of Home Economics, University of Nebraska at Omaha, Omaha, Nebraska

Miss Mary E. Killian, Professor Emeritus, former Director of Food Service and Institutional Management, Wisconsin University—Stout, Menomonie, Wisconsin

The late Mr. Harry J. Fawcett, Author and Past President, Club Manager's Association of America, Kansas City, Missouri

Mr. Herman A. Breithaupt, Author, Chef Instructor, and former Department Head, Chadsey High School, Detroit, Michigan

The late Mr. Ward B. Arbury, Chairman 1969-1971, The Statler Foundation, Buffalo, New York

Mr. Frank Blazek, Managing Director, New Tower Hotel Courts, Omaha, Nebraska

Mr. Raymond C. Matson, Past President, National Restaurant Association, Omaha, Nebraska

Mrs. Twyla Hawkes, Secretary, Boys Town Counseling Center

There are many others whom I would thank individually if space permitted. However, I especially wish to mention the many boys of Boys Town who unknowingly provided courage, inspiration, and direction.

Joseph A. Villella

part I

history and growth of the food service industry

chapter 1

history of the industry

In days gone by, pilgrims and travelers were given food and lodging at night stops, monasteries, estates of nobles, and inns. Night stops were comparable to modern truck stops or trailer camps. Inns were found in every town and village and along every post road. Until the middle of the last century, the inn was the major lodging place for travelers.

The innkeeper was by nature a happy person who loved people and was, most often, a respected figure and leader in the community. Although the inn generally furnished food, drink, and entertainment to local inhabitants as well as to travelers, the business of feeding people was more closely associated with that of lodging than it is today.

With the coming of the railways and the disappearance of post houses, country inns declined. Those in towns and cities began to be replaced by hotels capable of accommodating a large number of guests. Taverns serving refreshments persisted, and a few dining rooms that specialized in fine cooking were established.

The ease of travel brought additional changes in social life. The waves of people coming and going required a larger number of facilities to handle them. They also created a demand for more variety in eating and lodging.

As we approached the twentieth century, a great expansion in the restaurant business began. By the early 1930s, the number of restaurants of all varieties had more than tripled. This was partly because changes in social life increased the number of people who depended upon restaurants for their board and partly because dining out had become a popular form of entertainment.

Today approximately 4 million people are employed in all forms of the restaurant business.

THE INDUSTRY TODAY

Never in history has there been such an array of places for dining out. The variety, smartness of design, convenience of location, quality, and prices available in our country today are unparalleled. Never has so much money been spent by Americans on food eaten away from home.

Understandably enough, this expansion has created new jobs in the food service industry. As a result, there is an unprecedented need for educated young people to fill these positions.

Young men and women must be taught the principles and standards of planning, selecting, buying, caring for, producing, and serving food. This will bring them in contact with a profession that enjoys the unusual position of providing and extending daily satisfaction and enjoyment known by civilized people in all parts of the world. A professional warmth exists in all trade functions, be it a luncheon, an anniversary, a birthday, a graduation, a promotion, or a wedding. Such affairs are continuously being held. The satisfaction of adding to the good times of patrons and of being accepted by people everywhere is endlessly rewarding.

The eating-out boom has come at a period of increasing opportunity. In the past two decades the need for facilities has grown, and it will continue to grow steadily. Even if there is some temporary overexpansion, the industry is basically sound. There are a number of important reasons why this is true:

1. Increased use of the automobile and airplane is making people mobile. This trend will continue as more highways are completed, parking is improved, and air travel becomes easier.
2. The population is increasing—from 130 million in 1940 to a projected 222 million in 1980. This is chiefly the result of:
   a. A more liberal immigration policy
   b. A death rate that is lower than our birthrate
3. Graduated taxation and a long period of prosperity has brought a wider distribution of wealth. Even the current period of inflation

does not decrease the number of people eating out. It just increases the popularity of less expensive restaurants.

4. Over 50 million workers are receiving paid vacations. This is more than ever before. These people have an increasing tendency to take their time off in the winter as well as the summer.
5. More and more families are finding two incomes necessary. This often means that neither adult is home in time to cook very often. This increases the use of convenience foods and restaurant facilities.
6. Certain industrial developments have added to demand for newer, bigger, and better dining facilities. One-story plant layouts have brought new industrial areas outside the existing urban centers. Downtown restaurants are not convenient to the workers, executives, and technicians working in such places.
7. The coming and going of executives and technicians between various plants and research laboratories is creating need for additional lodging and dining in new areas.

WHAT IS THE FOOD SERVICE INDUSTRY?

It is big business. More than 38 billion meals are eaten outside the home every year. It gets bigger all the time. By the middle 70s, it is estimated that at least one of every daily meal will be eaten away from home. The industry's greatest need today is to attract young people seeking career opportunities.

In a city, an eating-out facility always caters to a particular group of customers. The measure of how well this group is being served is directly related to the success of the establishment. The customer is always free to determine where to go, how much to eat, and also how much to spend. The various kinds of establishments include: hotels, motels, clubs, coffee shops, dining rooms, buffets, dormitories, cafeterias, in-plant, department stores, colleges, camps, exhibitions, steamships, and airlines.

Who Can Work in the Food Service Industry?

There are more than seventy different types of jobs in the food service industry. There is a job to fit almost every level of intelligence and interest. Many opportunities are available to young people with exposure to and training in the industry.

There are three important qualities to have: 1. like people 2. appreciate food 3. like the idea of being of service to people. Some possible jobs are: chef, cook, baker, steward, butcher, host, hostess, waitress, bartender, head waiter, waiter, busboy, cashier, food checker, and wine steward.

GROWTH OF THE FOOD SERVICE INDUSTRY

Eating-out facilities grow along with the population. Although economic cycles have some effect on the food service industry, it is not as sensitive as other businesses. The industry saw its most rapid growth period starting in the late fifties and continuing into the sixties. Americans now spend more than 45 billion dollars a year for food eaten away from home. Approximately 4 million people are employed in jobs and positions in food services. Shorter workweeks and more industry growth will increase this number. That will mean more opportunities for beginners, for those with trade school experience, and for college graduates. Projection figures indicate that growth will reach a new high within this decade. More than 750 million meals are served outside the home each week. Some important reasons for the large growth in the past decades are: (1) ease of travel (2) increased population (3) wider distribution of wealth (4) more leisure time (5) new industrial development.

Recent reports predict a steady yearly climb in dollar volume. By their estimates an all-time high will be reached in 1977. A 47 billion-dollar volume of business is projected for the food service industry in that year. This does not take into consideration the institutional or non-public food service operations. Nor does it reflect the additional impact of the "living away from home" industries.

Reports prepared for the National Restaurant Association point out that the number of people employed in the industry will climb to about four million by the middle 70s. By that time, approximately 250,000 employees will be needed each year to provide replacements and fill new openings. About 75,000 of them will be needed for jobs that do not exist today.

It is not uncommon in families of average income for people to eat one of every three meals away from home today. This includes the child in school who carries a cafeteria tray at the tender age of five. This is new. This is today's pace and it is expressed in all walks of life. More people are eating away from home than ever before. This can mean only one thing in the years to come. Youngsters who are taught to carry a cafeteria tray before they are taught to read will be eating away from home throughout their life. By the time these young people are in their teens, they will have had more meals away from home than their parents did at the same age. In some cases they will have had more than their parents or grandparents had in a lifetime.

Remember, approximately 250,000 job openings are expected annually in the restaurant industry through the mid-1970s. The food service industry needs to meet this rapid growth with people who can manage, prepare, and serve food. This need will continue for many years.

There are now more than 380,000 individual establishments. That is nearly one eating place for every 540 people. This does not take into consideration the new establishments that continue to open every week.

The Food Service Industry Is Big Business

The food service industry is comprised of not only all commercial eating and drinking places in the country but also all those businesses with food service as a secondary activity. This includes drug stores, department stores, hotels, and factories as well as institutional and charitable places such as hospitals and colleges.

Among the retail trade industries, public eating and drinking places ranked fourth in sales for 1971. They followed only food stores, automotive stores, and general merchandise stores.

It requires more than 34 billion pounds of food yearly to satisfy the appetite of the American eating-out public. The food service industry uses nearly 20 percent of all the food produced in the United States. Food purchases by public eating and drinking places alone were estimated to be nearly 10 billion dollars in 1969. The principal suppliers for independent eating places are distributors, not growers or manufacturers. However, the source varies by product and by the primary type of food service offered.

Food service equipment purchases total over 700 million dollars annually. In addition, the food service industry is a major market for furniture, furnishings, floor covering, maintenance materials, cleaning supplies, air conditioning, and construction.

Chain restaurants are taking a greater share of the restaurant market every year. In 1969, chains of eleven or more units captured 9.6 percent of the total restaurant sales. This was a boost of nearly 18 percent over the 8.3 percent of the market they had in 1968.

Franchised outlets are proliferating. Now nearly 25 percent of all U.S. franchise companies are involved in some phase of food service.

The states with the largest number of public eating and drinking places are California, New York, Pennsylvania, Illinois, Texas, Ohio, New Jersey, Wisconsin, Michigan, and Florida.

States recording the largest total sales volumes for eating and drinking establishments are California, New York, Illinois, Pennsylvania, Ohio, Texas, Michigan, New Jersey, Florida, and Massachusetts.

Employment and Productivity

Approximately 4 million workers, managers, and proprietors are employed by the food service industry today. One survey shows that the typical restaurant hires nine persons. Colleges generally engage the greatest number, averaging seventy-five per school. Hospitals average thirty-six employees.

Part-time personnel are important to the food service industry. Four out of ten employees work less than thirty-nine hours per week.

Women make up nearly 56 percent of all those employed by public eating and drinking establishments.

ORIGINS OF COOKERY

All cultures have cooking values that are characteristic of their region and the way in which the people live.

Since people first discovered that meat placed on a fire was tastier and much easier to eat, they have sought better ways to prepare what food they had. This was the fundamental discovery. They added to it the use of water, utensils, pots, pans, etc. No matter how simple or how fancy the implements or vessels were, their only purpose was to make food more palatable.

The basic methods of cooking are the same throughout the world. They have changed little throughout history. The art of cooking, however, differs greatly depending on the customs of a particular society and the foodstuffs available there. The ancient Chinese, the early Greeks, the Romans, the Gauls, and others all developed methods of cookery that employed varied uses of foodstuffs, herbs, and spices.

France is generally acknowledged to have developed the most refined cuisine in the western world. Since it was here that the rules and principles of cooking were established, French words, expressions, and names are used more universally in regard to cooking than those of any other language.

The origin of French cooking, as we know it, is associated with the arrival of Catherine de Medici in France. In 1533 she married the Duc d' Orleans, who later became Henry II of France. Under her direction a staff of cooks were brought with her from Florence, Italy.

In the spirit of the Renaissance, Italian chefs had developed a new culture in cooking. It was then considered the best in Europe. The powerful and aristocratic de Medici family had long enjoyed the excellence of Italian cooks.

The French chefs of the time were also recognized by their contemporaries as fine cooks. They enjoyed a good deal of consideration and recognition, but the Italian masters were able to teach their French counterparts some subtle refinements. These were then imparted to the French cuisine. Using the raw materials of fine foods that were present in the barns, vineyards, gardens, and pastures of their country, the French cooks were able to prepare tremendous feasts. The dishes were served with great style and ceremony.

Although French books on cookery appeared in the early sixteenth century, the first work that set down a system and order of cooking principles was done by a great French chef named La Varenne. He was chef of the Marquis d'Uxelles. His book was entitled *Le Cuisinier Français*. It appeared in 1651.

Another notable chef of the period was Massailot. It was Massailot who clearly defined the instructions that were to be followed. The title of his work was *Le Cuisiner Royal et Bourgeois* which appeared in 1691. During this period, the seventeenth century, chefs and pastry chefs began to study cooking as a science and to think of their work as a profession.

These writings are evidence that dishes and culinary practices were growing in variety. In the homes of the wealthy, a great many dishes were served at each meal.

This period also brought the big changes in equipment. The lack of refinement of the early years gave way to an appreciation of fine utensils.

Before this time little attention had been given to the manner in which food was served. All the food had been heaped together on a platter.

As noble families and households took an active interest in the cooking of foods, it was not uncommon that favorite dishes would be given the names of noble ladies by chefs and pastry chefs. These dishes sometimes originated in the household and other times outside the household. No matter where they were first created, it was common to have a dish named for some person.

This interest of the nobility in the culinary arts had the effect of increasing the profession. The times were marked by the serving of splendid banquets with elaborate displays of cold foods. Magnificent dishes were produced for official dinners, suppers, and buffets.

Kitchens in this period were quite unlike the kitchens of today. Charcoal and wood were the common fuels. Their fires restricted air movement and created uneven lighting. A limited selection of kitchen equipment and utensils made the preparation of food even more complicated, but certainly not less enjoyable or rewarding to the master working on a favorite dish.

Eighteenth-century France was rich in the discovery of embellishments to the culinary arts. Louis XIV was a great eater. He especially loved a variety of soups. With the help of Maria Theresa, wife of the king, more order was introduced to the royal table. Dishes of foods were served separately and more variety developed. Soups, seafoods, game, meats, vegetables, pastries, preserves, fruits, and sweets came to be prepared in a variety of ways and served in one meal. The order in which food was eaten was governed by protocol and the ceremony of service was carried out under established rules of etiquette.

Elaborate-floor length table cloths were used, and several napkins would be given in the course of the dinner. Although the fork had been introduced earlier in Italy, it was not until the period of Louis XIV that it joined the knife and spoon and came into general use. The reigns of Louis XV, 1715 to 1774, and Louis XVI, 1774 to 1792, saw a continued development of the culinary arts.

Most of the sauces on which modern French cuisine is based were developed during or shortly after the period of Louis XIV.

The first restaurant opened in Paris in 1765. During the period of the French revolution, the number of restaurants increased greatly. Many of them attracted the talents of the great chefs who had formerly been employed in the households of royalty and nobility.

The art of cookery grew during the wars and revolutions of the nineteenth century. Finally, in the beginning of the twentieth century, cookery emerged as a grandiose and well-developed art. The pleasures of the table became one of the most important qualities to the formula of good living.

August Escoffier was born in 1848. He was reputed to be the greatest chef since Careme and probably left more of an imprint on the preparation part of our industry than any other French chef. Escoffier associated himself with Cesar Ritz at the London Savoy Hotel's opening. It was said that during his stay there the cooking was finer than at any luxury hotel in the world. Mr. Escoffier wrote quite a number of books. *A Guide to Modern Cookery* is his best known in America. It was published in England in 1907. Translated into many languages, it has been the bible of most European chefs coming to America.

The number of restaurants multiplied and became more varied in the food and service they offered. As greater numbers of people had an opportunity to taste the delicate meals that had formerly been served only in the households of nobility, refinements in culinary arts became universal. Naturally, the expressions used to describe them were in French. These French words and phrases are understood throughout the civilized world.

It would be nearly impossible to list all cooking terms. The words in the glossary at the back of this book are a partial listing of the many terms that are encountered in any work situation.

chapter 2

natural resources

An abundance of food resources encourages the flourishing of good cookery.

While American cookery does not have the oldest traditions, it does represent a rich sprinkling of peoples and backgrounds. This mixture has produced one of the most extensive eating cultures of the world. As people from all nations came to this country, they brought with them their native foodstuffs and methods of cooking. These people did not venture easily into new and different foods. They preferred to remain close to their old-world dishes. This had the effect of preserving the national foods of different countries.

American food has been influenced not only by the people from numerous other lands but also by regional differences. This country is blessed with mile upon mile of coastal waters ranging in temperature from subtropical to frigid. There are also strong inland rivers, high mountains that provide days of sunshine followed by crisp cool nights, fertile plains, and vast grazing lands. All these produce their respective bounties. The coastal areas, the South, the Great Plains states of the midwest, and the sun-drenched lands of the far west all have their own dishes, both plain and fancy, to contribute to the variety of flavors found in American cookery.

Food supplies in this country have made great strides in the last twenty years. More food items than ever are available today. These years have seen a 100 percent increase in items on hand.

There will continue to be an abundance of food in America, although there will be more mouths to feed. The population is calculated to reach 222 million by 1980. This is an increase of 15.5 per-

Figure 2-1. A modern American farm.

cent over the 192 million people of 1964. A continual growth of food and farm product exports is also expected. That will create more food production demands.

The growth is based on:

1. The food production capacity of the U.S. in the mid-1960s, which was far greater than the actual output of farm products.
2. The potential for much more extensive use of land resources. Approximately 55 million acres of cropland were withheld from production by government programs designed to adjust farm output to market needs.
3. Public and private research that continues to turn out new procedures and processes in farm technology. For example: the use of electronic computers in farming and farm-related business and industry; the development of weather programs for the farmer; advice on what crop to plant, what seed to use, the rate of land use, and what pest-control practices to use.

New marketing improvements coupled with fast delivery of fresh food items have been largely responsible for the profuseness of food supplies. These days, less food goes bad on its way from the farm to the consumer. Marketing improvements include:

1. sanitary packing
2. better containers
3. faster transporting
4. on-the-scene packaging to reduce spoilage
5. better storage facilities

Motor truck transportation has been greatly improved by better roads, bigger loads, and refrigeration trailers.

Chemicals play an important role in the preservation of food. If chemicals were not used for pest control, within a few years the farmer's production of crops and livestock might decrease by 25 to 30 percent. A further loss from insects would be incurred in stored products. This could range from 5 percent for vegetables to 15 or 20 percent for grains. (Figure 2-2 shows crops being dusted.)

Figure 2-2. Crop dusting for pest control increases productivity and preserves food.

Chemicals aid in controlling 10,000 kinds of insects competing for our food. In addition to insects it is necessary to combat 1,500 plant diseases and 250 animal diseases.

chapter 3

types of operations

INTRODUCTION TO FOOD SERVICE OPERATIONS

In presenting the topics that follow, the sprawled out, variable, and ever-changing nature of our industry has been constantly in mind. To present one phase of the industry is but to raise a question about the rest.

I have chosen to present this work from the standpoint of the more inclusive or larger operations. These are not necessarily larger in the sense of numbers fed or in the dollar volume of sales, but rather in the sense of departments working in harmony to produce quality foods and provide service to the dining public. This will allow the methods of operation to be observed without being confused by combining the duties of many employees in the hands of one. Such a situation may be found in the smaller operation.

Frequent reference is also made to hotels. They represent the more inclusive type of operation. A medium-sized hotel will have a variety of departments that are required to provide food services.

All food service facilities have routines that are the result of their particular phase of the business. An endless array of sound practices and applications can be observed in various segments of the industry. However, a study of how different food departments and stations are related to the whole can best be made by examining a hotel-type operation. Depending on the nature of the food operation and its volume of

14

business, there are many successful work combinations that may be made by varying the number of man-hours devoted to a task.

Hotels today vary in type and purpose and in their form of ownership.

TYPES OF HOTEL AND MOTEL OPERATIONS

TRANSIENT HOTEL AND MOTEL.   Primarily serving the traveler, rooms may be let on a per-day basis, often without reservations. Some transient hotels also cater to convention business or less-expensive family trade.

Figure 3-1.   The Plaza Hotel in New York City—a first-class semiresidential and transient hotel.

RESIDENTIAL HOTEL.   Sometimes called apartment hotels. Full hotel service is available in this type of establishment. Rates are usually on a monthly basis but sometimes on a yearly basis. Rooms may be rented singly or by the suite, furnished or unfurnished. A few rooms may be held for visiting guests of residents.

SEMIRESIDENTIAL HOTEL.   Has some resident guests as well as facilities for transients. Room rents may be on a daily, weekly, or monthly rate. Full hotel services are available to guests for dining. This appeals to a short-term resident guest.

RESORT HOTEL.   Located in a recreational area. The resort operations offer more services than the other types of hotels because the guests are there for rest and recreation. The rates are fixed by the day or week. Today some resort hotels remain open all year. In the off-season these hotels cater to travelers and convention bookings. Resort hotels include lodges in state or national parks, dude ranches, health spas, and winter resorts.

Resorts offer a variety of job possibilities in food service. The facilities found in resorts are similar to those available in a fine hotel or club. In addition to sleeping rooms, suites, and cottages, resorts may have fine dining rooms, coffee shops, and snack bars. A variety of food

Figure 3-2.   The Broadmoor Hotel, a resort in Colorado Springs, Colorado.

services may also be available at outdoor dining facilities, such as at the beach or on a terrace.

Resorts sometimes appeal to couples working together. In some instances employees work a winter resort in one part of the country and then move to a summer resort in the spring. This arrangement appeals to people who enjoy the recreational and sports activities available in the off-work hours. Resorts are usually located on the coastlines, mountains, inland lakes, scenic locales, areas where mineral waters are found, and small islands off the mainland. For the enjoyment of its guests, a resort facility may offer activities such as professional entertainment, horseracing, shops, sightseeing, varied sports, and sailing. It may also have a park or country club as a part of the facilities. Meals may be available on the American, European, or modified American plan.

CLUB HOTEL. A private club facility that has hotel features. Dining rooms, lounges, and recreation facilities may be very complete. Hotel rooms may be available to members and their guests.

MOTOR HOTEL. The mobile pace of our society has brought the motor hotel into its own. No longer is this the roadside inn of yesterday. These spick-and-span establishments are often referred to as "horizontal hotels." Most are transient operations having very smart new facilities. Some resorts are being built with the motor-hotel appearance of low buildings. Rooms are sold by the day. Reservations may be made in advance. Most motor hotels are connected to a referral reservation system that offers free advance reservations to other points. All hotel services are available. The motor hotel is informal in operation although it may appear formally impressive. They are new and have much appeal with the public who like the informal feeling, the convenience, and some economy. Economy results from the combination of cheaper land with less expensive labor. Motor hotels are most often outside the city limits so that they can employ a less costly type of construction than that required by a high-rise structure. Maintenance costs are less in these horizontal-type buildings, and their locations mean lower taxes. In some cases the owner is also the manager. The above savings bring down the percentage of occupancy needed to a simple break-even point, resulting in lower costs that may be passed on to the patrons.

AMERICAN PLAN HOTEL. One rate is quoted for room and for meals together.

Figure 3-3. The Holiday Inn, a motel in Forsyth, Georgia.

MODIFIED AMERICAN PLAN. Includes one or two meals with the rate that is quoted for the room.

EUROPEAN PLAN HOTEL. A separate rate is quoted for room. All meals are charged and paid for individually.

Private Clubs

EARLY CLUBS. The early Greek and Roman civilizations had forms of clubs with membership practices that are similar to membership practices in our clubs of today. These clubs of ancient times were formed for various reasons: religious motives, bathing, dining, speaking, and political purposes. Cicero's speaking clubs, for example, were formed for the purpose of having a free verbal interchange of ideas. These symposiums were for the mutual enjoyment of the members.

As social clubs began to come to the fore in nineteenth-century England, some began to develop a pattern that would influence the cultural level of their community. The members' growing interest in the arts and sciences, together with changing social values, created a need for permanent quarters for the group's exclusive use. In some cases houses were acquired for this purpose. These were the forerunners of today's "clubhouses." In other cases parts of buildings were leased for club purposes. Today this is also a common practice.

Clubs in America

Private clubs in America have become a big business, offering many services and conveniences to members and their families. Tangible benefits are derived in the form of quality foods, beverages, and fine appointments in decor and furnishings. Intangible values are received in the form of satisfaction of hours well spent in the company of compatible people with similar interests. Most private clubs are member owned and, outside of meeting their operating expenses, attempt to make no profit in the course of the year.

Private clubs in America in the 1850s were patterned on the idea of an English gentleman's club. They never carried this pattern to the extremes of the English club where, in the old days, members wore their hats everywhere except the dining room. The American gentleman found that his club, and not his home, became his castle.

Most clubs in America have bylaws that provide that they are not operated for profit. In exchange for this, their dues and fees structure are exempt from income tax.

Soon after the turn of the century, the popularity of the country club rose in America. Following this came a variety of private club facilities, each varying to some extent in purpose or objectives. The growth and expansion of our times has been reflected in the growth of private clubs. Some of the more common types of clubs are:

GOLF CLUB.   Primarily a club that has very good golf, but many have other recreational facilities. It has snack and beverage services to accommodate players and their guests. Most have complete restaurant services.

CITY CLUB.   This facility may be a building of a few stories or may be several floors (usually the top floors) of a large high-rise. This type of club is for the social and recreational enjoyment of its members. Its purpose may be to further the arts and sciences. In some areas it becomes the nucleus of all social and cultural activities of a community. It may have any or all of the social facilities found in a large first-class hotel. It may also have a number of indoor recreational facilities such as squash, swimming, and steam rooms. Types of city clubs may be: athletic clubs, university clubs, luncheon clubs, fraternal clubs, and military clubs.

COUNTRY CLUB.   Similar to the city club in that the same type of service is rendered, but the country club operations also have an extensive outdoor program. The additional services would include activities such as golf, swimming, boating, horseback riding, etc. Country clubs are for the social, cultural, and recreational enjoyment of their members. These types of clubs are usually open only during the summer months. Extensive programs are developed during the open season so that as much as possible is offered to the membership. The club may also have a counterpart in a city club. In that case essentially the same membership either owns or operates the two clubs all year around for their enjoyment and convenience. In some cases the ownership may be different but the membership is much the same. Country clubs are usually located outside the city limits. Some may serve a more specific purpose such as a swim club, golf club, tennis club, military club, hunt club, or fraternal club.

NIGHTCLUB. A general term applied to the type of establishment that serves food and liquor, has a floor show, and has music and room for dancing. It is usually open at night. "Nightclub" is a popular name given to this type of public restaurant with entertainment. It is not a private club open to members only.

NONPROFIT NATURE. A private club is a nonprofit organization that is designed to operate as a corporate entity. If there are any excess funds left after operational expenses, they are returned to the corporation for the benefit of the members. These funds cannot be returned to the members individually. That usually means that any surplus is used for the general betterment of club facilities and equipment.

It is common practice in the industry to hire valued employees on a yearly basis even though a clubhouse may not be open the entire year. This, of course, has the effect of keeping these employees within the organization. The knowledge accumulated by the employee on likes and dislikes of the individual members makes her or him a tried and trusted member of a very large "family" of club members.

Military and Government Feeding

A young person faced with military service may further his or her education in food services while in the armed forces. The large variety of food services found in civilian life is also found in military life. There are various types of schools that will provide special training in food services to young people in the military. The student should keep in mind that the armed forces have almost all possible types of facilities. There are dining rooms, cafeterias, snack counters, coffee shops, and quality foods served on board ships and during flights. The training provided in

Figure 3-4. The final evaluation meal at a U.S. Navy cooking school (*official U.S. Navy photograph*).

all the branches of the services is excellent. The student is taught the fundamentals and most up-to-date techniques of food cookery and baking and has the opportunity to work with the latest equipment.

In addition to the meals provided to personnel on military installations, many of the camps, posts, or bases, etc., have N.C.O. clubs and officer's clubs. These offer the same service and convenience as a private club in civilian life. The military services represent the largest food operation. They serve millions of meals each day and control more independent units than any chain or franchise institution in the country.

Much time is spent by the armed forces on advanced food research and development for processing methods, standards, design, and equipment. Tightly controlled menus are prepared yearly by skilled dietitians.

GOVERNMENT SERVICES INC. This is a nonprofit government body that services only government agencies. This organization has three divisions—cafeterias, snack and vending areas, and national parks. Individual locations are leased from the General Services Administration.

OFFICER AND N.C.O. CLUBS. These represent a big business. They do millions of dollars in volume in a year and employ thousands of workers, both civilian and military. These military facilities are operated in a business fashion using the business methods required by any successful hotel or large restaurant. The skilled personnel, necessary to run living facilities, kitchens, bars, dining rooms, snack areas, and private social functions, are as much needed in these clubs as in any large metropolitan establishment.

Military clubs came into being for reasons similar to those that prompted the growth of city and country clubs. It was the desire to associate socially with persons of the same interests or background. Military clubs provide recreation facilities for members and their families. They also promote the general well-being and social-cultural enjoyment of their members.

Base, camp, or post clubs are known for their good food, drinks, service, and atmosphere.

POST EXCHANGE SERVICES. The post exchange services offer civilian employment in all parts of the world where there are military bases and posts. This self-supported system operates snack bars, cafeterias, and other eating outlets without public appropriation in most areas around the world where American forces are found.

The exchange services are the largest food service organization in terms of units operated. They are among the top three in dollar volume. When military personnel have time off from their duties, they patronize those post facilities that offer good food at attractive prices. Also, such facilities provide an efficient and well-operated convenience for members of the service and their families. The post exchange services control more than 2,500 individual installations and do a volume in excess of 200 million dollars per year. These installations may be found in various parts of the United States as well as around the world.

Military personnel use the post exchange for purchases of all sorts of merchandise besides food services.

Dormitories

Colleges and universities in this country have seen a large growth not only in numbers of students but also in the facilities that new numbers demand. Many new high-rise buildings for student housing are seen on campus today. More students are living on the campus than ever before, and this means more meals are being served in these hotel-like dormitories. Some of these buildings are built with beautiful design and good construction. The equipment in food services is often the best available. One dormitory may be large enough to house several hundred or even several thousand students. Each dormitory usually has large facilities to serve the students three meals a day.

Dormitory students pay a yearly fee for their room and board. A large university in America may have as many as 40 dormitories, more than 22,000 beds, and more than 1,000 people engaged in food production and services on a campus. Dormitories may have either separate receiving, storage, and kitchen areas or a central receiving, storage, and preparation kitchen that services and supplies all dormitories with prepared foods and bakery items.

Colleges

Today's colleges are feeding more people than ever before in dormitories, snack areas, union buildings, visitor living areas, etc. The installations in these areas are often exceptional. Many jobs are available to food service workers.

Some colleges operate their own facilities and others are leased to professional caterers.

CAMPUS FEEDING IS A BIG BUSINESS. As many as 50,000 meals or more can be served daily in all these feeding areas. Sales volume runs into the millions.

The individual feeding outlets may be designed to receive, store, and prepare foods in each unit. The alternative is to have one or more commissary areas receive the raw materials and do the cooking for the various outlets on campus.

FRATERNITY AND SORORITY HOUSES. Fraternity and sorority houses are located on a campus that provides living accommodations to its student members. These quarters employ their own food service staff and facilities. Many of these houses may be found on a campus. Each usually employs professional back of the house personnel. Much of the front of the house work is done by the members.

Take-Home

The mobile pace of society today has brought another phase to the food service world. Today a great many restaurants have take-out service as an additional operational feature of the house. Other take-home establishments operate with no dining space available to patrons and prepare a limited selection of foods that are taken elsewhere for consumption.

Franchise specialty houses have done a grand job in this area. They can be found among the top fifteen companies in dollar-volume sales in America. These companies do heavy merchandising and very effective advertising to keep sales at a high level.

Cafeterias

Cafeterias have seen a big change in recent years. Today cafeterias have very tasteful appointments. Some have party rooms and others offer special service sections for fast service. The scramble system is a newer feature in the cafeteria line. This resembles a large self-service supermarket. Patrons do not stay in line but go to special sections for specific foods and then pay a cashier at a central point. Cafeterias may be independent units serving the public (located in the heavy traffic areas of downtown or suburban centers) or they may be a part of a large institution or establishment employing or housing great numbers of people. The ease of selection, the informality, and the turnover ability makes a cafeteria popular when handling large numbers of people at one time.

Steamships

The largest, fastest, and most luxurious ships are on the seas today. The same graceful appointments and convenience found in the finest first-class hotels are available for the shipboard patron's enjoyment. Acres of indoor and outdoor facilities are at the traveler's disposal for play and relaxation. The fine food served throughout the day is of prime importance.

Outdoor luncheon buffets, tidbit snack areas, dining room service, lounge areas, and cabin service all require the same skills found in the finest hotel or continental restaurant. Cruise ships may operate during spring, summer, and autumn. Trans-ocean ships make voyages throughout the year.

The excellent cuisine on board includes many special delicacies from the ports and countries visited. These include exotic and internationally famous dishes.

Airline Flight Kitchens

Food facilities in a large airline may range in variety from an employee cafeteria to fancy flight snacks or very complete gourmet dinners. "Flight kitchen" is the term given to a commissary-type kitchen that does all the buying, storing, and preparing of food that is served on

Figure 3-5. Meal being served aboard an American Airlines 747 Luxuryliner.

board air flights. No matter what time of the day or what type of meal, all the foods and beverages are prepared in the flight kitchens. The food is transported in efficient warmers and refrigerators, all of the latest design. The airlines have put a strong emphasis on exquisite meals and luxury service. A large number of meals are served daily from these flight kitchens. Flight kitchens have developed the technique of producing in quantity but with a flair for quality in the individual product. The providing of extras has become part of the image of the airlines. Flight kitchens of a less elaborate nature may also be found in the military services. Some airlines operate their own food preparation divisions. Others are not engaged in preparing foods. They rely instead on catering firms to provide the prepared meals for their traveling guests.

Hospitals — Institutions

Privately owned, state, and federal hospitals have the need of food services for patient and guest accommodations. Their kitchen designs must be very functional. Food service equipment is often the latest. With menu selection available to the patient, more planning and utilization of equipment is necessary. Private, city, county, state, and federal hospitals located in the various states represent a dollar volume that runs into the millions yearly. The state hospitals in California alone serve over 60,000 meals a day and have more than 20,000 beds.

The hospitals may include food service for:

1. bed patients
2. patient self-service (cafeteria)
3. guest facilities (snack bar, cafeteria)
4. staff and employee facilities (cafeteria, vending units)

Waiting on bed patients requires a different approach to the service of food than do the other types. The other hospital services offered are discussed with slight modification in other parts of the book. A diet kitchen may exist in the hospital to give special attention to those meals prepared for patients who may be on therapeutic diets. There are basically two operating patterns of providing food service to bed patients. Combinations of these can be made utilizing some features of both.

1. *CENTRALIZED TRAY SERVICE.* The food is prepared, cooked, and placed on a tray in a central kitchen. A tray assembly unit is used to fill the trays. The menu of each tray is filled as it moves down the line. The tray is checked and transported to the patient. Trays and utensils are returned to the central area for cleaning.

2. *DECENTRALIZED TRAY SERVICE.* This may take two forms:
    a. All food is prepared in a central kitchen and transported in bulk in a food cart to the floor pantries where the individual meals are assembled. Utensils may be washed in a central kitchen or pantry. Clean utensils are stored in floor pantries.
    b. Convenience foods are used with a microwave oven. The service is essentially the same as above with the exception that food is frozen in either bulk or individual portions. Microwave ovens are located in the floor pantry for instant warming of the entrée.

In-plant Feeder

In-plant feeding is a by-product of the war years. These industrial feeders provide a meal on the job so that workers can have the benefit of a hot meal and the convenience of having it in the building. Manufacturing plants, office buildings, exhibition halls, and other establishments have this type of operation. Company cafeterias, canteens, mobile units, and vending machines are typical installations that may be run by the company or contracted to an outside catering firm. Contract employee feeding is a very important function for industries and institutions.

Figure 3-6.   An in-plant cafeteria at a J.C. Penney warehouse.

These food service management systems offer various types of services to businesses, industries, schools, colleges, hospitals, and recreation centers. These systems vary from installation to installation depending on the particular needs of the concern.

Some in-plant feeders have branched into a package program. They provide food and lodging for work crews in construction areas that are far from city or community conveniences. This type of program has taken professional feeders to distant parts of the world.

The following is a list of possible systems of operation:

MANUAL SYSTEM.   In this type of installation, menu and services are varied to suit the wishes of the client and the local tastes of the customers. A complete selection of soups, entrées, and desserts is available. The service may be simple cafeteria-style or dining room table service.

VENDING SYSTEM.   This type of installation may range from an automatic snack bar to complete menu service with a full-time supervisor and staff. One food service management system has 122 completely equipped and competently staffed service centers across the country to support over 100,000 vending machines.

Reliable service is provided twenty-four hours a day, seven days a week.

COMBINATION SYSTEM. This approach is suggested when the client's situation requires a combination of manual and vending systems. This type of installation offers a combined menu. The primary mealtime service is manual, supported by automatic vending units at break periods and for the smaller shifts. An excellent selection of attractively packaged sandwiches, salads, desserts, pastries, and beverages is available through the vending machines. The contract feeder provides supervision for the personal touch.

SUPPORT SERVICES. These include the professional talents of nutritionists, designers, master chefs, food production supervisors, and electromechanical experts all working as a team to keep up the top-quality around-the-clock service that is expected.

FACILITIES PLANNING. Services are available to help the client choose the desired and most useful allocation of space. These professional planning departments develop the attractive dining areas to meet the needs of the client. The designers, equipment specialists, and decorators also work with architects in the preliminary stages of new buildings. This early planning ensures that the layout and decor of the production and the dining areas will provide the best traffic flow and achieve the client's desired objective.

CULINARY TECHNOLOGY. Modern research and new techniques in planning menus are constant concerns. New products, new recipes, and new methods of packaging receive thorough testing. Dietitians conduct comprehensive programs of taste panels and food-preference surveys to find the right foods in the right locations of the country.

SPECIAL SERVICES. Attractive coffee-cart service and the special talents needed to provide a delicatessen cafeteria in an office building are among the other special services available. One such feeder has a staff of 27,000 serving 10,000 clients and providing meals for 4,000,000 people every day.*

* Automatic Retailers of America.

Department Stores

Department stores offer a large variety of food service to customers. Dining rooms, cafeterias, and snack counters may all be found in department stores. In most instances these facilities were added as a convenience to the store patron. The "captive" shoppers want to eat as quickly and conveniently as possible. The location of downtown department stores means that hundreds of office workers in the area also enjoy the closeness of these quick eating facilities.

Many innovations have come into department store food services. The open-wall feeding of shopping center malls has brought cocktail lounges, fast-service island stands of attractive design, fancy dining rooms, and coffee shops with an outdoor atmosphere. They have also provided a take-out convenience for pastry items, specialty foods, etc.

Catering Firms

Catering services vary. These firms are entirely in the business of providing social functions with food, beverages, and services. Similar services are also available in restaurants or hotels that have a specialized catering department. The food is prepared either in the kitchens of a private caterer or in the large kitchens of the restaurant or hotel. The food may be transported and served at an office building, a factory, a church, a school, or a private home. All the equipment, supplies, and food that is necessary is provided by the firm that is doing the catering. Generally caterers serve one-time affairs that are handled and paid for on an individual basis. However, many caterers provide daily luncheon service for the officer or executive dining rooms of banks and other firms. Some caterers also provide evening meal service as well.

Restaurants

The dictionary meaning of the word "restaurant" is: "(1) A place where refreshments or meals are provided; (2) A public dining room."

These definitions take in all the operations about which we are writing. The refreshments or meals may be produced on the premises or, as is sometimes the case with private clubs, offices, banks, etc., that are not catering to the public, the food may be brought in from commissaries. In other words, some restaurants do not have a kitchen on the premises where the food they serve is produced. Instead, the food is produced in a commissary and brought to the restaurant for service.

Generally speaking, restaurants are either table-service or self-service. Some restaurants offer both types of service.

TABLE-SERVICE RESTAURANTS. In this kind of restaurant the food is selected by the patron from a menu. The order is given to a waiter who serves the meal. The elaborateness of that service, the decor and furnishings of the room, and the provision of music or entertainment depend entirely on the clientele patronizing the establishment and, of course, its menu prices.

Figure 3-7. A restaurant in a hotel—the Oak Room at the Plaza Hotel, New York City.

Restaurants may be part of a hotel or club or an independent operation in a heavy traffic area. Large shopping centers and suburban communities provide such a setting. Some follow ethnic designations such as French, Italian, German, Swedish, Hawaiian, etc. Their menus usually feature dishes of the homelands that evoke nostalgic memories. In this type of restaurant the decoration, costumes of the servers, music, and entertainment are part of the atmosphere of the setting.

SPECIALTY RESTAURANTS. Good table service also characterizes the restaurant that features steak, seafood, pancakes, pizza, or fried

chicken. Many of these also feature carry-out service. Frequently they are chain operations or franchises. Most of the specialty steak restaurants carry a rather complete menu.

COFFEE SHOPS AND SANDWICH SHOPS.   At one time these were common adjuncts to the restaurant service in most large hotels. A few prospered in locations close to hotels. Many now prosper in downtown business areas. Both table service and counter service are available in most of them. In some hotels today, their coffee or sandwich shop is the only restaurant service provided even though they may still offer banquet service. Snack foods as well as complete meals are available in coffee shops.

SELF-SERVICE RESTAURANTS.   These may range from complete self-service to a modified table service. Modified service may mean the beverage and the dessert are served at the table. Self-service restaurants include cafeterias, buffets, and smorgasbords. In some cities the largest proportion of restaurant patrons use the self-service type of restaurant for at least one meal daily.

The cafeteria menu is presented daily on signs that are hung on the wall in view of the customers. Prices are also usually posted on these signs, but they may be placed alongside the food at the steam table or counter. A cafeteria menu is usually complete with all the components of a full meal. The foods, while visible to the patron, are protected by glass until served by counter employees. Rigidly enforced sanitary laws ensure this practice. Patrons get napkins and silverware first as they walk toward the beverage station. Hot dishes, cold items, and desserts are then selected and placed on the tray. In most establishments the checker who totals the selections collects the money as well. Sometimes the checker gives the customer a bill to be paid to a cashier on the way out. Of course, patrons of a cafeteria pay only for the food selected.

BUFFET RESTAURANTS.   In recent years we have noted some very successful buffet restaurants. These differ from the cafeteria only in that the buffet is on a fixed-price basis. One price covers the entire meal, including seconds if desired. The selection of food items may be as large as the best cafeteria, and it is usually beautifully displayed. Quite frequently, the food selections may include large decorated pieces such as hams, turkeys, various cold fish items, and roast beef rounds or ribs sliced to order.

Figure 3-8. A buffet at Hotel Las Brisas, Acapulco, Mexico.

Buffet service can also usually be obtained from a regular or a specially prepared menu in most clubs and hotels. Some larger restaurants have private rooms where this service is available.

SMORGASBORDS. This is a Scandinavian name that literally means "hors d'oeuvres." However, for a good many years a number of these restaurants have been serving meals practically on the same basis as buffet restaurants. Smorgasbords are usually characterized by self-service, fixed price, and lots of hors d'oeuvres but not as many entrées.

Railroads

A variety of food facilities are featured in railroad travel. Snack counters, club cars, and dining cars provide the more extensive type of service on the various lines of a railroad. Some foods are prepared en route.

Others are prepared in advance and simply held for service while en route. Because of the amount of travel time, employees spend several days off at their home base prior to their next departure.

Construction Camps

As in the military, wherever people are sent so must the kitchens go. This type of food outlet may be handled by the construction firm or by an in-plant feeder as previously discussed. The food supplied is of a high quality. The service is of a relatively simple nature.

Drive-ins

For dining in the automobile, essentially a short-order light lunch variety of foods is offered. Some drive-ins have additional parking space available. In that case patrons may leave the car and enter a service section where a large selection of food items is available. The food served in the drive-in is prepared and served in such a way that a minimum of utensils and supplies is needed. Special equipment and methods of operation make this a unique segment of the food service industry.

Many drive-ins have inside dining rooms as well so that these establishments have two front of the house operations as well as their production department.

Institutions

An institution may range in variety of food service from a simple facility serving several hundred meals a day to a large complex serving several thousand meals daily. The larger facility may have a coffee shop for visitors as well as snack units. The larger institution may also have a large storeroom, bakery, and butcher shop in addition to the kitchens.

HOMES FOR THE ELDERLY.   Homes for the "retired set," that is, for the elderly, are more inclusive and have more to offer than ever before. These institutions may include apartment living or life in a "manor." Hospitals, nursing homes, and custodial homes are included in this group of organizations. A variety of additional services are also available in these operations. These may range from a registered nurse to a small clinic or a beauty salon.

Those homes that provide three meals daily quite often use the services of a staff dietitian to develop menus that will fulfill the nutritional demands of elderly residents and patients. The dietitian also handles special diets. Homes for the elderly provide tray service, cafeterias, and family service dining rooms. They may be located in a one-story building or a high-rise.

Schools

The school lunch program has made it possible to serve a hot meal to every child in school. This means large school lunch operations offering varied employment for full-time employees as well as short-hour part-time employees. School lunch operations may do their own cooking in individual kitchens, or a central commissary may prepare the food for several schools and then truck it to the various satellite schools in the district. There the food is heated and served up. A large school system in one American city serves more than fifty million meals in one year.

chapter 4

ownership and management

TYPES OF OWNERSHIP

A food operation, whether an independent enterprise or part of a large hotel or similar institution, exists in one of the following types of businesses:

A *sole proprietorship* refers to the type of organization that is owned and operated by a single person.

A *partnership* is an association of two or more people involved in the ownership of a business.

A *silent partner* is one who has an agreement with other partners to share in profit or loss but who has no voice in the operation of the business.

Limited partners are liable for the limited amount agreed upon when the partnership is formed.

A *corporation* is a business owned by stockholders doing business together as one entity. Stockholders elect a board of directors who establish policy and hire the needed management.

A *franchise* is the right assigned an individual, partnership, or corporation, to use a name or formula. Franchisers receive assistance in the operation of a food business in a specific area. In return they usually pay a fixed fee and a continual percentage of the gross volume. This type of business has brought owners and operators into the field primarily because of the professional assistance given. Some of this includes professional site planning; proven construction plans with architectural assistance; and financial counseling to secure the best mortgage, central purchasing power, professional supervision during opening as needed, and a steady clientele through a continual national advertising program.

Franchise operations have seen a real growth in recent years. They have brought doctors, lawyers, business people, etc., into the food

Figure 4-1. A franchise operation in Nebraska.

service world. Pizza parlors, pancake houses, steak houses, drive-ins, and motor hotels are but a few examples of franchise businesses.

An operating company may own the land, buildings, and furnishings of the property and may have a franchise with a national chain. Under a franchise arrangement the local investor buys the franchise from the national company. This gives the investor the services listed on page 35. The local investor builds and equips the facility using the trade name in accordance with specifications provided. The local investor pays a percentage of the gross income and other small fees to the national firm. This amount pays for national advertising and general promotion as well as any operational assistance that might be needed from time to time. The national company maintains certain standards in all phases of the operations in order to maintain a consistent pattern of service. The national name across the country works well in producing increased business in drop-in activity as well as developing local patronage.

Chain operation is a popular term given to several operations that have either the same name or different names but the same ownership. The owner may be an individual, a partnership, or a corporation. The individual places of business may be in separate locations with the home office in still another area. Operational practices are established by the home office. Management is engaged by the home office. Local management is often preferred, in which case training programs are available to teach the operational practices and policies. Facilities housing the individual establishments may be leased or they may be owned by the parent company.

In a *lease arrangement* the operating company develops a contract with the owner of the property. The contract defines the conditions of the transaction and the purposes for which the premises will be used. Usually the owner of the facility provides the land and building and, sometimes, heating and cooling equipment. The operating company provides the furnishings and movable equipment. The lease fee is usually based on a minimum or a preagreed percentage of sales, whichever is the largest.

MANAGEMENT TITLES

Management responsibilities vary from midmanagement to upper management levels. Management responsibilities vary also from house to house. The following are some of the more common management titles in the various phases of the food industry.

Types of Hotel Managers

The hotel industry has several management titles that are used extensively to designate areas of responsibility. These position titles are not listed in Chapters 5 and 7 which deal with job classifications. They are as follows:

The *manager* is the person actively in control of the operation.

The *managing director* is actively in control of the operation and also a director of the operating company.

The *general manager* has administrative and general duties in a large hotel. Almost all current operations are supervised by administrative assistants and department heads. Many supervise two or more hotels.

The *resident manager* usually lives in the hotel. She or he may be in charge of one property of a chain, each one of which a general manager may oversee. In a larger hotel, the resident manager may be on duty in the evening hours when other managers are not.

The *executive assistant manager* is directly responsible to the general manager and assists in all areas of operation in the establishment. He or she may work closely with several assistants and coordinate their functions in administering the policies and practices of the establishment.

Assistant managers are responsible to the general manager. They are usually assigned several departments that they supervise directly in addition to general and administrative coordination of house operations.

Management in the Military

The military services have a commissioned officer who is directly responsible for the operation and performance of the dining hall facilities where the daily meals are served. In the navy these officers are called supply officers. In the Army, Marines, and Air Force, they are mess officers. The mess officers' responsibilities are of a general nature. They are concerned with the everyday administrative functioning of the facility.

Noncommissioned officers are directly concerned with the daily mechanics of providing food and service in the dining halls. They oversee the preparation and service, make work assignments and reports, and maintain the necessary records.

CLUB OFFICERS. Club officers are commissioned officers who are

directly responsible for the operation of the officers' clubs. They may be directly involved with the daily operations and function as operating heads in the same way as club managers. In some installations a civilian manager is hired to perform the operational duties of club management. In this instance the manager would definitely be engaged with the daily operations. The club officer would then be concerned with the general administration of the club. It is possible that a good club officer with sound management practices may spend an entire career in the military running officers' clubs at various posts, bases, or stations around the world.

MANAGERS OF N.C.O. CLUBS. This management position is for the management of a noncommissioned officers' club. Almost all military installations have this type of operation. This club has a governing board that establishes the policy that the manager administrates. It is possible for a qualified noncommissioned officer to spend an entire length of stay in the military in this position engaged in the management of noncommissioned officers' clubs.

COMMISSARY MEN. This is the title and basic rank given to the people in charge of a navy or coast guard kitchen and dining hall. The size of the kitchens and dining halls varies and so do the grades of commissary men. There are several noncommissioned officer ranks available under this classification. Additional ranks range upward to that of *warrant officer.* These responsible jobs involve overseeing the production and service of daily meals. Compensation is scaled according to grade. Additional fringe benefits, including housing and maintenance, become available in the higher grades. Special training is available to those engaged in the preparation of food similar to other branches of the military.

MESS SERGEANTS. This is the title and basic rank given to persons in charge of the direct operating functions of preparing and serving food in the Army, the Marines, and the Air Force.

The size of the operation and number of people supervised in this area differs from installation to installation. Rank likewise varies several grades for this noncommissioned officer's job. There is a great diversity of food service and facilities around the globe wherever the military is stationed that require large numbers of supervisory personnel. Research is constantly going on in an effort to develop better food products and new ways of doing the old job of feeding large numbers. Schools are available in the military where special training is provided to those engaged in the preparation of food.

Catering Services

CATERING MANAGERS OR MAITRES D'HOTEL. Generally these people are in charge of making arrangements for and executing banquets. They must see that the establishment is supplying all the items and services it has agreed to provide. This position may involve the supervision of several dining areas in addition to the banquet department. Catering managers may consult daily with other department heads such as the executive chef or steward concerning banquet menus, daily menus, and other operating problems. They make arrangements with clients for social functions either by telephone, in person, or by mail. Acting as a buffer between the food service department and the public, they handle and adjust complaints concerning service or quality of food. The distribution of information to the chef, steward, banquet manager, and other employees concerned with the execution of a private affair is also part of their job. They must inspect the finished arrangements and may be present at the time of a banquet, supervising service and greeting guests. Their duties may also take them into the food preparation and bar departments. In that case they will have to keep more records. The responsibility for making a profit will be theirs.

Catering managers are usually employed in large restaurants or hotels of the more formal type. The organization of an establishment and the ability of the individual may determine what, if any, additional authority will be delegated to this position.

In some concerns all these phases are combined and the position is titled "food manager" or "restaurant manager." Then the maitre d'hotel would be responsible for food service only.

In popular usage the term "maitre d' " is used to describe the work duties of a headwaiter in a smaller establishment who is responsible to the manager.

Restaurant Managers

Restaurant managers have charge of and operate an entire restaurant. They may also operate the beverage and other related departments. There may be a supporting staff for this position in large establishments where there is more than one kitchen and several dining areas. In smaller operations restaurant managers work directly with service and production personnel.

Managers of Other Operations

The titles listed below are given to the people in charge of an entire food preparation and service operation. These titles are most often used in single-purpose units. Examples of such units are cafeterias, drive-ins, take-out services, pancake houses, and coffee shops. The individuals are called cafeteria managers, drive-in managers, and so on.

ASSISTANT MANAGERS.   These people work directly under the manager. They may assist the manager in general but may also have some duties they specifically assume. They are in charge of the operation when the manager is not there.

NIGHT MANAGERS.   These people have the same general duties as the manager. The position is found in those businesses involving long serving periods, such as a twenty-four hour operation. As the name implies, these employees work the night shift. They are responsible to and report to the manager.

CLUB MANAGERS.   As previously discussed, private clubs offer a varied selection of food facilities. These may include the very simple snack-type foods found at pool side to the very elaborate foods of social functions. Elaborate functions of all types take place perhaps most consistently in the private clubs in nearly all communities. The position of club manager requires an unusual talent in handling people as well as the ability to manage the various departments engaged in providing recreation, food, beverage, and service to the membership. The club manager's responsibilities vary with the club. A small club may have one dining area while large clubs may have snack areas, dining rooms, party rooms, banquet rooms, cocktail lounges, and room service. The club manager is responsible for the caliber of the operation and also the proper functioning of all operating departments and personnel.

CHAIN EXECUTIVES.   These positions are usually associated with large chain-type operations. They do not ordinarily involve direct contact with food preparation and service, although a thorough knowledge of these facets is required. The work performed is usually administrative and travel from house to house may be an important part of the duties.

FOOD SUPERVISORS (Hospital).   These individuals supervise personnel in the overall operation of the food preparation area as directed and defined by a dietitian. They are responsible for the quality, quantity, and presentation of food. The formulation of menus and development of procedures and practices in the preparation areas and for food handlers are part of a food supervisor's job. They prepare work schedules, develop work patterns, and maintain inventories. They also conduct training classes or assist an instructor in explaining procedures. They orient new employees in department regulations and leave regulations, give job descriptions, and explain job requirements. They may, if assigned, prepare some foods and assist in dishing up and assembling trays. They may also, if so directed, prepare time schedules for food service workers. The position is responsible to the chief cook and dietitian.

FOOD SERVICE MANAGERS (*Institution, Hospital*). These people have complete charge of buying, storing, preparing, and serving all food. They must have knowledge of kitchen operation, food preparation, and appropriate methods of serving. They must be proficient in food cost control. If supervision of a large kitchen staff is involved, they must have the ability to work with and direct people. There may be a staff of highly skilled people to assist with the management of the food service department. A food supervisor and a dietitian may also be on the staff. A larger operation could have several dietitians, each performing specific duties. The title of "food service manager" is found in more general use in contract feeding firms that have developed a contract with an institution's administration. They then provide all the management personnel with experience in the proper and efficient operation of the food service department.

ADMINISTRATIVE DIETITIANS (*Institution, Hospital*). These individuals may perform the same general duties as the food service manager and have the same staff available to assist with the managerial duties. The title of "administrative dietitian" is more frequently used in those installations that are operating their own food service departments.

FOOD SERVICE DIRECTORS (see *Food Service Managers*).

part II

the front of the house—
job titles, departments,
stations, and equipment

chapter 5

the front
of the house—
job titles

No matter how large or how small or what type of food service outlet is under consideration, there are always two areas within the "house," as all establishments are called. The two areas are called the "front" and the "back," or the front of the house and the back of the house.

The front of the house is like the stage in a theater. It is the part that is always visible to the public. The back of the house is like the area behind the scenes and is not always visible to the public.

These two areas, although dependent on one another, perform entirely different functions. They require different abilities in the workers needed.

The front of the house is the service department that brings the finished product to the patrons. The back of the house is the production department. There the raw material is converted to the finished product.

The word "house" has a special meaning in the industry. Different jobs in the back of the house are: chef, broiler cook, steward, pastry chef, food checker, kitchen steward, etc. Some departments in the back of the house are: pantry; main cooking—hot ranges; storeroom; butcher shop, etc. These departments may fabricate (not to the final stage) or convert to the finished product. The back of the house will be discussed in further detail in Part 3.

FRONT OF THE HOUSE

Some front of the house jobs are: manager, hostess, waiter, busboy, captain, headwaiter, cashier, hostess, bartender, etc. Some front of the house departments are the bar and the lobbies and dining rooms.

The front of the house areas may be very simple or very elaborate, but the purpose they serve is the same. They provide satisfaction and comfort in the home away from home. The objective of the patron is the governing factor whether one type of facility is used or another. The front of the house personnel are continually striving to see that the facilities provided by the house are rendering the proper comfort and satisfaction to the patrons.

Front of the house personnel are constantly under the watchful and ever-present eye of the public. Because of this attention, they are reminded by management of the importance of personal appearance. Also under the watchful eye of the public and management is the quality of service that is being rendered by the personnel in this area of the house. The front of the house personnel are as much on stage as the performer. Front of the house personnel are taught to do their work according to the patterns of operation of the particular establishment. Their technical performance, combined with a certain amount of social grace, becomes a professional norm that governs the department. When this quality is present, it is felt by all patrons. It is as important as good food that is properly prepared.

Job Titles (front of the house)

To assist in the understanding of the jobs performed by the front of the house, this book will list the duties of the employees that work in this area and include a description of the work performed. Mention will also be made of the lines of responsibility from management to the working level.

The restaurant industry is multiphased. It includes operations that take many forms and range from the small "mama-papa" business to the very large organization. Some run food volumes into the millions of dollars yearly and employ thousands of people. Therefore, the job descriptions and duties that are listed are norms. Real jobs will vary according to the particular business.

Uniforms are worn by some front of the house personnel. This is established by house policy. Uniforms may be provided by the house or, in some cases, purchased by employees.

BAR BOYS OR GIRLS.   The work of bar boys or girls is that of being general helpers to the bartender. The work includes carrying supplies and equipment such as fruits, soft mixes, paper supplies, and some silverware from the storeroom to the bar. They may also carry ice and assist in washing glasses. Other similar duties are performed if the bartender so directs. This position is responsible to the captain or hostess.

BAR WAITERS OR WAITRESSES.   They take the patrons' orders and serve the beverages mixed by the bartender. They collect payment from patrons and settle accounts with the bartender or cashier. At times they may suggest and describe cocktails, highballs, or liquors. This position may be responsible to the headwaiter or hostess.

BARTENDERS.   They greet guests that come to the bar, take their orders, and mix and serve the alcoholic drinks. They may receive payment and make change. Bartenders are responsible for the appearance of the bar

Figure 5-1. A waitress taking an order in the coffee house at the Waldorf-Astoria Hotel, New York City.

and for seeing that sufficient supplies are on hand. They may perform miscellaneous tasks, such as washing and drying glasses, and set up snack foods during cocktail hours. They may also assist with periodic inventories. In a small establishment, they may oversee the cocktail lounge and serve drinks in slow periods of the day. This position may be responsible to a head bartender or wine steward.

HEAD BARTENDERS. These people supervise, instruct, and assist bartenders in mixing and serving drinks and in keeping the bar areas in a neat, orderly condition. They may schedule the working hours of all the bartenders in the establishment. The position is responsible to the wine steward or catering manager (maitre d'hotel).

BUS BOYS OR GIRLS. They assist the waiters or waitresses by performing routine duties. These duties include taking finished courses and used dishes to the kitchen, replacing soiled table linen with clean linen, bringing additional butter to the guests, filling water bottles and glasses, and bringing clean silverware to the dining room. These workers may also perform other tasks as assigned such as setting tables, polishing silverware and serving pieces, cleaning and sweeping the dining room, and dusting furniture and fixtures. The position is responsible to the hostess or captain.

MAITRES d'HOTEL. In popular usage today the title of "maitre d' hotel" is reserved for the person in charge of the dining room in a hotel or restaurant. In this capacity he or she supervises a team of captains, waiters, and junior waiters.

In the past the position of maitre d'hotel was always held by persons of high standing, sometimes from noble families. In this capacity they would formally oversee all the household departments and attend to the details of the visiting heads of state and royal families. Every detail of the kitchen, dining room, wine cellar, and living facilities would come under their watchful eyes.

Maitres d'hotel in a restaurant today are people with many qualities of professional knowledge. They must understand the wants of their guests and, equally important, the workings of the kitchen. They are required to be capable administrators, psychologists, confidants, diplomats, and executives. They are well-groomed men or women with a good education. A free-flowing knowledge of foods and wines is necessary as is the art of using this knowledge to assist patrons in making their selections. The position is responsible to the general manager, restaurant manager, or catering manager, depending on the size and organization of the establishment.

FOOD CONTROLLERS.   These people are responsible for compiling the statistics of food costs, sales, and profit and loss. They also develop the procedures of portion control and item usage. This position is usually found in a large establishment. Food controllers may take inventory on foodstuffs with the chef or steward and work closely with both of them on matters of buying and producing. They may assist in writing the menu with the chef. The position is responsible to the auditor or manager.

FOOD VENDING MACHINE OPERATORS (or Routemen).   This position may be that of an independent business person working alone. In that case they place their own machines in various installations in a community. A few of the types of installation are motor hotels, schools, offices, and factories. The establishment in which the machine is located receives a percentage of the volume for having the machine on the premises. The maintenance of the machine is the concern of the routeman.

Food machine operators, or routemen, may be paid employees of coin-machine firms that handle a single type of unit or a large variety of coin-operated machines. The duties are a variety of tasks that include locating new machine sites; developing good public relations for the firm by handling complaints at the time of servicing; making adjustments to the unit to ensure good quality control of the product; making small adjustments that may be necessary to the proper functioning of the machine; and lastly handling cash funds and the keeping of any required records.

These and other duties that may be assigned vary, depending on the size of the operation. The routemen are "front people" in the sense of being onstage. When performing duties that require the replenishing or the simple adjusting of a machine they are "production people." The daily duties of this position require driving from site to site and working indoors and outdoors.

MERCHANDISING SUPERVISORS.   These relatively new positions are chiefly found in the large chains and in some of the larger restaurants. These people essentially perform the function of selling more of the organization's product, which is food. They develop new menu designs, art displays, and advertising programs and, in general, look for new ways to attract customers.

PERSONNEL DIRECTORS.   This position is found in the large chain-type operations and very large restaurants, hotels, and clubs. Personnel directors may be in complete charge of locating, hiring, and training employees. They handle all personnel matters and work on maintaining good relations between the house and the employees in general.

MENU PLANNERS. They are employed in large restaurants. These people conduct research on menu planning and develop all the menus used by the organization. They are concerned with the seasonal nature and regional differences of foods. An educational background in dietetics or foods and nutrition is required.

DIRECTORS OF RECIPE DEVELOPMENT. This position is found in large restaurants and chain-type operations. These are people with high technical training or experience who work in test kitchens creating new recipes. A strong knowledge of food preparation is essential.

CAR HOPS. Waiting on customers in automobiles, car hops serve beverages or food and sometimes both. The refreshments are brought to the automobiles. Later the charges are collected and the soiled silverware, dishes, equipment, and tools are removed. The car hop is responsible to the drive-in manager.

CASHIERS. These people receive food checks and payments from waiters or from departing guests and ring up the amount indicated on the cash register. They make the change for guests or waiters. If the check is a charge in a hotel, they make out a voucher so that it can be posted to the individual account as soon as possible. Cashiers may perform other tasks, such as keeping control on food checks or selling cigars, cigarettes, tobacco, and candy. This position is responsible to the auditor.

FOOD CHECKERS. They check food orders going out of the kitchen for quality and quantity; itemize costs on the register and total the check; keep a record of silver and equipment sent out of dining room on room service; and compile and tabulate the types of food served. They complete and turn a cash report in to the general cashier showing the cash and charge receipts from that shift. Food checkers are responsible to the auditor.

HEAD BUSBOYS OR BUSGIRLS. These people have the responsibility of instructing and assigning work schedules to the busboys and busgirls. They work closely with the hostess, headwaiter, and chef. In some installations they may spend a considerable amount of time in the kitchens carrying soiled dishes, etc. This work would bring them in close contact with the chef. The position is responsible to the hostess or headwaiter.

HEADWAITERS, HOSTS, OR HOSTESSES.   These people greet guests as they enter the dining room. They count how many there are in the party and ask if the party has preference as to where they would like to sit. The headwaiter then motions to the waiter captain and tells her or him where to seat the guests. If the captain is not available, a headwaiter may escort guests to a table and give each one a menu. He or she may be requested to take orders from guests and then transmit them to the waiters. Headwaiters are in charge of the dining room and all personnel working there. They are responsible to the catering manager, if there is one, or the manager or owner.

Where there is no headwaiter, hostesses or hosts greet guests as they enter a coffee shop or dining room, escort them to the tables, and present menus or, in coffee shops, place menus on the table in front of the guests. They are in charge of the dining area and have the responsibility of seeing it is in order and properly staffed at all times. They arrange the work schedules of employees. The position is responsible to the catering manager or manager.

HEAD ROOM SERVICE WAITERS OR WAITRESSES.   These people are in charge of and responsible for the room service department. They make sure that orders are taken properly, inspect food and equipment before it is taken to guests' rooms, keep a record of employee work time, and see that employees are properly trained. The position is responsible to the catering manager.

WAITER CAPTAINS.   Under the general supervision of the headwaiter, waiter captains are in charge of one section of a dining room. They instruct, supervise, and give help to the waiters and busboys when needed. After guests have been greeted by the headwaiter, waiter captains receive and escort them to a table of proper size. They seat patrons so that each waiter will have an equal number of people to serve. They present the menus and take orders as soon as the patrons are ready. They give the orders to the waiter assigned to the table and then withdraw to receive the next guests. They watch all the tables under their jurisdiction to detect any dissatisfaction and may make adjustments in response to complaints. Waiter captains may suggest wines to be served. They are responsible to the headwaiter.

WAITERS OR WAITRESSES. They serve foods and beverages to patrons in the various dining rooms and coffee shops. Where busboys are not employed, they prepare tables or counters for serving meals and reset after every usage. They learn the specials of the day from the hostess or manager upon reporting to their work stations so that these items can be suggested to the patrons. They may present the menu. They obtain the order from the patron, write it on a small check, and place the check in the proper place in kitchen if the order is not relayed verbally. They secure the food from the kitchen, serve the patron, and present the bill for payment. They may collect the money or direct the patron to the cashier. At a lunch counter no setup is necessary. Guests are provided with the necessary utensils according to the order. The position is responsible to the headwaiter, hostess, or manager.

ROOM SERVICE WAITERS AND WAITRESSES. These people handle the dining service when a guest is served in the room. They also present the check for foods ordered. They may be paid in cash or the guest may sign for the order. They return to the room after a reasonable period of time, put the carrier or wagon in the storage place, and take the dirty dishes to the dishwashers. The position is responsible to the catering manager.

WATER–COFFEE BOYS OR GIRLS. These people fill water glasses when guests are seated at the table and later serve them coffee. The position is responsible to the hostess or headwaiter, who may assign other miscellaneous duties.

BANQUET MANAGERS. They arrange details of banquets and provide the necessary physical equipment needed to put on the party. They also provide temporary banquet workers. During the banquet they may greet the host, hostess, and guests. They also act as headwaiter to make certain that everything is as ordered. They see that all party rooms are in order at all times and check before and after an affair to make sure that the patrons receive exactly what they have paid for. In some cases this may mean using a party room for several functions in the course of one day. Banquet managers may sell and arrange a special party. They present the bill for signature or payment when the party is over. When authorized, they may pay the part-time employees at the end of the evening.

Banquet managers are usually employed by large hotels. They are responsible to the catering manager, maitre d'hotel, or executive assistant manager, depending on the way the establishment is organized.

SETUP WAITERS OR WAITRESSES.   In addition to performing some waiter or waitress duties, these people may work between meal hours in the dining area. During this period they see that table settings, service stands, and the various working supplies in dining areas are available and in place for the next meal. The position is responsible to the hostess, host, or headwaiter, depending on the type of organization.

LIQUOR CONTROLLERS.   Liquor controllers are responsible for compiling statistics of liquor costs, sales, profits, and losses. They inventory the bars as needed, sometimes daily, and prepare the daily consumption report that is forwarded to the auditing office. They issue merchandise to all bar areas but usually do not buy liquor. Instead, they forward purchase orders to a central purchase agent, who may order for several hotels in a chain. The position is responsible to the auditor or manager.

SOCIAL DIRECTORS.   These people have charge of social affairs. They take care of the guests' comfort, entertainment, and amusement. They arrange social functions such as recreational outings, luncheons, fashion shows, dinners, stage shows, card-playing sessions, and dances. The social director is responsible to the manager.

SALES MANAGERS.   These people are responsible for the development and operation of the sales department. They maintain files on past group business. They work with the social director and promotion office on advertising for programs. They develop sales contacts and may do some traveling to other areas to bring new business into the establishment. The position is responsible to the manager.

DIETITIANS.   The title of "dietitian" refers in its broadest sense to several groups of professional people. A dietitian may be:

1.   an administrative dietitian
2.   a therapeutic dietitian
3.   a teacher
4.   a research worker
5.   a food consultant
6.   a public health nutritionist

We will concern ourselves with the duties performed by administrative dietitians and therapeutic dietitians.

Administrative dietitians are in charge of large-scale food service operations. They use the principles of nutrition and good management in the operation of an entire food department. The facility may be an institution, school, university, hospital, or other private or governmental establishment. The duties performed may include selecting, training, and overseeing workers and supervisors; buying, preparing, and serving food; selecting, buying, and using equipment and supplies; designing the layout of the working department; and maintaining required reports and records. Depending on the type, size, and organizational structure of the food operation, dietitians may direct a dietary department, establishing policy and coordinating the dietary services. In this capacity, dietitians are responsible for the successful operation of a department within a predescribed budget as well as the direction of department activities to conform with activities of other departments. Administrative dietitians may in general perform the same tasks as a food service manager and have the same staff available to assist with the managerial duties. The title of "food service manager" is usually used by contract feeding firms. If they have a contract with an institution, the firm provides all the management service and experience in the proper and efficient operation of the food service department.

Therapeutic dietitians plan and supervise the preparation of meals for patients who require special diets. The nutritive value of foods is the most important consideration in preparing such diets. Therapeutic dietitians may consult with a physician and with the patient to learn his or her preferences in planning a diet. They may also discuss diet care with the patient's family upon her or his leaving the hospital. In small institutions administrative dietitians may also perform the work of therapeutic dietitians. This position may be responsible to an administrator, business manager, or food service director, depending on the size and type of institution.

chapter 6

departments, stations, and equipment in the front of the house

The front of the house activities differ from house to house, but common to all is personnel providing service to the dining public in a defined area. In some establishments the serving area is a back of the house function. The front of the house layout, design, and operating activities differ in the various kinds of operations. Front of the house facilities may be one of the following or they may be a combination of several:

CAFETERIA.   A self-service facility serving one or all meals. Items are sold on individual basis. Very little service is rendered by personnel. The service area, which is the cafeteria counter, may or may not be a part of the dining room.

COFFEE SHOP.   An informal dining area where light refreshments or complete meals are provided. Usually both counter service and table service are available. The preparation and pickup area may be seen by the public; however, the public does not come in contact with it. The facilities may also be arranged in such a way that none of the back of the house functions are visible.

DINING ROOM.   An eating area in a large establishment or an independent operation. The front of the house is clearly defined in both these settings. If the dining room is an independent restaurant, the service is usually more elaborate and the selection of food more inclusive. With this also comes higher prices and more luxurious surroundings.

Figure 6-1. A hotel dining room in California.

DRIVE-IN. An eating establishment laid out so that patrons can be accommodated while remaining in their automobiles. A wise operator quickly realizes that the area defined for car parking is the front of the house. The same rules that pertain to tidiness, uniforms, training, and quality of service rendered are as vital in this operation as in any of the others mentioned.

CATERING SERVICE. An establishment that provides food and services for social affairs. Most often the food is served but not cooked in the home, school, factory, etc. Then again, the serving and dining areas may be in one location. Generally the area where the guests are dining is considered the front of the house.

IN-PLANT FEEDING. A service that prepares and dispenses food to a regular group of plant workers. The area where dining takes place is the front of the house.

HOTEL BANQUET DEPARTMENT. A hotel offers the largest variety of front of the house facilities for the dining public. A busy hotel considers routine the daily handling of large numbers. The following kinds of social events take place in the banquet department of a hotel:

1. a private breakfast	7. a breakfast buffet
2. a private luncheon	8. a cocktail party
3. a private dinner	9. a buffet
4. a cocktail supper	10. a dinner dance
5. a wedding reception	11. a festive dinner
6. an afternoon tea	

SPECIALTY ROOMS. A specialty room, for example a Hawaiian room, may offer authentic food and decor of a distant land.

PARTY ROOMS. Areas used for private functions. Special menus are usually prepared although service from regular menus can be arranged in these rooms, depending upon the size of the party. Party rooms are available in most restaurants. They are operated similarly to a hotel banquet department but on a smaller scale. These rooms are front of the house areas.

COCKTAIL LOUNGES. If a dining room is filled and guests must wait for a table for dinner, they are usually invited to have a cocktail in the lounge until their tables are ready. At that time they will be paged. It serves this function as well as the usual one of providing social enjoyment to patrons. This is a front of the house area.

In general, wherever the public is dining is where the front of the house is located. This is the place where the employees are onstage.

Supporting Facilities in the Front of the House

In addition to the front of the house areas that are designated as the areas for dining, there are supporting stations and facilities that must not be overlooked. These facilities are located and designed in such a way as to make the handling of guests most efficient. Some of these facilities are:

CHECKROOM.   This department is used for checking the wraps of the dining guests. It is also used for holding small packages, umbrellas, and overshoes. This is a front of the house area.

CASHIER.   All food checks and, sometimes, cocktail checks are paid at this station. Some establishments have this department in the back of the house. That depends upon the size of the establishment. If this is the case, the waiter will collect the payment and return the change to the guests.

REST ROOMS.   The public rest rooms are usually in the front of the house. Facilities for personnel are in the back of the house.

OFFICES.   The "working" offices are most often behind the scenes. The work routines of a busy office add little to a dining setting.

CATERING OFFICES.   These offices are "show" offices. They are usually found in a large hotel or club. This office functions as a selling office. Pictures of social affairs, flowers, silver pieces, and attractive appointments are important to this post. The catering office is a front of the house area.

ROOM SERVICE.   This may range from a refreshing beverage to a snack to a complete meal. Service may vary from a tray to a portable table to a bed tray. Employees in this area perform a front of the house duty.

SERVICE STAND OR STATION.   This is a unit that houses all the working supplies needed by service personnel in the performance of their duties. It may be small or large and it may include ice, water, and refrigeration. The station may be simple in design and totally visible or hidden behind a partition or decorative screen.

GIFT SHOP.   An added convenience for the dining patron. It is usually located close to the checkroom. Patrons that are waiting may use this opportunity to mill and browse.

FRONT OF THE HOUSE
EQUIPMENT

Equipment that varies in purpose, design, and material will be found in the front of the house. Chairs, tables, service stands, linens, china, silver, glassware, carts, beverage-dispensing units, hot and cold food-holding units, and eating counters are some of the pieces of equipment.

Since food service operations have different objectives, a large selection of equipment is available. For one operation a piece of equipment may be used just as it comes from the factory. In another establishment the same piece of equipment may require a special finish to fit into the decorative scheme and overall setting of the dining area.

Figure 6-2.   A formal table setting.

A piece of equipment for the front of the house may be ordered in a special color, choice of fabric, type of light fixture, and construction material.

Service units in a dining area may be designed to hold such items as silverware, glasses, china, linens, and placemats in reserve. A fresh water hookup may also be included. These units can also be provided with hot and cold compartments for holding food and beverage items at the proper temperature. This type of insulated compartment can keep food at an ideal temperature for maximum retention of nutrition and appetite appeal.

A large manufacturing plant that wants to serve well-cooked, appetizing food to large numbers of people in a short period of time would require equipment specifically designed for this purpose. An attractively appointed dining room with fine cuisine and impeccable service would require still different pieces of equipment. This is true of all accommodations found in the front of the house. Chairs, tables, tabletops, coffee servers, china, glassware, and other dining room pieces are chosen from a large selection. A chair in use in a fast turnover coffee shop that has a simple menu would generally differ from a chair in a dining room with fine service, a formal atmosphere, and a leisurely pace of dining.

Figures 6-3 through 6-13 show some of the equipment used in food service operations.

In a small operation, food is generally hand-transported from the back of the house to the dining area. Often the waiter or waitress just has to go a few steps to the kitchen to pick up an order. However, in larger operations, food and utensils often have to be transported over a distance and in large quantities. Figure 6-3 illustrates some of the carts that might be used. The bussing cart (a) is used for storing and bussing items in the dining area. The service wagon (b) is used for cooking near the table or keeping foods warm in the dining area. For cold foods, such as seafood cocktail, an ice cart (c) is sometimes used. The dessert or pastry cart (d) is wheeled to the table for the customer to make a choice. The food carrier (e) uses canned heat to keep food warm while being transported to a room where it will be eaten. This kind of carrier is often used for hotel room service.

In large establishments it is sometimes necessary to keep foods or beverages hot for a period of time. In Figure 6-4 some of the common warmers are shown. The samovar (a) dispenses hot liquids such as coffee or tea. The chafing dishes (b), (c), and (d) are often used for buffets. The rechaud lamp (e) is commonly used for heating. Part (1) is an intensifier and (2) is a snuffer for use in this lamp.

Figure 6-3.   Food carts.

Figure 6-4.   Serving pieces with warmers.

Figure 6-5 shows covered servers for keeping food warm while transporting it. The coffee hottle (a) fits on and into the cup. Covers such as those shown in (b) are useful for dishes from breakfast through dinner.

Meat is for the most part carved in the kitchen and served on individual plates. However, some restaurants prefer to carve the meat to the customer's order either buffet style or at individual tables. Some meat holders (Figure 6-6) used in the front of the house are (a) a wooden plank on which the meat (or fish) can be broiled; (b) a ham holder for carving; and (c) a roast holder.

Some wines are best when served chilled. In fancy establishments wine coolers such as the two shown in Figure 6-7 might be used. Item (a) is on a stand for serving from a place near the table and (b) is for use on the table.

Figure 6-8 shows a dish for serving cold foods, such as seafood, fruits, or soups. The base has ice in it and the food is put in the upper dish or liner.

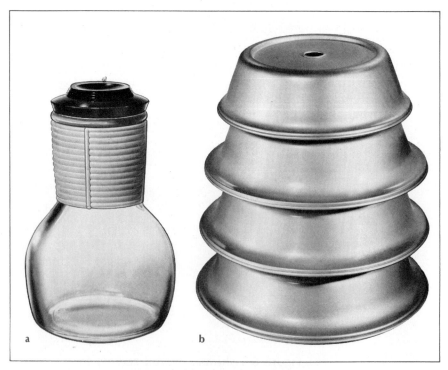

Figure 6-5.   Covers and insulated servers keep foods hot.

Various styles of pitchers (Figure 6-9) are used for both hot and cold liquids. Some typical ones are (a) a coffee server; (b) a water or juice pitcher; and (c) a gravy boat.

Large serving dishes (Figure 6-10) are useful for buffets or large dinner parties. Item (a) is a lazy susan. Items (b) and (c) are Escoffier dishes which come in a variety of sizes and shapes. The tray often serves also as a lid.

Figure 6-11 through 6-13 show some items that are used at each table.

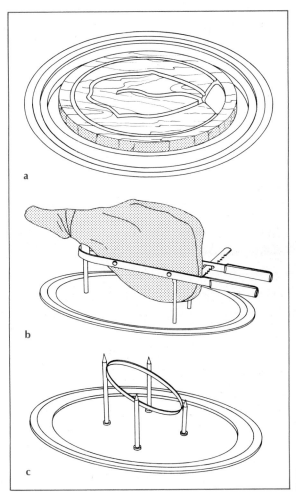

a

b

c

Figure 6-6. Various dishes for serving meats.

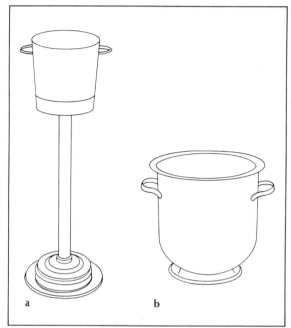

a   b

Figure 6-7. Wine coolers.

Figure 6-8. A dish for serving cold foods.

a

b

c

Figure 6-9.   Hot and cold pitchers.

a

b

c

Figure 6-10.   Large serving dishes.

Figure 6-11. Some individual table items are (a) sugar and creamer; (b) oyster cracker dish; (c) bread basket; and (d) celery tray.

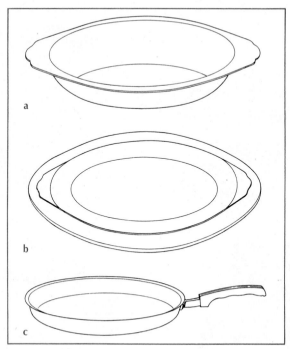

Figure 6-12. Main dishes are sometimes cooked and served in the same dish or pot. Casseroles or egg dishes are often served in an (a) au gratin dish. A sizzle platter (b) sometimes has a wood liner or board. A crepe suzette pan (c) can be used for making this dessert at a side table right near the guests.

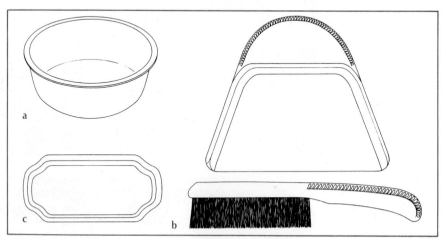

Figure 6-13. After-dinner items include (a) a finger bowl; (b) a bread crumber; and (c) a cash tray.

part III

Cookware

the back of the house—
job titles, departments,
stations, and equipment

chapter 7

the back
of the house—
job titles

The workers in the back of the house are the chef, pastry chef, broiler cook, steward, butcher, timekeeper, etc.

Some of the departments in the back of the house are the hot range, pantry, cold meat, storeroom, ware washing, bakery, butcher shop, preparation rooms, service bar, etc. The back of the house is basically the production area of the establishment. This is where the raw materials are first delivered, cleaned, stored, and ultimately prepared for the patron. Sometimes this is all done in a matter of minutes. The kitchen and its related stations and departments are arranged to do a particular job. There is no such thing as a universal kitchen. Kitchens vary according to stations and departments. They are designed to make specific job objectives easier to accomplish. The kitchen is usually the largest and the busiest place in the back of the house. This is where the front and the back of the house personnel come in contact with one another and work together to please the waiting patron. It is in this area that the orders are turned in, prepared, and picked up. A back of the house that is well designed is planned so that work is done in a steady flow of movement. There is little or no backtracking or cross motion.

There may be as few as one to five or as many as several hundred working in this area.

JOB TITLES IN THE BACK OF THE HOUSE

For a clearer understanding of the jobs performed by the back of the house personnel, we have listed job titles with a description of the duties of and the order of responsibility of a particular job.

70

Work clothes or uniforms are worn by these employees. Uniforms are customarily supplied by employers.

EXECUTIVE CHEFS. These people are usually employed in the bigger operations doing a large volume of business. The type of establishment may or may not be formal, but it always feeds large numbers of people daily. The duties performed by executive chefs depend on the structure of the organization within the establishment, the management policy, and individual ability. They generally supervise and coordinate the buying, storage, and preparation of all food. Administrative ability is important in this capacity. Executive chefs oversee the work of chefs, cooks, and other kitchen employees. They may supervise as many as several hundred workers. They keep all payroll records, etc. The position is responsible to the general manager, food service director, or owner, depending on the type of food operation in which the executive chef is employed.

CHEFS OR FIRST COOKS. Chefs work closely with the executive chef. In some establishments they are known as "sous chefs." They may be in charge of a kitchen or a department in a large installation and have to supervise and assist from one to ten cooks. In a smaller operation where there is no executive chef, those duties are covered by the first cook, who is often referred to as a "working chef." The position is responsible to the executive chef or manager.

COOKS OR SECOND COOKS. These workers prepare varied foods. They also supervise the production crew in preparing, cooking, and serving meats and vegetables as directed by the chef or the manager. In a small establishment or one in which the owner is very active in food preparation, the second cook performs some of the duties of the chef.

COOK APPRENTICES OR HELPERS. These are workers that assist the cook in the general handling and preparation of food. They receive instructions from the cook to whom they are assigned and help prepare and cook foods. Cook apprentices work in various departments as directed. The position is responsible to the chef.

DINNER COOKS. The duties of dinner cooks vary among establishments. This position is found mostly in middle-sized places of business. These people prepare, cook, season, and portion all foodstuffs for the noon and or evening meal. They handle all the stewing, roasting, broiling, braising, and other cooking of meat. The dinner cook is responsible to the chef.

FRY COOKS.   Cooks in this position prepare meats, fish, fowl, fruits, eggs, and vegetables in a pan of deep or shallow fat. They are responsible to the chef.

GARDE-MANGERS OR COLD MEAT PERSONS.   These people prepare and work with all cold meat, fish, and poultry dishes. They prepare appetizers or hors d'oeuvres such as canapes. They make all salad dressings and mayonnaise according to recipe. They work with leftover foods to make appetizing dishes. In some situations they will open and serve clams and oysters and prepare other fish for service. They may also act as the fish butcher. If a house serves paté maison, the garde-manger prepares it. The position is responsible to the chef.

KITCHEN MEN OR WOMEN.   These workers scrub and scour worktables, refrigerators, and other equipment and general work areas. The position is responsible to the kitchen steward or chef.

ASSISTANT GARDE-MANGERS OR SANDWICH PERSONS.   These people assist the garde-manger. They usually perform simple tasks such as slicing and grinding meat and making sandwiches. They are responsible to the chef.

STEWARDS.   In some establishments where there is no buyer or purchasing agent, stewards purchase foodstuffs and kitchen supplies either on their own responsibility or after review with the executive chef. Stewards inspect the delivery of these items and maintain the necessary controls for efficient issuing of food to cooks. In general stewards are in charge of all back of the house personnel not engaged in cooking. They attempt to keep a sufficient supply of foodstuffs on hand and work closely with the chef to see that no waste occurs. They may maintain detailed cost figures of purchases and turn in a daily purchase report to the auditing department. They may summarize each day's issues and report item costs daily to auditing. In larger establishments stewards may have other supervisors to assist, such as a kitchen steward and a banquet steward. In some larger places of business they may oversee the making and serving of salads, fruits, juices, relishes, coffee, and other foods prepared in the pantry. The position is responsible to the chef or to the manager.

KITCHEN STEWARDS.   These people work under the general supervision of the steward. They supervise employees in the food department who are not actively engaged in food preparation such as dishwashers, pantry workers, storeroom help, etc. Kitchen stewards are responsible for cleanliness, economy in operations, and efficiency of workers. They see that all dish warmers or cold counters have the china, glass, and silver required for each meal's service. They work closely with the chef and are responsible to the steward.

BANQUET STEWARDS.   They supervise the temporary banquet employees and see that food is delivered to dining room as soon as possible. They help control idle talking, noise, and confusion on the part of waiters and kitchen personnel while they are in the back of the house. In general, they see to it that all banquet kitchen equipment as well as the kitchen itself is returned to a clean and ready stage following any function. They may have to bring some equipment from the main kitchen and must make sure it is returned when it is no longer in use. The position is usually responsible to the steward.

ICE CREAM MEN OR WOMEN.   These people mix, prepare, cook, and freeze ingredients to make all frozen desserts. They may also cook the sauces, fruits, and syrups that are used with them. The position is responsible to the chef. In many establishments they are one of the pastry chef's or baker's crew.

SHORT ORDER COOKS.   These people cook to order and serve steaks, chops, cutlets, eggs, and other quickly prepared foods to waiters or to counter customers. They may also serve foods from a steam table that were cooked in the main kitchen. They work in cafeterias, lunchrooms, grills, coffee shops, or snack areas. The position is responsible to the chef.

VEGETABLE COOKS.   These people take care of all fresh vegetables, cleaning and cutting them. They cook all fresh, frozen, dehy-

drated, and canned vegetables. Some vegetables they may prepare for direct consumption and some they may prepare for other
cooks to complete or use in cooking. The position is responsible
to the chef.

BREAKFAST COOKS.   They prepare and cook to order all breakfast
items that are fried or broiled. During the day they may assist the
fry cook or broiler cook. They are responsible to the chef.

BROILER COOKS.   These people work mostly on the broiler cooking
meat, fish, and poultry. They also garnish and prepare the broiled
food for service to patrons. They are usually employed in the
larger, more high-class hotels or restaurants. They may work on
gas, charcoal, or charbroil stoves. The position is responsible to
the chef.

COOKS' HELPERS.   These people assist in the various departments of
the kitchen, as the chef or supervisor directs. They work under
supervision on a variety of tasks. The nature of the work brings
them in contact with all the working departments in the preparation and production areas. This is an excellent way for a young as-
pirant to begin the training process.

SAUCE COOKS.   These people prepare and cook all the sauces that are
to be used in the kitchen. They also prepare the meat, fish, and
poultry stock broths, as well as soups. This job is usually found in
the larger, more formal hotels and restaurants.

SWING COOKS.   These people substitute for or assist all the cooks in
the kitchen. They relieve cooks during illness, vacations, days off,
or rush periods. This job is usually found only in the larger establishments. Responsibility is to the chef.

BUTCHERS (Meat Cutters).   These people obtain meat from the
steward and are responsible for all meat prior to cooking. They
cut, trim, and prepare meats for all forms of cooking. They are
responsible for all storage and handling of meat so that it is
used to its best advantage. They prepare and have all items that
are on the bill of fare ready for cooking. They also do this for any
special function that is scheduled. In some establishments they
make corned beef and sausages besides butchering all cuts of

Figure 7-1. Executive chef and Meat cutter preparing for a banquet.

meat for cooking by others. The position is responsible to the chef.

BUTCHERS' HELPERS. These people assist the butcher in meat cutting. If no chicken and fish butcher is employed, they may work in this area as well. They also deliver meat from the ice box to the cooking department. The position is responsible to the chef.

CHICKEN AND FISH BUTCHERS. These people usually work under the direction of the meat butcher and are responsible for cutting the food into portions. They clean, trim, and cut seafood and fowl into the individual orders. The position is responsible to the chef.

KITCHEN RUNNERS. Their exact duties vary, depending on the nature of the establishment and its physical layout. They carry food by hand or truck from the storeroom to the kitchen or from the kitchen to various departments or other points in the kitchen. They also do odd jobs such as storing leftover foods, cleaning equipment, preparing vegetables, preparing fruit juices, etc. The position is responsible to the chef.

KITCHEN MANAGERS. These workers are general supervisors over all the production personnel in the kitchen areas. They are usually responsible to the restaurant manager. The position exists chiefly in those operations where a chef or steward is not employed. They supervise the buying, storing, and preparation of all food. They may also make menus and utilize leftovers. They take regular inventory and reorder when necessary. Kitchen managers are responsible to the restaurant manager.

FOOD SERVICE DIRECTORS. These workers exercise general supervision over all production areas in one or more kitchens. They are also responsible for all the service that may be needed on counters and in the dining rooms. This position is usually found in a large institution. Food service directors are responsible for the buying of food, its storage, its preparation, and the service necessary to handle large groups. Very little cooking is done to order in this type of operation. A formal college education in dietetics or comparable subjects is desirable. The position is usually responsible to the business manager of an institution such as a university or hospital.

OYSTER MEN OR WOMEN. These individuals shuck oysters and clams. They prepare shrimp, crab, and lobster for cocktail usage. This position is found in a specialty house or large hotel. In other kitchens this work may be done by the butcher or pantry person. Oyster persons are responsible to the chef.

PANTRYMEN OR PANTRYWOMEN. These workers draw from the storeroom all the raw materials needed to prepare all the fruit or vegetable salads, seafood cocktails, canapés, and other cold dishes. Pantry workers serve these items to waiters and waitresses. If there is no cold meat department, they slice and portion cold meats and cheeses. They also serve desserts and side dishes such as bread and butter. They make sandwiches and prepare garnishes for other departments.

HEAD PANTRYMEN OR PANTRYWOMEN. These people supervise and assist pantry workers in the handling and processing of all cold food in the pantry. They are responsible to the chef. Pantry heads draw all materials for fruit, fruit juice and cereal service, raw salads, bread, rolls, butter, milk, and cream. In some establishments they also dispense cheese and ice cream desserts that are not specially prepared by others. Coffee, tea, and their substitutes may also be served from here.

PASTRY CHEFS. These people supervise the preparation of desserts, pastries, frozen desserts, fondants, fillings, and fancy sugar decorations. They will have pastry cooks working under them. If the establishment has the equipment to produce its own breads and rolls, they will also supervise bakers. Pastry chefs oversee the bread and pastry needs of all kitchens and departments in a large hotel, club, or restaurant. This position is a creative one and requires the ability to coordinate the activity of others. Pastry chefs are responsible to the chef.

PASTRY COOKS. These workers mix batters as needed and produce the normal day-to-day items such as butters, spreads, cookies, pastries, and cakes. They help in the making of fancy pieces. They may make pies. They usually supervise a pastry cook helper who works the dough, cleans the equipment, and does other miscellaneous duties. The position is responsible to the chef.

PASTRY COOK HELPERS. These people work closely under a pastry cook. They carry supplies to and from the bakery. They see to the cleanliness of all the equipment in the bakery and make certain that all items are usable and ready. They perform routine tasks that they are taught to handle. The position is responsible to the pastry chef.

PIE MAKERS. These people make all the pie fillings. They usually work in large restaurants where there is no pastry cook. They are responsible to the pastry chef or the chef.

RECEIVING CLERKS. These employees are generally a storeroom manager's first assistant. They run the storeroom in the manager's absence. They receive and store all deliveries, making sure that each is entered in the storeroom receiving book. This is particularly important when deliveries are made without an invoice. Most establishments provide a form of their own on which such deliveries must be entered. To avoid subsequent misunderstandings this should be done at the receiving dock. Receiving clerks assist in taking inventory and keep the storeroom manager posted on which items may need reordering. In some institutional operations where no steward is employed, these workers receive, store, distribute, and keep records of deliveries made on items that have been purchased by the dietician, chef, purchasing department, or manager.

POT WASHERS. These people thoroughly clean all cooking utensils, pots and pans, and portable kitchen equipment. They also return these things to stations where they are used. Pot washers work under the direction of the kitchen steward.

PURCHASING AGENTS. These people purchase some foodstuffs, kitchen supplies, and equipment. They usually work in a very large chain and supplement the purchases of the local steward by making large contracts for several products. They work very closely with all the chefs and stewards. The position is responsible to the manager or a corporate officer in the home office. As the name implies, this person is in charge of the purchase of all supplies with the exception of capital goods such as furniture and fixed equipment. When purchasing agents are employed, they have supervision over any purchases made by the steward or replenishments ordered by the storekeeper. They usually provide specifications for the receiving department to check the goods received. The position is responsible to the management.

SOUS CHEFS. These are assistants to an executive chef in a larger restaurant or hotel. They supervise the cooks in the preparation and cooking of food. They see that food is properly prepared. They are in charge of the kitchen in the absence of the executive chef. During serving hours they may be stationed in front of the cooking range calling in orders. They also check as the plates are filled to see that food is prepared as ordered. They watch for garnishments and give instructions and criticism as needed. A sous chef would not be employed where the chef in charge is a working chef doing some of the cooking. The position is responsible to the executive chef.

NIGHT CHEFS. These workers remain on duty at night and have charge of the kitchen at that time. They are working chefs supervised by the executive chef. The position is responsible to the executive chef. In many establishments, when demand for service decreases, the night chef prepares the fancy vegetables or potatoes that are required in the following day's menus.

BAKERS. These people bake bread, rolls, muffins, and biscuits for use in dining rooms of hotels and restaurants. They make dough according to recipes and then cut and shape the dough by hand or machine. In smaller establishments where there is no pastry chef, the baker may also make the pies, cakes, and pastries. The position is responsible to the chef.

BENCH MEN OR WOMEN. These workers knead, cut, and shape dough, preparing it for baking. The position is found in larger establishments and is responsible to the pastry chef.

OVEN MEN OR WOMEN. These workers bake the dough and shelve it. The position is found in large establishments.

NIGHT BAKERS. These workers mix the dough and shape it for the following day's baking. The position is found in larger establishments and is responsible to the pastry chef.

COFFEE MEN OR WOMEN. These people usually work in the pantry. They make all hot beverages during the rush periods. They clean and maintain the equipment used. The position is responsible to the chef.

WINE STEWARDS. These people are in charge of storing wines and liquors and issuing them upon properly signed requisitions. When authorized by the purchasing agent or management, they may purchase beverages directly from outside salespeople. They may assist in the liquor control duties of the auditing department. They inspect and approve bills for payment. They oversee setups for party bars. They supervise the wine room and see to proper storage conditions. The position is responsible to the manager.

CELLAR MEN OR WOMEN. These workers receive and store beverages in storage rooms and fill requisitions to the front or service bars. They maintain a running inventory of stock. They advise the wine steward when additional supplies are needed. They may prepare some special syrups and maintain the gas and syrups in the dispensing units of the bar. The cellar person is responsible to the wine steward and may perform other duties as the steward directs.

DISHWASHERS (Machine or Hand). These people receive, sort, and scrape all china, glassware, and silverware that is returned from the dining areas for washing. When cleaned, they return the wares to warm or cold cabinets and shelves for their next use. Dish washers work under the kitchen steward.

GARBAGE MEN OR WOMEN. These people are employed in large establishments. They collect garbage from work stations and transport it to the garbage room on hand trucks. They dump the garbage on a raking table or the floor and examine it for lost silverware, etc. They clean the garbage cans and the garbage room with hot water and steam. They are responsible to the kitchen steward.

GLASS WASHERS. These people sort, scrape, wash, and rinse all glassware such as pitchers, plates, and dishes. Washing is usually done by machine. These workers are found in the larger establishments. They are responsible to the kitchen steward.

SILVER MEN OR WOMEN. These workers wash, burnish, and remove tarnish from flat and hollow silverware. They may sharpen cutting knives, buff silverware, and also take care of other special equipment. The people working in this position are also responsible to the kitchen steward.

SANITATION MEN OR WOMEN. This is a title given to those who work as porters, dishwashers, kitchen persons, and pot washers. It is their job to keep dishes, cooking utensils, equipment, and floors clean. They return all wares used in cooking and serving food or beverages to the proper location for their next use. A large variety of modern machines simplify the work procedures of these jobs. Many young people begin their careers in the food industry by working in these departments. From here they can observe the workings of different departments. Sanitation men and women are usually directed by the kitchen steward. The steward makes sure that on any day and every day a health department inspection would approve of the kitchen's sanitary conditions.

STOREROOM PERSONS OR STOREKEEPERS.   These individuals are responsible for receiving, inspecting, counting, and storing all food and other articles delivered to their domain. This may be a dock or an area in the storeroom. They are responsible for filling all requisitions and, under the instructions of the house auditor, for keeping a journal in a book or loose-leaf ledger of all goods received and delivered. The names of the purveyors, the costs, descriptions of articles, and other required information are recorded. Storekeepers take monthly inventories with the auditor and help maintain a current inventory. They may order supplies if authorized. They wear work clothes and a white frock most of the time. They are responsible to the steward.

chapter 8

departments, stations, and equipment in the back of the house

DEPARTMENTS AND STATIONS IN THE BACK OF THE HOUSE

The back of the house may consist of several very specialized departments with highly skilled people working in each. These employees are trained to do a certain phase of food preparation work. They spend very little time, if any, doing other types of cooking. The work areas may include several departments and stations or only one or two, depending on the size of the operation and the complexity of the food services offered. We will consider departments that are found in the back of the house. In some operations, a department we describe as independent may be combined with another. This depends on the size and type of service being offered. An example of this would be a combined pantry and cold meat department.

For ease of understanding, each department, and the food it prepares or stores, is listed under two groupings: food and nonfood departments.

Food Departments

PANTRY. Salads, desserts, milk, dips, appetizers, fruits and juices, cereals, crackers, butter, and ice cream are dealt with here.

MAIN COOKING (Ranges or Hot Line). This is where meats are roasted, broiled, fried, steamed, baked, or boiled. Soups, vegetables, and sauces are also prepared here.

82

BAKERY. In most establishments this is a production department only. All breads, pastries, and baked specialty items are made here. These products are served mostly from the pantry.

STOREROOM. Edible and nonedible supplies including canned items, dry foods, frozen foods, etc., are kept here.

DIET KITCHEN (in Large Hospitals). This is where food is prepared for patients on therapeutic diets.

MEAT PREPARATION (Butcher Shop). All beef, pork, lamb, veal, poultry, sea food, etc., are prepared for cooking here.

VEGETABLE PREPARATION ROOM. The cleaning, slicing, and preparing of vegetables such as onions, carrots, potatoes, lettuce, etc., are done here.

ICE CREAM ROOM. In most establishments this is a production department for ice creams, sherbets, bombs, and frozen cream specialty desserts. Ice cream products are usually served from the pantry.

The departments that are listed below are generally those that are found in the larger operations or in specialty houses. In the smaller operations, the products of these departments are made in the pantry with the exception of the cooking of shellfish. That would be done in the main cooking section.

COLD MEAT (in Some Places Called "Garde Manger"). All cold meats and sauces, appetizers, meat salads, sandwiches, and cold hors d'oeuvres are handled here.

SALAD PREPARATION ROOM. An area for the preparation of large amounts of salads and relishes.

DESSERT PREPARATION ROOM. Desserts from the bakery and ice cream rooms are finished here.

SANDWICH ROOM. This area is found frequently in institutions where large numbers of sandwiches are prepared daily.

OYSTER KITCHEN. The cooking of shellfish and the opening and serving of all raw shellfish are done here.

COFFEE STATION. This is not a department but, because of its importance in size and location, it is included in this section. The coffee station is placed so that coffee can be picked up as service personnel leave the kitchen. In some operations it may be a part of the pantry.

SERVING FACILITY. The serving facility may be a part of the back of the house station or department where the food is prepared and dished up for service personnel to pick up and present to the guest. The serving facility is also found in a cafeteria where the food is placed on the plate before the patron.

BANQUET SERVING PANTRY OR KITCHEN. The banquet serving pantry is that area where banquet foods are served. The food is cooked in the central kitchen and then transported to this area for dishing up. The banquet serving area is equipped with special equipment, utensils, china, and glassware that are used only for parties. The area may also be a special banquet kitchen where all the food is cooked and served and all the utensils, china, and glassware are washed and stored.

ROOM SERVICE. Most hotels and motor hotels have some form of room service. These vary from a very limited to an extensive selection of food items that are served in the guest rooms. Food served to a patient in a hospital room is also a form of room service. In the hospital the selection may or may not be made by the patient. In any case it is served systematically from the kitchen with many other meals. In the hotel the order is taken by a special operator who records and relays it to the room service waiter. Hotel and hospital room services may differ in the way the order is taken, in the reason for a choice, and in the preparation. However, the concern of keeping the food warm or cold is similar when transporting to patients or guest rooms. It is important in both cases to be courteous and to provide efficient service.

THE MAIN KITCHEN. The main kitchen may contain all or some of the above departments, depending on the size of the operation. (See Figure 8-1.)

Figure 8-1. The various preparation areas of a large institutional kitchen.

The kitchen should be located so that it is as close as possible to the dining room. It should be a very short distance from the area where the food is finally dished up and taken to the patron for his or her pleasure and enjoyment. The size of the kitchen and the equipment placed in the kitchen depend upon the type of food that is to be produced, the type of service that is to be given, and the number of people to be served.

There is one basic principle that is so many times overlooked. If the working space is either too big and scattered or too small, the business of catering to guests cannot be carried on effectively, efficiently, or profitably. Too frequently the kitchen is the last place to be designed. As a result, what space is left in the overall planning is given to the kitchen.

The best relationship develops between service personnel and patrons when there is no time wasted in running for food or supplies. The happy and productive quality that is so important in the dining room flourishes when there is a well-planned flow from raw material to finished product. At times all this is accomplished in a matter of minutes. Limiting the steps that have to be taken and providing the necessary equipment make the difference between happy patrons and employees and patrons and employees that are both dissatisfied.

The kitchen is, without a doubt, the most fascinating part of a hotel, restaurant, or institution. Upon entering the kitchen one sees a surprisingly lively picture of activity. It takes knowledge of kitchen organization to find one's way about this center of action.

Here one sees the artist at work, the worker at his or her job, and the manager surrounded by swift and continual human movement. Here is where food is transformed from raw material to finished product in the shortest possible time. It takes an individual with a talent for organization to meet the many demands of such an establishment.

The size and installations of the main kitchen depend on the foods that are being served, the number and size of dining rooms being serviced, and the type of service to be provided in the dining rooms or other serving areas.

Nonfood Areas in the Back of the House

The service bar is used in dispensing soft and alcoholic beverages to the dining area.

The wine room is the storage and controlling area for all beverages.

The garbage room is the collection point for garbage. Containers from all departments are emptied and sanitized. Care is taken to retrieve silverware, glasses, and china that may get into the containers.

The silver room is for repairing, cleaning, burnishing, and storing all surplus flatware and hollow ware.

The glass washing area is for washing and sterilizing all glassware.

The china and silverware washing area is for washing, rinsing, and putting away tableware.

The pot washing area is for cleaning cooking equipment and utensils.

The chef's office is the area where the chef writes menus and does other paperwork.

The cloakrooms, toilets, and showers are for employee needs and convenience. Every establishment must have facilities for the employees to wash their hands before returning to their stations.

The employee dining room is for the dining needs and convenience of employees. The employee dining room may provide, in addition to meals, facilities for off-duty employees to purchase soft drinks, etc., from vending machines.

The receiving area is outside the storeroom where material is deposited for checking.

The silver storage area is where extra silver is kept.

The china and glass storage is the area for storing the reserve supply of china and glass.

The loading dock is an area set aside for deliveries that are to be made. Outgoing items also leave from this point.

BACK OF THE HOUSE EQUIPMENT AND UTENSILS

Kitchen Equipment

A great variety of equipment is available today to aid the food service operator. Some are improved versions of what has been available before. Others are new and having revolutionizing results. The choice of equipment depends on the scope of the operation and the space available. For how many people must a meal be prepared? Is a large selection of food prepared or a large quantity? It is important that the equipment have certain features.

1. It must have a smooth surface and be easy to clean.
2. Parts that touch food need to be removable for cleaning.
3. Moving parts of machine have to be covered for safety.
4. Switches should be easy to reach and easy to handle.
5. Safety devices that protect against overloading must be installed.
6. There must be no cables, pulleys, or counter weights to go out of adjustment.
7. There is nothing that will rust, corrode, chip, warp, or peel.
8. All nuts, bolts, or rivets must be kept tight so as to avoid leakage.

There is one crucial fact to remember when buying equipment: Know what you are getting before you place the order.

COUNTER MODELS. Almost every type of equipment found in today's kitchens is available in counter models. Units are made that can be readily combined into series that provide a versatile, efficient, and streamlined arrangement. These are suitable for either front or back of the house use. Broilers, fryers, open tops, grills, etc., can all be provided in a neat unit that is easily accessible and to which additions can be made to grow with an establishment's needs.

WHAT TYPE TO BUY. Beginning with equipment for storage, refrigeration, mixing, cooking, baking, roasting, serving, and dishwashing, equipment can be tailored to a particular operation. This does not mean that every piece of equipment has to be made to order. The buyer knows what is needed and has so much to select from that she or he can be certain of getting the right items.

REMEMBER. Decide first what you are going to serve—what is going to be on the menu. Then buy the equipment that will do that job.

ELECTRIC, GAS, OR STEAM? Modern cookery demands can be met by different methods of heating and most equipment can be ordered to suit a particular house. Steam is very valuable in a large operation and is most readily available. If it is not, steam can be obtained either electrically or by gas heat.

COOKING UTENSILS. Because of the more frequent use and higher temperatures of commercial cooking, pots and pans are generally of heavier gauge metal than those found in a well-equipped home. They come in a variety of shapes and sizes.

Illustrations of the most common utensils are shown in the succeeding pages. Many have been especially designed to meet the exacting demands of the great feeding industry.

METALS. Utensils of aluminum, copper, and stainless steel are chiefly used today.

Aluminum is very light. It is cheap and easy to clean. Some special hotel ware may be reinforced by a bimetal layer on the bottom for longer life and better heat conduction. Handles should be riveted. Steel wool should not be used to clean aluminum. It will injure the surface.

Copper has always been popular because it distributes heat better than any other metal. However, copper is expensive. It is retinned on the interior to prevent the forming of the greenish poisonous pigment that results from the action of acetic acid on copper.

Stainless steel is being used more and more. It never requires retinning and its original cost is offset by its long life. It keeps forever. The metal is very hard and is also heavier than other materials.

Iron or *steel* pans are very suitable for small frying pans. This is because of the hardness of the material and its fine pored construction. These pans require special care. Avoid washing them out. Wipe them out instead with soft paper. If the pan must be washed out for some reason, it should be greased. It is most important to keep the metal greased.

All utensils must be carefully handled so that their new, clean appearances and shapes are maintained.

METAL CONDUCTIVITY.   Copper has much greater conductivity than any other material used in utensils.*

Copper	100.00%
Aluminum	54.2%
Cast iron	11.9%
Steel	11.8%

Types of Equipment

In addition to the handling of equipment, its arrangement for efficient use is also important. Figure 8-1 shows a large kitchen combining the many preparation areas. Figure 8-2 shows one preparation area with all utensils and pots for that area neatly stored and ready for use.

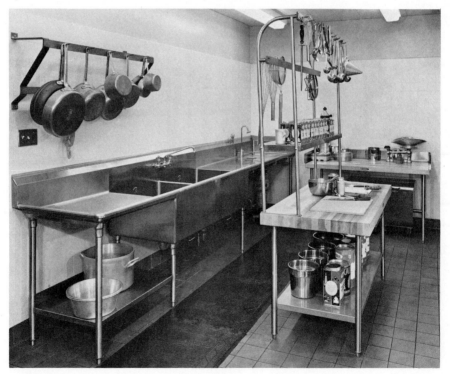

Figure 8-2.   A preparation area showing efficient utensil storage.

* Taken at 100 degrees C, the boiling point of water. Source: *Handbook of Chemistry and Physics,* 34th Edition.

Figure 8-3.   The range section in the hot line of a kitchen.

Figure 8-3 shows the range section in the hot line of a kitchen. This is just one of the hundreds of possible variations. Cooking equipment is updated constantly by the many manufacturers. Figure 8-4 shows some of the common cooking devices that might be used in various operations. The most common range has an open-burner top and an oven below. The one shown in the figure (a) has a backsplash and an elevated shelf. An oven that saves time is the convection oven (b) which has a circulating system that distributes the heat by blower. This oven reheats in a few minutes. The rack arrangement inside permits five times the capacity of a conventional oven. This oven bakes and broils with less shrinkage and better texture. The increasingly popular microwave oven (c) heats food in a matter of seconds or minutes. The microwave energy penetrates the food creating warmth and heat. The stack-type oven (d) is used for baking large quantities. The pizza oven (e) is able to heat to a higher temperature than a conventional oven. The broiler (f) has a shift lever that raises or lowers the grid. The overhead compartment is for warming. The grill (g) has an oven similar to the one shown in (a). In smaller operations many items are grilled, such as eggs, bacon, hamburgers, frankfurters, etc. Steam cookers (h) and (i) range in

Figure 8-4. Various types of large cooking appliances.

f   g

h

Figure 8-4 (*Continued*).

i

j

k

Figure 8-4 (*Continued*).

Figure 8-5.   Toasters and bun warmer.

size from the large batteries of steam units used in institutions to the counter model (i) used for meat and vegetables and quick reheating of foods. For frying foods in large quantities items (j) and (k) might be used. The large skillet (j) has a tilt action for easy removal of food. The deep-fat fryer (k) has large baskets in which the food can cook and then be put up to drain.

Depending on the meal, bread will be served in a variety of ways. Often it is either warmed or toasted in a device such as the ones shown in Figure 8-5. The bun warmer (a) is a common kitchen item. The toasters (b) and (c) are examples of the different sizes and types available.

Good coffee is a must for any successful restaurant. Figure 8-6 shows two types, (a) having an individual pot capacity and (b) capable of brewing on a large scale.

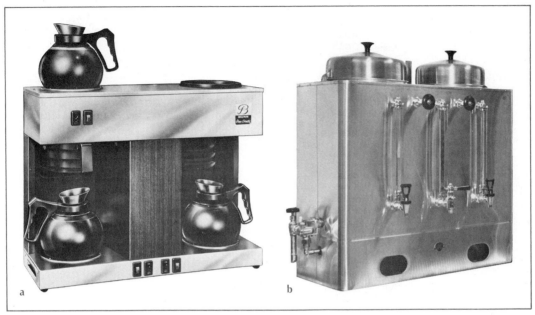

a   b

Figure 8-6.   Coffeemakers.

Food often has to be transported hot or cold, as in schools, hospitals, and large cafeterias. The carts shown in Figure 8-7 are all equipped with temperature-control devices.

Figure 8-8 shows several types of mixers with some attachments. Depending on the intended use, the mixers shown or other similar varieties will be used. Mixers vary greatly in capacity. The counter model (a) holds twelve quarts while the floor model (b) holds eighty. Item (c) shows an attachment for vegetable slicing being used with a tray support. Item (d) shows the vegetable chopper attachment off the machine. Meat can be ground by attaching a meat chopper (e) to the mixer. Bread and roll dough can be mixed with dough arms (f) and (g). The pastry knife attachment (h) can cut flour and shortening together for making pie dough. The wire whip (i) is used for light mixings. In addition to the mixers and attachments used in kitchens, some small machines can perform the same purposes. The Buffalo Chopper (j) is a food cutter used in both general food areas and some specific departments.

Some food service establishments cut their own meats. (Chapter 18 discusses the handling of meat in detail.) Four items that might be used for butchering or cutting (Figure 8-9) are (a) a meat saw; (b) a meat grinder; (c) a slicer; and (d) a tenderizer.

Figure 8-7. Carts equipped with temperature-control devices. The cart with the dispensing spigot is most often used in hospitals. The tall cart is a kitchen or bakery cart and the other two are banquet carts.

Scales (Figure 8-10) are useful and often necessary in large kitchens. They come in various sizes ranging from the floor model (a) to the counter model (b).

Small Utensils

Among the most important small utensils for the kitchen are knives.

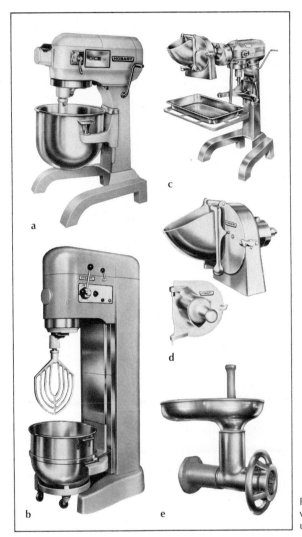

Figure 8-8. Mixers come in various sizes and with many useful attachments.

Knives come in an extraordinary number of sizes and shapes, each kind usually geared to a specific use. Figure 8-11 shows some of the common types of knives. The small paring knife (a) is used to trim the skin, rind, outside part, etc., off of fruits and vegetables. The boning knife (b) is used to separate meat from bone. Bread is often sliced in machines but for hand slicing a sharp knife such as the one shown in (c) would be used. The French knife (d) has a reinforced heel and is used for several

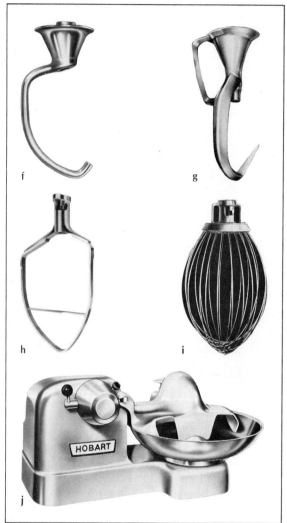

Figure 8-8 (*Continued*).

purposes such as chopping, dicing, etc. The butcher's knife (e) has a clip point. The meat cleaver (f) is used for hacking apart such items as chicken. Spatulas are flat, dull-edged, flexible knives used for spreading or mixing soft substances. The one shown in the figure (g) is for frosting. Wider spatulas are used for turning (h). The pie knife (i) cuts

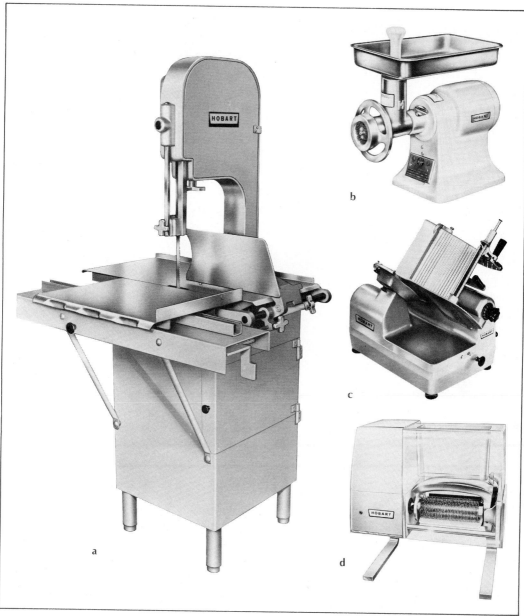

Figure 8-9. Machines for handling meat.

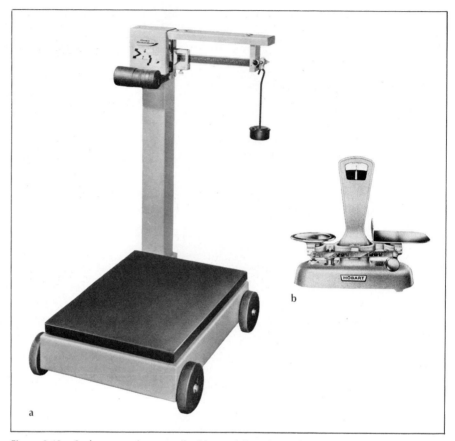

Figure 8-10.   Scales range from small table models to large floor models.

through the pie and then is slipped under the piece for serving. Two important utensils used along with knives are cook's forks (j) and a sharpening steel (k). Knives must be kept sharp to be useful. A dull knife can make a mess of an otherwise fine dish.

Other items used for cutting (Figure 8-12) are (a) a cheese cutter; (b) an egg slicer; (c) a butter cutter; (d) a tomato slicer; and (e) a potato cutter. For large-scale chores, items such as the electric potato peeler shown in Figure 8-13 can save valuable time.

As with knives, the different shapes and sizes of spoons are designed for varied purposes. Figure 8-14 shows just a sample of the many varieties available. The skimmer (a) is used for skimming liquids.

Figure 8-11.   Knives come in a variety of shapes, each one usually assigned to a specific use. The knives in this illustration and their uses are discussed in the text.

Figure 8-12.   Food cutters.

Ladles (b) come in a wide variety of sizes from a tiny one-ounce for gravies, sauces, etc., to the larger ones used for soup. Bowl spoons (c) can be either plain or slotted as can the squared-off pan spoons (d).

Some small utensils used for meat (Figure 8-15) are (a) a hand meat tenderizer; (b) steak weights; (c) a hamburger pattie mold; and (d) a meat thermometer.

With the ever-increasing use of canned foods, can openers are essential to any kitchen. The one shown in Figure 8-16 can be used for almost any size can up to the very large.

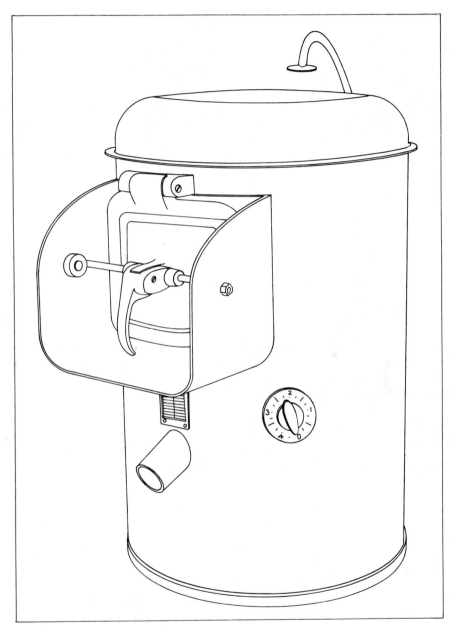

Figure 8-13.   Electric potato peeler.

The food dipper shown in Figure 8-17 is used for taking up liquids.

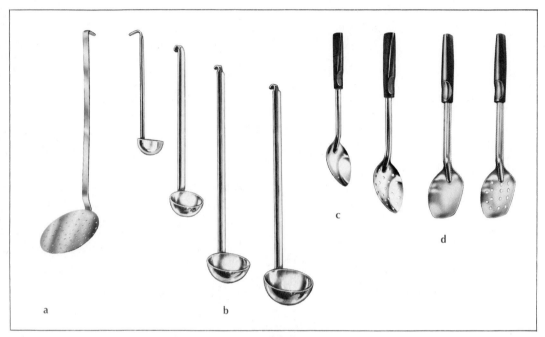

Figure 8-14.   Skimmer, spoons, and ladles.

Figure 8-15.   Some small utensils used for meat.

Figure 8-16.   Can opener.

Gelatin and aspic dishes are often made more decorative by setting them in fancy molds. Three such molds are shown in Figure 8-18.

A scoop such as the one shown in Figure 8-19 is used for dry food items such as sugar, flour, beans, etc.

Many foods are best used in a shaker or have to be strained through a utensil. Figure 8-20 shows several shakers and strainers: (a) is a salt shaker for use in the kitchen, not in the dining area; (b) is a sieve; (c) is a spaghetti strainer; and (d) is a colander used for straining. Figure 8-21 is a fruit juicer. The fruit is placed between the top presser and the bottom strainer. The strainer holds the pulp and pit on top while allowing the juice to pass through.

Figure 8-17.   A food dipper.

Figure 8-18.   Various molds for gelatin and aspic dishes.

Figure 8-19.   A scoop.

Figure 8-20. Shaker and strainers.

Pots and Pans

Pans for frying (Figure 8-22) should be heavy to allow heat to spread evenly. Different materials are used. The steel frying pans (a) do not require as much care as the cast-iron skillets (b) but they are also not quite as heavy. Restaurants that make a specialty of serving omelettes usually have pans such as the one shown in (c) that are kept in good shape. The sauté pan (d) has deep sides to avoid spilling and splattering.

Baking and roasting pans (Figure 8-23) come with or without lids depending on the intended use.

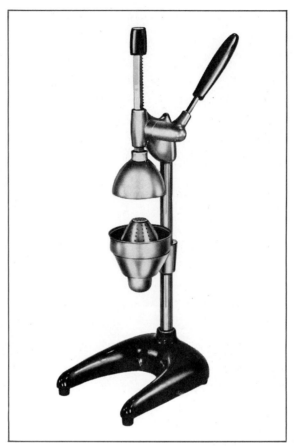

Figure 8-21.   A fruit juicer.

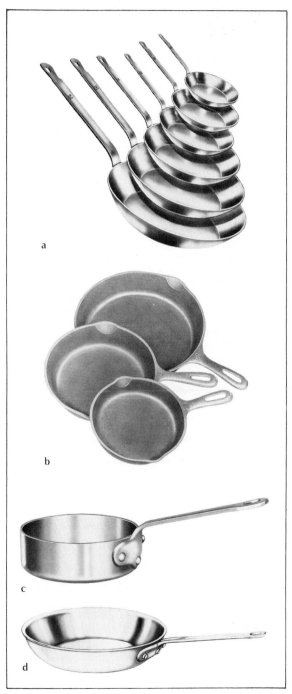

Figure 8-22.   Various frying pans.

Figure 8-23. Various pans used for roasting and baking.

Figure 8-24.   Some common pots and pans.

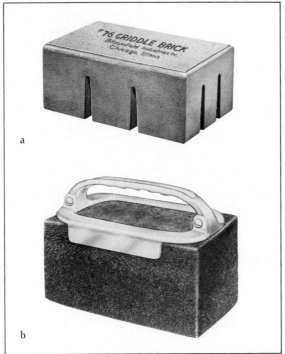

a

b

Figure 8-25. A griddle brick and a griddle stone.

Figure 8-24 shows just a few of the many pots available. The metals described earlier in this chapter are used in manufacturing almost every kind of pot. The saucepans or sauce pots (a) and (b) usually come with a cover but may often be used without one. A double boiler (c) is used for foods that do not go directly on the flame. Water is kept in the lower section and the food is put in the upper part. The boiling water cooks the food without touching it. The stock pot shown in (d) has a tap for removing the liquid easily.

Figure 8-25 shows a brick and stone used for cleaning griddles.

Bakery Equipment

The bakery is usually a separate area or room in a large establishment. Baking requires different tools than the rest of the kitchen. Figure 8-26 shows a typical bakery setup with a stacked oven, bakery cart, work-table, ingredient bins, and many other items which are shown in the illustrations that follow.

Pastry chefs and bakers wear caps as do personnel in other parts of the kitchen. Figure 8-27 shows three typical caps.

Figure 8-26.   A typical bakery setup.

Figure 8-27.   Some common baker's caps.

Baked goods are often manufactured in a plant and then transferred to restaurants, institutions, etc. Some large establishments have their own bakeries as do some smaller restaurants that specialize in fine

Figure 8-28.   Cart for transporting baked goods.

pastries. For transporting baked goods a number of carts are available. A common type is the cart shown in Figure 8-28 which has holders for trays to hold the baked goods in a level position.

Worktables should have the characteristics described earlier in this chapter. Figure 8-29 shows a sturdy table useful for baker's work and an ingredient bin for holding large amounts of the necessary ingredients such as flour at one time.

Pastry is often displayed not only in bakery shops but also in restaurants where the patrons are tempted to choose from a large and appealing variety. Figure 8-30 shows a refrigerated display case.

Bread and rolls are naturally the staple product of bakeries. Some equipment for handling these items are shown in Figure 8-31: (a) is a

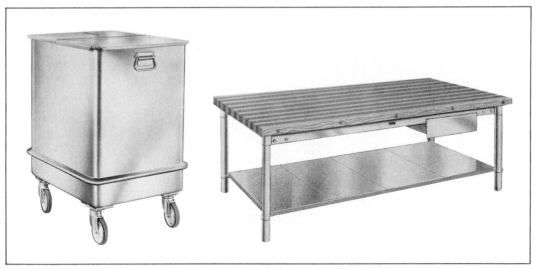

Figure 8-29. A baker's worktable and a bin for holding large amounts of ingredients.

Figure 8-30. A refrigerated showcase for baked goods.

Figure 8-31.   Items for handling bread and rolls.

bread slicer; (b) is a roll and bun slicer; and (c) is a bun divider used for dividing dough into equal parts. Dough is often mixed in large quantities and then used in a variety of baked products. Figure 8-34 shows two popular models of mixer (a) and (b), and a dough conditioner (c). Figure 8-33 is a doughnut machine.

Figure 8-34 shows mixing bowls ranging from a capacity of $\frac{3}{4}$ of a quart and a diameter at top of $6\frac{7}{16}$ inches to a capacity of 80 quarts and a diameter of $30\frac{1}{2}$ inches. Mixing bowls come in many other sizes and shapes. Unlike many other kitchen items, bowls are not usually designed for specific uses, only for specific quantities.

Baking pans and racks (Figure 8-35) often are designed for specific uses to provide a bakery with uniformity of product. The loaf pans in (a)

Figure 8-32. Machines used in mixing dough.

are attached to facilitate making four loaves at once. The tins shown in (b) and (c) are for frankfurter rolls and muffins, respectively. The spring-form pan (d) comes with or without a center tube. The latch on the side of the pan is opened after baking to make the removing of a cake very easy. The cake pan shown in (e) is similar to the springform in that the middle is removable but in this pan you push the middle up. Angel food cakes are usually baked in such a pan. The plain round cake pan (f) is used for many kinds of cakes. The cookie sheet (g) is long and flat to allow the baking of many cookies at one time. The rack or grate (h) is used for cooling and icing baked goods.

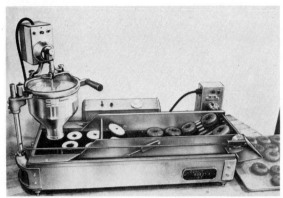

Figure 8-33.   A doughnut machine.

Figure 8-34.   Various mixing bowls.

Figure 8-35.   Various baking pans and an icing grate.

Figure 8-36.   Some small bakery items.

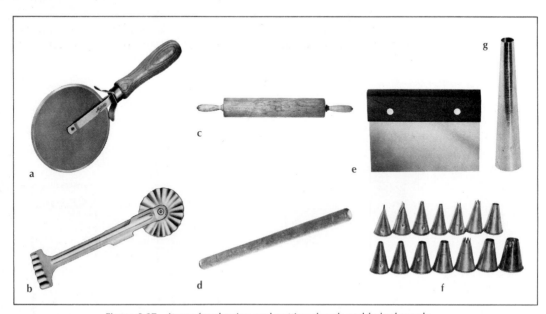

Figure 8-37.   Items for shaping and cutting dough and baked goods.

Figure 8-38.   A cake stand.

Some small bakery utensils (Figure 8-36) include (a) pastry brushes; (b) a wire whisk; and (c) a measuring cup with lip. Some small utensils for shaping and cutting dough and baked goods (Figure 8-37) are (a) a pastry wheel; (b) an edger for pies; (c) and (d) two types of rolling pins; (e) a bench scraper for removing bits of dough from the worktable; (f) pastry tubes for shaping and decorating pastry; and (g) a cream roll horn.

Cake stands are used for displaying and serving the finished cake. Revolving stands such as the one shown in Figure 8-38 are used when decorating cakes.

part IV

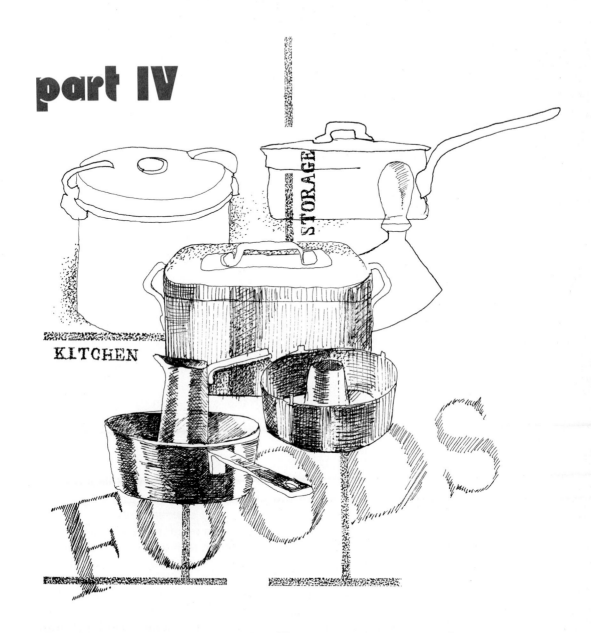

layout and design of
food service facilities

chapter 9

layout and design

LAYOUT

At various points in this text we have discussed the importance of the proper location of a department; the selecting and placing of a piece of equipment within a department; the location of various departments one to the other; etc. The departmental units have been recognized as separate definable working units of a whole.

In this section dealing with the layout of an establishment we will bring out the interdependence that exists between the front of the house, the back of the house, and the operating departments and stations within these two areas.

Efficiently operated departments compliment each other. They provide the production or service required by the complete operation. Departments and stations are designed to function as parts of a single effort to achieve the objectives set by the establishment.

The location of each department in relationship to the whole is vitally important. If the design and layout of facilities are well conceived in the planning, costly corrections after construction will be avoided.

A good operation does not just happen. Prerequisites to a smooth, functional, and profitable food service facility are the proper utilization of space for equipment; the proper allocation of work space for workers; convenient utensil storage; and defined work patterns for personnel to assist them in performing their respective duties from the handling of raw materials to the finished food product.

General guides have been developed within the industry. They provide assistance in determining such things as the amount of square footage necessary in the back of the house. The size of this area is directly related to the number of people to be fed in the front of the house. This varies to some extent, depending on the type of operation and the service provided. Information is also available on the production or cooking load for each item of equipment as well as for determining the amount of illumination required by the different areas in the house.

Building materials in walls, ceilings, and floors are not the same. Various materials accomplish different objectives. For example, the walls, ceiling, floor, and lighting in the dishroom may differ from other areas in the kitchen because of levels of moisture and noise and the general type of work that is done in this area. Additional information, as the location of a cafeteria in a large factory for maximum employee usage, is also available. It should be considered when designing that type of operation. In developing a layout, consideration is given as well to the general and fundamental conditions of exploring floor space on one level that can be used for the back of the house and front of the house areas. It should be developed so that, as near as possible, a continual movement of raw materials to finished product is achieved.

What Is a Layout?

A layout may be anything from a rough preliminary to a developed and completed drawing. It may be the design of a department or a complete operation including all the departments. A layout will show:

1. The location of pieces of equipment in relation to the area, using every inch of kitchen space to best advantage
2. The flow of food through the kitchen; how it moves from the raw to the completed state; where it is ultimately presented to the patron in the dining room
3. The location of personnel work sites in relation to the equipment and the pattern of the food flow

The layout is the best means of showing the use of space, equipment, and people prior to the final drawings. By studying the layout, the most efficient locations for the departments and equipment can be found. Such things as outlets, water drains, aisle space, traffic bottlenecks, etc., will be indicated in the layout.

If the dining area is well planned and beautiful but the kitchen is overstocked with equipment and very limited in working space, the operation, at best, will be inefficient. If the kitchen is too large or located too far from the dining area, the result, again, will be inefficiency. The time to discover all these things is in the layout stage.

THE KITCHEN LAYOUT

The kitchen is the heart of an operation. This is the center of activity. The kitchen sends its pulsations throughout the house. One of the most important functions of the kitchen is to convert the raw materials into finished product in the shortest possible time. Quality food properly prepared in this area will start a chain reaction that will be felt throughout the house. When all is well in the kitchen, when this is being done quietly and efficiently, the personnel reflect the satisfaction they get from a job well done. And they, in turn, pass it on to the dining patron.

In order to be able to produce quietly, smoothly, and quickly, the working space of the kitchen must be designed to meet the demands made upon it by the dining area.

The location of the kitchen, the departments within the kitchen, and the selection of equipment within the department all require much study. They must be carefully planned if a quiet kitchen with a smooth flow of food and traffic and a quick method of turning raw materials into a finished product are to be achieved.

IMPORTANT FACTORS TO CONSIDER IN A KITCHEN LAYOUT

1. What is it you want to do?
    a. Produce food in as efficient a manner as possible.
    b. Eliminate noise and confusion in production and service areas.
    c. Control operating expenses.
    d. Develop pleasant working conditions for personnel and pleasant dining facilities for patrons.
2. How do you accomplish these goals?
    Plans for the development of production areas originate with operators who work with their staffs. Quite often they prepare preliminary drawings prior to calling in professional assistance, but they may rely entirely on outside people to prepare the layout.
3. Who can help you?
    a. An architect can advise on building codes, changes in construction, and possible ways of building. Architects may also provide specialists from their staffs to assist in developing a plan to handle the work loads. Such a plan would include space alloca-

tion, selection of equipment, and location of departments. Architects provide the services of a draftsman to produce drawings and a supervisor to oversee construction. The costs for this service may be a fixed fee or a predetermined percentage of the overall construction costs.

b. A consultant is someone to whom you go for advice. Our industry has a number of these, mostly people who have retired after many years of operating food establishments. These are people who are reputed to have the know-how. Often, in laying out a new operation or correcting some fault in an older one, their services and advice are most valuable.

c. A restaurant equipment dealer is able to offer assistance in layout and to construct equipment according to your specifications. Architects and consultants may also recommend items of kitchen equipment. These, of course, are a saving over those that must be fabricated to order. Most equipment dealers carry all items necessary for restaurants.

THE FINAL LAYOUT

As the preliminary layouts are discussed with the owner, architect, consultants, fabricators, etc., many thoughts and ideas are brought out. A unified pattern becomes apparent as the meetings and consultations progress.

When several working layouts have produced a final layout or drawing, specification sheets are drawn up and coded by numbers to coincide with numbered locations on the layout.

Along with the final layout, or plan, and specifications of equipment, additional mechanical plans and specifications are also worked out. These mechanical plans will show the types of electrical, heating, plumbing, and air-movement services available to the various pieces of equipment. Each service requires a drawing of its own.

In larger installations, contracting for the food service equipment may be a part of the general contract for the building. In other installations the contract may be left to the lessee who will operate the facilities. It may also be a separate contract developed by the architect.

Several layouts with specifications of equipment can be prepared in order to have them submitted for bids to purchase.

OTHER CONSIDERATIONS

Other items that should be explored during the stages of preliminary sketches, drawings, and layouts are:

1. air-conditioning needs
2. warm-air requirements
3. fresh-air movement
4. adequate hot-water supply
5. adequate number of properly located floor drains
6. adequate number of properly located electrical outlets
7. level of floors for proper draining
8. entranceways
9. stairways
10. rest rooms
11. dressing rooms

After all the drawings are made, all the construction is over, and every piece of equipment is in place, the operation is not yet complete. Watch for public acceptance. Study this living element to see whether your calculations and performance are right. The diners will always tell, but one has to watch and listen. This principle also holds true for production and service personnel. A good worker will always develop a pattern of work that will bring to light imperfections in the operation. Once again, management has to look and listen.

Remember: As long as you have people steadily coming through your doors, your plan is approved.

FLOORS AND WALL MATERIALS

What materials are to be used on the floors? The answer to this, as well as to other alternatives that arise when formulating plans for a good layout, is variable. It depends entirely upon the answers to such questions as:

1. How much money can be allocated to floor material?
2. How much use will the floor receive?
3. What kind of use will it receive? Heavy production, corridor, display, etc?
4. Is all use foot traffic?
5. What care does the material require?
6. Will the floor be installed on a new site or an old one?
7. Is more than one type of flooring required?

Basically, the type of flooring material used is determined by how much wear and tear an area will receive. The general formula is: the heavier the nature of work and usage, the heavier the floor.

This formula progresses in degrees. The floor of the dining room, where the patron is served, is covered with soft carpeting. Traffic may be heavy in the dining area, but the nature of the work performed is relatively light. It is not uncommon to see the heavy traffic or congestion areas of lobbies or foyers surfaced in stone or tile because of the unusual number of people gathering at certain times.

1. *Cement floors* are used in receiving, storage, and corridor spaces. They are not good for the kitchen. Cement floors are sealed and may be painted periodically. A more durable finish and color can be achieved by troweling specially designed materials into the cement when it is fresh.

2. *Terrazzo* is used in corridor space, not in kitchens. It will not stand up to grease. It is also good for dining areas.

3. *Quarry tile* is the best material for general kitchen areas of heavy usage. It is also used in some dining areas.

4. *Asphalt tile* can be used in light-production kitchen areas and general work areas. It is not completely resistant to grease. Asphalt tile is good in dining areas.

5. *Vinyl flooring* can be used in light kitchen work areas where no heavy production takes place. It is also good in light-usage corridors. A lot of water on the floor will expand the seams. Vinyl is good for dining areas.

In selecting a material for flooring, consideration is also given to the maintenance required and the ability of the respective materials to stand up to the use of detergents and other cleaning aids.

Wall Materials

The same general concepts that pertain to the materials for the floors apply to the choice of materials for walls. The areas of heaviest usage can have the same quarry tile installed on the walls as are used on floors. A lighter-bodied tile will chip. Quarry tile is practically chip-proof under normal working conditions.

It is important that wall materials are easily cleaned. For this reason a light-colored glazed tile is very popular. A more recent decorative treatment of a wall in a working area is tile on the lower half of a wall and wallpaper on the upper half.

chapter 10

layouts of
several kinds
of operations

It must be remembered that each new kitchen or restaurant may present problems that require alterations, additions, or opportunities for changes. These changes may be able to bring about cuts in costs and improvement of operations.

Each operation has its own needs in terms of layout. However, there are usually many similarities among the various kitchens of any one type of operation. Figure 10-1 shows a food flow chart. This traces the movement from raw materials to finished product. It also shows the flow of china, pots, utensils, and garbage. Figures 10-2 and 10-3 show typical layouts of individual operating stations and departments. Figure 10-4 illustrates a blending of stations and departments as might be set up in a typical school kitchen. The layouts show where important equipment might be located for the most efficient operation. These layouts will help you visualize where various jobs are performed, how the food production progresses through a typical operation, and how your potential job or jobs might fit into a whole operation.

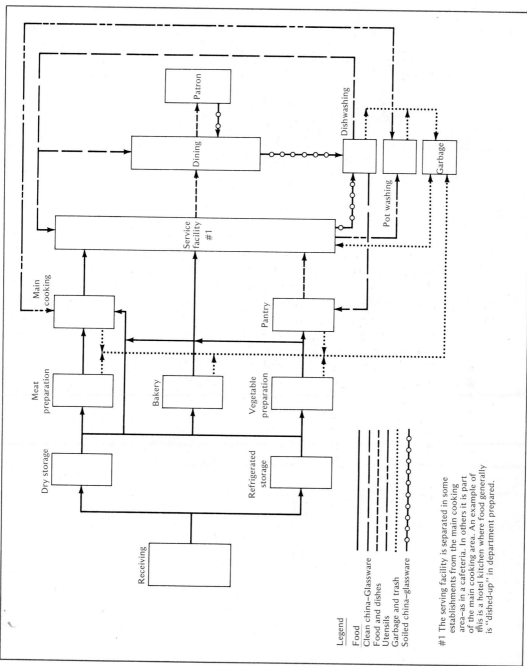

Figure 10-1. Food flow chart.

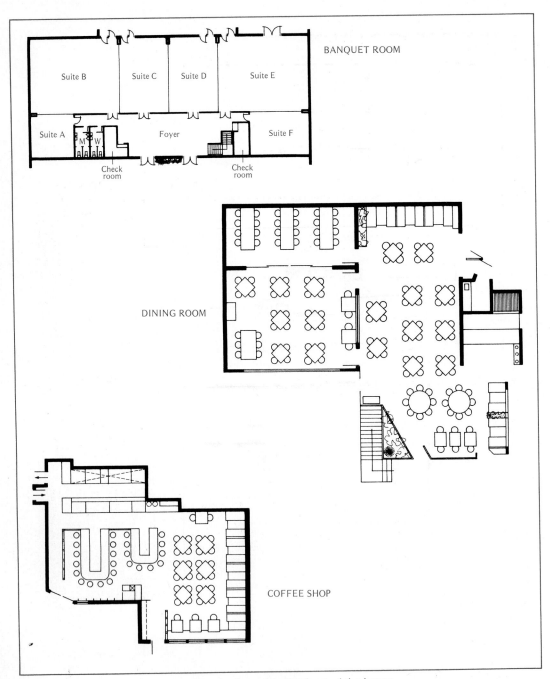

Figure 10-2.   Food service layouts in the front of the house.

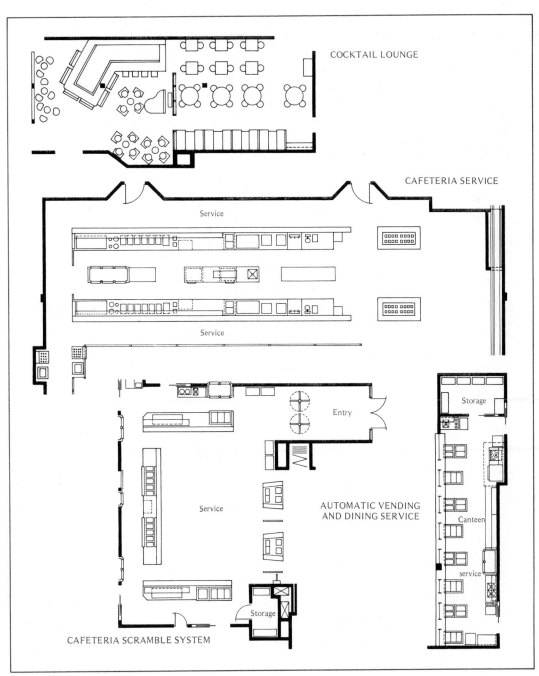

Figure 10-2. (*Continued*).

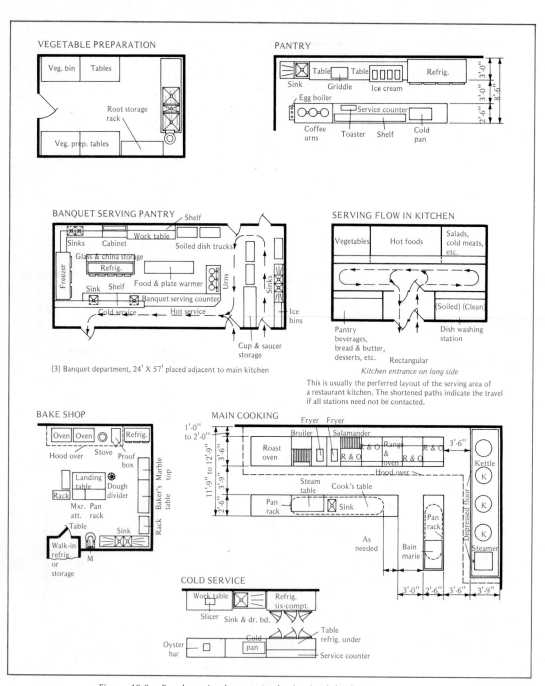

Figure 10-3. Food service layouts in the back of the house.

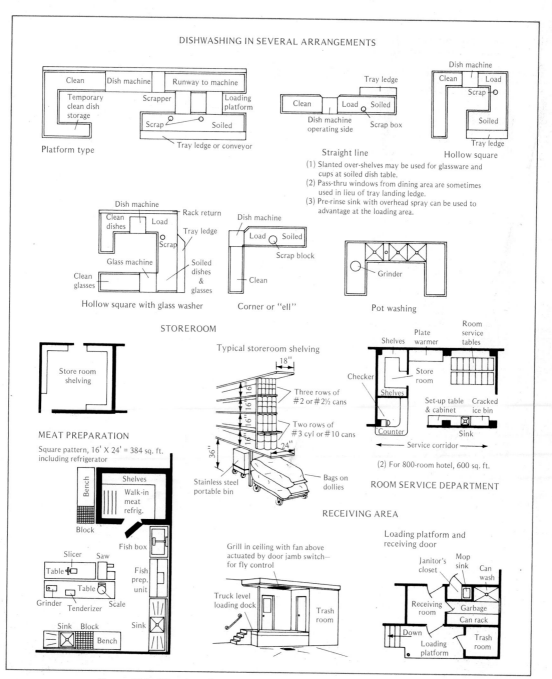

DISHWASHING IN SEVERAL ARRANGEMENTS

Platform type

Straight line

(1) Slanted over-shelves may be used for glassware and cups at soiled dish table.
(2) Pass-thru windows from dining area are sometimes used in lieu of tray landing ledge.
(3) Pre-rinse sink with overhead spray can be used to advantage at the loading area.

Hollow square

Hollow square with glass washer

Corner or "ell"

Pot washing

STOREROOM

Typical storeroom shelving

Three rows of #2 or #2½ cans

Two rows of #3 cyl or #10 cans

Stainless steel portable bin

Bags on dollies

MEAT PREPARATION

Square pattern, 16' X 24' = 384 sq. ft. including refrigerator

(2) For 800-room hotel, 600 sq. ft.

ROOM SERVICE DEPARTMENT

RECEIVING AREA

Grill in ceiling with fan above actuated by door jamb switch— for fly control

Loading platform and receiving door

Figure 10-3. (Continued).

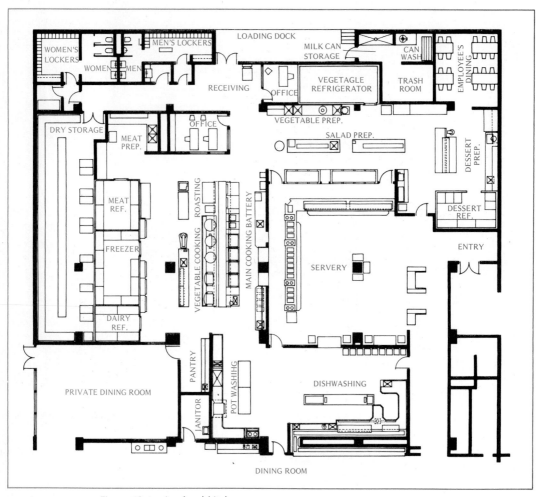

Figure 10-4. A school kitchen.

part V

health,
hygiene,
and sanitation

chapter 11

sanitation in food establishments

Since the beginning of history, foods and drinks have been used as vehicles for permanently removing a person from life. From the courts of the Caesars, down through the Borgias and Medicis of the Middle Ages, and even in modern times food, one of the most essential elements to life, has also been used to terminate it.

This despicable criminal act is not the only danger. Lack of knowledge of the properties of food, its preparation, and its preservation have resulted in much pain and physical distress, if not death.

Therefore, it is necessary for anyone thinking about working in the food industry, particularly in careers dealing with the preparation and serving of meals, to become thoroughly acquainted with the requirements of sanitation.

In its book *Today's Health Guide*, the American Medical Association gives this advice: "Select a clean establishment, many of these bear well-known labels of recognized quality. Substandard food establishments should obviously be avoided. Health authorities in many states post ratings in a prominent place in the establishment. Such a rating does not guarantee excellence in food, but it does guarantee that equipment and general sanitation meet minimum requirements."

The same publication says, "to avoid food infection or poisoning the best safeguard to follow is to avoid ground or mixed combinations of foods not cooked immediately before being eaten, such as meat spreads (chicken—ham); potato; seafood; and egg salads; cream or custard filled pastries; cold sliced meats, including cold cuts; cream dishes; undercooked meats—particularly poultry and pork; and custards."

While the American Medical Association has numerous observations about infections that can arise from handling and preparing food, they also say: "Proper cooking renders most foods safe. A good rule: Always keep hot foods hot and cold foods cold prior to eating."

Years ago, as many old-timers will recall, people would spend a convivial evening in a public restaurant. The restaurant's food was accompanied by an assortment of wines and hard liquor and preceded by cocktails, snacks, and hors d'oeuvres in the homes of friends. The dispersing patrons, returning to their homes, would cry "food poisoning" upon the slightest symptom of stomach distress.

We are not discounting the possibility that in some cases they were correct. It is a well-established fact that, as the physicians testify, what is one man's meat is another's poison. In many cases such complaints were honestly made when the food was both wholesome and properly cooked.

Seldom in such cases was the group affected. Sometimes only one or two became ill. But, human nature being what it is, the restaurant got the blame and sometimes very bad publicity, whether it deserved it or not.

Today, happily, there are few such complaints and they are getting fewer. Operators are ready and willing to conform to local, state, and federal regulations. Furthermore, they exact strict adherence to these regulations by everyone in their employ.

This leads us to what is perhaps the most important part of this book—the problem of sanitation.

REGULATING AUTHORITIES AND INSPECTION REPORTS

The regulations concerning the health practice standards are governed by one of two departments of government:

1. The U.S. Public Health Service if the establishment is serving guests who are enroute to another place. This includes airlines, railroads, and steamship lines.
2. The city, county, or state health department. This department sees to it that an establishment operates according to the prescribed health standards that have been established by law. The following services may be performed by the local health department:

   a. issuing of licenses to restaurants
   b. inspection service on a routine basis

      c. educational services for the training of personnel
      d. providing of materials and information on correct practices
      e. special assistance if needed by an establishment

The objectives of local or U.S. public health departments as they pertain to food serving establishments can be generally outlined as follows:

1. to educate food service personnel about the need for sanitary precautions and about the role they play in the health of a community
2. to educate operators on how to prevent disease that may be carried by food
3. to show how bacteria may enter food and cause illness
4. to ensure compliance, by individual operations, with established practices. These practices are recognized as the most sanitary method of handling all forms of food in preparation and service

An establishment's first consideration is to operate within the law. We cannot quote all city and state requirements for restaurant operators, but the following copy of the United States Public Health Service Food Service Sanitation Ordinance* may serve as a guide to the typical requirements expected of food service operators.

UNITED STATES PUBLIC HEALTH SERVICE FOOD SERVICE SANITATION ORDINANCE

(Recommendations)

An ordinance defining food, potentially hazardous food, adulterated, misbranded, food-service establishment, temporary food-service establishment, health authority, utensils, equipment, etc.; providing for the sale of only unadulterated, wholesome, properly branded food; regulating the sources of food; establishing sanitation standards for food, food protection, food-service personnel, food-service operations, food equipment and utensils, sanitary facilities and controls, and other facilities; requiring permits for the operation of food-service establishments; regulating the inspection (grading, regrading, and placarding) of such establishments; providing for the examination and condemna-

---

* Footnotes to this Ordinance have been left out to facilitate reading. A copy of the Ordinance and Code may be obtained from the U.S. Public Health Service, Washington, D.C.

tion of food; providing for the incorporation by reference the compliance provisions of the 1962 Edition of the "United States Public Health Service Food Service Sanitation Ordinance and Code"; and providing for the enforcement of this ordinance, and the fixing of penalties.

Be it ordained by _____ of the municipality of _____ as follows:

SECTION A. DEFINITIONS

The following definitions shall apply in the interpretation and the enforcement of this ordinance:

1. ADULTERATED shall mean the condition of a food (a) if it bears or contains any poisonous or deleterious substance in a quantity which may render it injurious to health; (b) if it bears or contains any *added* poisonous or deleterious substance for which no safe tolerance has been established by regulation, or in excess of such tolerance if one has been established; (c) if it consists in whole or in part of any filthy, putrid, or decomposed substance, or if it is otherwise unfit for human consumption; (d) if it has been processed, prepared, packed, or held under insanitary conditions, whereby it may have become contaminated with filth, or whereby it may have been rendered injurious to health; (e) if it is in whole or in part the product of a diseased animal, or an animal which has died otherwise than by slaughter or (f) if its container is composed in whole or in part of any poisonous or deleterious substance which may render the contents injurious to health.
2. APPROVED shall mean acceptable to the health authority based on his determination as to conformance with appropriate standards and good public health practice.
3. CLOSED shall mean fitted together snugly leaving no openings large enough to permit the entrance of vermin.
4. CORROSION-RESISTANT MATERIAL shall mean a material which maintains its original surface characteristics under prolonged influence of the food, cleaning compounds and sanitizing solutions which may contact it.
5. EASILY CLEANABLE shall mean readily accessible and of such material and finish, and so fabricated that residue may be completely removed by normal cleaning methods.
6. EMPLOYEE shall mean any person working in a food-service establishment who transports food or food containers, who engages in food preparation or service, or who comes in contact with any

food utensils or equipment.

7. EQUIPMENT shall mean all stoves, ranges, hoods, meatblocks, tables, counters, refrigerators, sinks, dishwashing machines, steamtables, and similar items, other than utensils, used in the operation of a food-service establishment.

8. FOOD shall mean any raw, cooked, or processed edible substance, beverage, or ingredient used or intended for use or for sale in whole or in part for human consumption.

9. FOOD-CONTACT SURFACES shall mean those surfaces of equipment and utensils with which food normally comes in contact, and those surfaces with which food may come in contact and drain back into surfaces normally in contact with food.

10. FOOD-PROCESSING ESTABLISHMENT shall mean a commercial establishment in which food is processed or otherwise prepared and packaged for human consumption.

11. FOOD-SERVICE ESTABLISHMENT shall mean any fixed or mobile restaurant; coffeeshop; cafeteria; short-order cafe; luncheonette, grill; tearoom; sandwich shop; soda fountain; tavern; bar, cocktail lounge; night club; roadside stand; industrial-feeding establishment; private, public, or nonprofit organization or institution routinely serving food; catering kitchen; commissary or similar place in which food or drink is prepared for sale or for service on the premises or elsewhere; and any other eating or drinking establishment or operation where food is served or provided for the public with or without charge.

12. HEALTH AUTHORITY shall mean the health authority of the municipality of _____, or his designated representative.

13. KITCHENWARE shall mean all multi-use utensils other than tableware used in the storage, preparation, conveying, or serving of food.

14. MISBRANDED shall mean the presence of any written, printed, or graphic matter, upon or accompanying food or containers of food, which is false or misleading, or which violates any applicable State or local labeling requirements.

15. PERISHABLE FOOD shall mean any food of such type or in such condition as may spoil.

16. PERSON shall mean an individual, or a firm, partnership, company, corporation, trustee, association, or any public or private entity.

17. POTENTIALLY HAZARDOUS FOOD shall mean any perishable food which consists in whole or in part of milk or milk products, eggs, meat, poultry, fish, shellfish, or other ingredients capable of sup-

porting rapid and progressive growth of infectious or toxigenic micro-organisms.

18. SAFE TEMPERATURES, as applied to potentially hazardous food, shall mean temperatures of 45°F. or below, and 140°F. or above.

19. SANITIZE shall mean effective bactericidal treatment of clean surfaces of equipment and utensils by a process which has been approved by the health authority as being effective in destroying micro-organisms, including pathogens.

20. SEALED shall mean free of cracks or other openings which permit the entry or passage of moisture.

21. SINGLE-SERVICE ARTICLES shall mean cups, containers, lids, or closures; plates, knives, forks, spoons, stirrers, paddles, straws, place mats, napkins, doilies, wrapping material; and all similar articles which are constructed wholly or in part from paper, paperboard, molded pulp, foil, wood, plastic, synthetic, or other readily destructible materials, and which are intended by the manufacturers and generally recognized by the public as for one usage only, then to be discarded.

22. TABLEWARE shall mean all multi-use eating and drinking utensils, including flatware (knives, forks, and spoons).

23. TEMPORARY FOOD-SERVICE ESTABLISHMENT shall mean any food-service establishment which operates at a fixed location for a temporary period of time, not to exceed 2 weeks, in connection with a fair, carnival, circus, public exhibition, or similar transitory gathering.

24. UTENSIL shall mean any tableware and kitchenware used in the storage, preparation, conveying, or serving of food.

25. WHOLESOME shall mean in sound condition, clean, free from adulteration, and otherwise suitable for use as human food.

SECTION B. FOOD

1. FOOD SUPPLIES: All food in food-service establishments shall be from sources approved or considered satisfactory by the health authority, and shall be clean, wholesome, free from spoilage, free from adulteration and misbranding, and safe for human consumption. No hermetically sealed, nonacid and low-acid food which has been processed in a place other than a commercial food-processing establishment shall be used.

2. FOOD PROTECTION: All food while being stored, prepared, displayed, served, or sold at food-service establishments, or during

transportation between such establishments, shall be protected from contamination. All perishable food shall be stored at such temperatures as will protect against spoilage. All potentially hazardous food shall be maintained at *safe* temperatures (45°F. or below, or 140°F. or above), except during necessary periods of preparation and service. Raw fruits and vegetables shall be washed before use. Stuffing, poultry, stuffed meats and poultry, and pork and pork products shall be thoroughly cooked before being served. Individual portions of food once served to the customer shall not be served again: *Provided,* That wrapped food which has not been unwrapped and which is wholesome may be re-served.

Only such poisonous and toxic materials as are required to maintain sanitary conditions and for sanitation purposes may be used or stored in food-service establishments. Poisonous and toxic materials shall be identified, and shall be used only in such manner and under such conditions as will not contaminate food or constitute a hazard to employees or customers.

SECTION C. PERSONNEL

1. HEALTH AND DISEASE CONTROL: No person while affected with any disease in a communicable form, or while a carrier of such disease, or while afflicted with boils, infected wounds, sores, or an acute respiratory infection, shall work in any area of a food-service establishment in any capacity in which there is a likelihood of such person contaminating food or food-contact surfaces with pathogenic organisms, or transmitting disease to other individuals; and no person known or suspected of being affected with any such disease or condition shall be employed in such an area or capacity. If the manager or person in charge of the establishment has reason to suspect that any employee has contracted any disease in a communicable form or has become carrier of such disease, he shall notify the health authority immediately.

2. CLEANLINESS: All employees shall wear clean outer garments, maintain a high degree of personal cleanliness, and conform to hygienic practices while on duty. They shall wash their hands thoroughly in an approved hand-washing facility before starting work, and as often as may be necessary to remove soil and contamination. No employee shall resume work after visiting the toilet room without first washing his hands.

SECTION D. FOOD EQUIPMENT AND UTENSILS

1. SANITARY DESIGN, CONSTRUCTION AND INSTALLATION OF EQUIPMENT AND UTENSILS: All equipment and utensils shall be so designed and of such material and workmanship as to be smooth, easily cleanable and durable, and shall be in good repair; and the food-contact surfaces of such equipment and utensils shall, in addition, be easily accessible for cleaning, nontoxic, corrosion resistant and relatively nonabsorbent: *Provided,* That, when approved by the health authority, exceptions may be made to the above materials requirements for equipment such as cutting boards, blocks, and bakers' tables.

   All equipment shall be so installed and maintained as to facilitate the cleaning thereof, and of all adjacent areas.

   Equipment in use at the time of adoption of this ordinance which does not meet fully the above requirements, may be continued in use if it is in good repair, capable of being maintained in a sanitary condition and the food-contact surfaces are nontoxic.

   Single-service articles shall be made from nontoxic materials.
2. CLEANLINESS OF EQUIPMENT AND UTENSILS: All eating and drinking utensils shall be thoroughly cleaned and sanitized after each usage.

   All kitchenware and food-contact surfaces of equipment, exclusive of cooking surfaces of equipment, used in the preparation or serving of food or drink, and all food-storage utensils, shall be thoroughly cleaned after each use. Cooking surfaces of equipment shall be cleaned at least once a day. All utensils and food contact surfaces of equipment used in the preparation, service, display, or storage of potentially hazardous food shall be thoroughly cleaned and sanitized prior to such use. Non-food-contact surfaces of equipment shall be cleaned at such intervals as to keep them in a clean and sanitary condition.

   After cleaning and until use, all food-contact surfaces of equipment and utensils shall be so stored and handled as to be protected from contamination.

   All single-service articles shall be stored, handled, and dispensed in a sanitary manner, and shall be used only once.

   Food-service establishments which do not have adequate and effective facilities for cleaning and sanitizing utensils shall use single-service articles.

SECTION E. SANITARY FACILITIES AND CONTROLS

1. WATER SUPPLY: The water supply shall be adequate, of a safe, sanitary quality and from an approved source. Hot and cold running water under pressure shall be provided in all areas where food is prepared, or equipment, utensils, or containers are washed.

     Water, if not piped into the establishment, shall be transported and stored in approved containers and shall be handled and dispensed in a sanitary manner.

     Ice used for any purpose shall be made from water which comes from an approved source, and shall be used only if it has been manufactured, stored, transported, and handled in a sanitary manner.

2. SEWAGE DISPOSAL: All sewage shall be disposed of in a public sewerage system or, in the absence thereof, in a manner approved by the health authority.

3. PLUMBING: Plumbing shall be so sized, installed, and maintained as to carry adequate quantities of water to required locations throughout the establishment; as to prevent contamination of the water supply; as to properly convey sewage and liquid wastes from the establishment to the sewage or sewage-disposal system; and so that it does not constitute a source of contamination of food, equipment, or utensils or create an insanitary condition or nuisance.

4. TOILET FACILITIES: Each food-service establishment shall be provided with adequate, conveniently located toilet facilities for its employees. Toilet fixtures shall be of sanitary design and readily cleanable. Toilet facilities, including rooms and fixtures, shall be kept in a clean condition and in good repair. The doors of all toilet rooms shall be self-closing. Toilet tissue shall be provided. Easily cleanable receptacles shall be provided for waste materials, and such receptacles in toilet rooms for women shall be covered. Where the use of non-water-carried sewage disposal facilities have been approved by the health authority, such facilities shall be separate from the establishment. When toilet facilities are provided for patrons, such facilities shall meet the requirements of this subsection.

5. HAND-WASHING FACILITIES: Each food-service establishment shall be provided with adequate, conveniently located hand-washing facilities for its employees, including a lavatory or lavatories equipped with hot and cold or tempered running water, hand-cleansing soap or detergent, and approved sanitary towels or other

approved hand-drying devices. Such facilities shall be kept clean and in good repair.

6. GARBAGE AND RUBBISH DISPOSAL: All garbage and rubbish containing food wastes shall, prior to disposal, be kept in leakproof, nonabsorbent containers which shall be kept covered with tight-fitting lids when filled or stored, or not in continuous use: *Provided,* that such containers need not be covered when stored in a special vermin-proofed room or enclosure, or in a food-waste refrigerator. All other rubbish shall be stored in containers, rooms, or areas in an approved manner. The rooms, enclosures, areas and containers used shall be adequate for the storage of all food waste and rubbish accumulating on the premises. Adequate cleaning facilities shall be provided, and each container, room, or area shall be thoroughly cleaned after the emptying or removal of garbage and rubbish. Food-waste grinders, if used, shall be installed in compliance with state and local standards and shall be of suitable construction. All garbage and rubbish shall be disposed of with sufficient frequency and in such a manner as to prevent a nuisance.

7. VERMIN CONTROL: Effective measures shall be taken to protect against the entrance into the establishment and the breeding or presence on the premises of vermin.

SECTION F. OTHER FACILITIES AND OPERATIONS

1. FLOORS, WALLS, AND CEILINGS: The floor surfaces in kitchens, in all other rooms and areas in which food is stored or prepared and in which utensils are washed, and in walk-in refrigerators, dressing or locker rooms and toilet rooms, shall be of smooth, nonabsorbent materials, and so constructed as to be easily cleanable: *Provided,* That the floors of nonrefrigerated, dry-food-storage areas need not be nonabsorbent. All floors shall be kept clean and in good repair. Floor drains shall be provided in all rooms where floors are subjected to flooding-type cleaning or where normal operations release or discharge water or other liquid waste on the floor. All exterior areas where food is served shall be kept clean and properly drained, and surfaces in such areas shall be finished so as to facilitate maintenance and minimize dust.

   The walls and ceilings of all rooms shall be kept clean and in good repair. All walls of rooms or areas in which food is prepared, or utensils or hands are washed, shall be easily cleanable, smooth and light-colored, and shall have washable surfaces up to the highest level reached by splash or spray.

2. LIGHTING: All areas in which food is prepared or stored or utensils are washed, hand-washing areas, dressing or locker rooms, toilet rooms, and garbage and rubbish storage areas shall be well lighted. During all cleanup activities, adequate light shall be provided in the area being cleaned, and upon or around equipment being cleaned.

3. VENTILATION: All rooms in which food is prepared or served or utensils are washed, dressing or locker rooms, toilet rooms, and garbage and rubbish storage areas shall be well ventilated. Ventilation hoods and devices shall be designed to prevent grease or condensate from dripping into food or onto food preparation surfaces. Filters, where used, shall be readily removable for cleaning or replacement. Ventilation systems shall comply with applicable State and local fire-prevention requirements and shall, when vented to the outside air, discharge in such manner as not to create a nuisance.

4. DRESSING ROOMS AND LOCKERS: Adequate facilities shall be provided for the orderly storage of employees' clothing and personal belongings. Where employees routinely change clothes within the establishment, one or more dressing rooms or designated areas shall be provided for this purpose. Such designated areas shall be located outside of the food preparation, storage, and serving areas, and the utensil-washing and storage areas: *Provided,* That when approved by the health authority, such an area may be located in a storage room where only completely packaged food is stored. Designated areas shall be equipped with adequate lockers, and lockers or other suitable facilities shall be provided in dressing rooms. Dressing rooms and lockers shall be kept clean.

5. HOUSEKEEPING: All parts of the establishment and its premises shall be kept neat, clean, and free of litter and rubbish. Cleaning operations shall be conducted in such a manner as to minimize contamination of food and food-contact surfaces. None of the operations connected with a food-service establishment shall be conducted in any room used as living or sleeping quarters. Soiled linens, coats, and aprons shall be kept in suitable containers until removed for laundering. No live birds or animals shall be allowed in any area used for the conduct of food-service establishment operations: *Provided,* That guide dogs accompanying blind persons may be permitted in dining areas.

SECTION G.   TEMPORARY FOOD SERVICE ESTABLISHMENTS

A temporary food-service establishment shall comply with all provisions of this ordinance which are applicable to its operation: *Provided,* That the health authority may augment such requirements when needed to assure the service of safe food, may prohibit the sale of certain potentially hazardous food and may modify specific requirements for physical facilities when in his opinion no imminent health hazard will result.

SECTION H.   ENFORCEMENT PROVISIONS

1. PERMIT: It shall be unlawful for any person to operate a food-service establishment within the municipality of _____, or its police jurisdiction, who does not possess a valid permit issued to him by the health authority. Only a person who complies with the requirements of this ordinance shall be entitled to receive and retain such a permit. Permits shall not be transferable from one person to another person or place. A valid permit shall be posted in every food-service establishment. Permits for temporary food-service establishments shall be issued for a period of time not to exceed 14 days.

    a. Issuance of Permits: Any person desiring to operate a food-service establishment shall make written application for a permit on forms provided by the health authority. Such application shall include: the applicant's full name and post office address and whether such applicant is an individual, firm, or corporation, and if a partnership, the names of the partners, together with their addresses shall be included; the location and type of the proposed food-service establishment; and the signature of the applicant or applicants. If the application is for a temporary food-service establishment, it shall also include the inclusive dates of the proposed operation.

        Upon receipt of such an application, the authority shall make an inspection of the food-service establishment to determine compliance with the provisions of this ordinance. When inspection reveals that the applicable requirements of this ordinance have been met, a permit shall be issued to the applicant by the health authority.

    b. Suspension of Permits: Permits may be suspended temporarily by the health authority for failure of the holder to comply with the requirements of this ordinance.

Whenever a permit holder or operator has failed to comply with any notice issued under the provisions of section H. of this ordinance, the permit holder or operator shall be notified in writing that the permit is, upon service of the notice, immediately suspended (or the establishment downgraded), and that an opportunity for a hearing will be provided if a written request for a hearing is filed with the health authority by the permit holder.

Notwithstanding the other provisions of this ordinance, whenever the health authority finds insanitary or other conditions in the operation of a food-service establishment which, in his judgment, constitute a substantial hazard to the public health, he may without warning, notice or hearing, issue a written notice to the permit holder or operator citing such condition, specifying the corrective action to be taken, and specifying the time period within which such action shall be taken; and, if deemed necessary, such order shall state that the permit is immediately suspended, and all food-service operations are to be immediately discontinued. Any person to whom such an order is issued shall comply immediately therewith, but upon written petition to the health authority, shall be afforded a hearing as soon as possible.

c. Reinstatement of Suspended Permit: Any person whose permit has been suspended may, at any time, make application for a reinspection for the purpose of reinstatement of the permit. Within 10 days following receipt of a written request, including a statement signed by the applicant that in his opinion the conditions causing suspension of the permit have been corrected, the health authority shall make a reinspection. If the applicant is complying with the requirements of this ordinance, the permit shall be reinstated.

d. Revocation of Permits: For serious or repeated violations of any of the requirements of this ordinance, or for interference with the health authority in the performance of his duties, the permit may be permanently revoked after an opportunity for a hearing has been provided by the health authority. Prior to such action, the health authority shall notify the permit holder in writing, stating the reasons for which the permit is subject to revocation and advising that the permit shall be permanently revoked at the end of 5 days following service of such notice, unless a request for a hearing is filed with the health authority, by the permit holder, within such 5-day period. A permit may be suspended for cause pending its revocation or a hearing relative thereto.

e. Hearings: The hearings provided for in this section shall be conducted by the health authority at a time and place designated by him. Based upon the record of such hearing, the health authority shall make a finding and shall sustain, modify, or rescind any official notice or order considered in the hearing. A written report of the hearing decision shall be furnished to the permit holder by the health authority.

2. INSPECTION OF FOOD-SERVICE ESTABLISHMENTS: At least once every 6 months, the health authority shall inspect each food-service establishment located in the municipality of _____, or its police jurisdiction, and shall make as many additional inspections and reinspections as are necessary for the enforcement of this ordinance.

a. Access to Establishments: The health authority, after proper identification, shall be permitted to enter, at any reasonable time, any food-service establishment within the municipality of _____, or its police jurisdiction, for the purpose of making inspections to determine compliance with this ordinance. He shall be permitted to examine the records of the establishment to obtain pertinent information pertaining to food and supplies purchased, received, or used, and persons employed.

b. Inspection Records: Demerit Values; Demerit Scores: Whenever the health authority makes an inspection of a food-service establishment, he shall record his findings on an inspection report form provided for this purpose, and shall furnish the original of such inspection report form to the permit holder or operator. Such form shall summarize the requirements of sections B. through G. of this ordinance and shall set forth demerit point values for each such requirement, in accordance with PHS Form 4006, which is a part of this section. Upon completion of an inspection, the health authority shall total the demerit point values for all requirements in violation, such total becoming the demerit score for the establishment.

c. Issuance of Notices: Whenever the health authority makes an inspection of a food-service establishment and discovers that any of the requirements of sections B. through G. of this ordinance have been violated, he shall notify the permit holder or operator of such violations by means of an inspection report form or other written notice. In such notification, the health authority shall:

(1) Set forth the specific violations found, together with the demerit score of the establishment.

(2) Establish a specific and reasonable period of time for the correction of the violations found, in accordance with the following provisions:

    (a) When the demerit score of the establishment is 20 or less, all violations of 2 or 4 demerit points must be corrected by the time of the next routine inspection; or

    (b) When the demerit score of the establishment is more than 20 but not more than 40, all items of 2 or 4 demerit points must be corrected within a period of time not to exceed 30 days; or

    (c) When one or more 6 demerit point items are in violation, regardless of demerit score, such items must be corrected within a period of time not to exceed 10 days.

    (d) When the demerit score of the establishment is more than 40, the permit is immediately suspended.

    (e) In the case of temporary food-service establishments, violations must be corrected within a specified period of time not to exceed 24 hours. Failure to comply with such notice shall result in immediate suspension of the permit.

(3) State that failure to comply with any notice issued in accordance with the provisions of this ordinance may result in immediate suspension of the permit (or the establishment downgraded).

(4) State that an opportunity for appeal from any notice or inspection findings will be provided if a written request for a hearing is filed with the health authority within the period of time established in the notice for correction.

d. Service of Notices: Notices provided for under this section shall be deemed to have been properly served when the original of the inspection report form or other notice has been delivered personally to the permit holder or person in charge, or such notice has been sent by registered or certified mail, return receipt requested, to the last known address of the permit holder. A copy of such notice shall be filed with the records of the health authority.

e. Grading of Food-Service Establishments: Every food-service establishment in the municipality of _____, or its police jurisdiction, shall display, in a place designated by the health authority, a placard approved by the health authority stating the grade received at the time of the most recent inspection of the establishment: *Provided,* That temporary food-service establishments shall not be subject to grading.

Grades of establishments shall be as follows:

Grade A. An establishment having a demerit score of not more than 10.

Grade B. An establishment having a demerit score of more than 10 but not more than 20.

Grade C. An establishment having a demerit score of more than 20 but not more than 40.

Notwithstanding the grade criteria established above, whenever a second consecutive violation of any item of 2 or 4 demerit points is discovered, the permit may be suspended (H.1.b.) or in lieu thereof, the establishment shall be downgraded to the next lower grade.

Immediately following each inspection, the health authority shall post the appropriate grade based upon the inspection findings, and shall issue an appropriate notice in accordance with subsection H.2.c. of this ordinance.

The permit holder or operator of any establishment, the grade of which has been lowered, may at any time request an inspection for the purpose of regrading the establishment. Within 10 days following receipt of a request including a signed statement that the conditions responsible for the lowering of the grade have, in the applicant's opinion, been corrected the health authority shall make an inspection and thereafter as many additional inspections as he may deem necessary to assure himself that the applicant is complying with the higher grade requirements; and, if the findings indicate compliance, shall award the higher grades.

3.   EXAMINATION AND CONDEMNATION OF FOOD: Food may be examined or sampled by the health authority as often as may be necessary to determine freedom from adulteration or misbranding. The health authority may, upon written notice to the owner or person in charge, place a hold order on any food which he determines or has probable cause to believe to be unwholesome or otherwise adulterated, or misbranded. Under a hold order, food shall be permitted to be suitably stored. It shall be unlawful for any person to remove or alter a hold order, notice or tag placed on food by the health authority, and neither such food nor the con-

tainers thereof shall be relabeled, repacked, reprocessed, altered, disposed of, or destroyed without permission of the health authority, except on order by a court of competent jurisdiction. After the owner or person in charge has had a hearing as provided for in subsection H.2.c.(4), and on the basis of evidence produced at such hearing, or on the basis of his examination in the event a written request for a hearing is not received within 10 days, the health authority may vacate the hold order, or may by written order direct the owner or person in charge of the food which was placed under the hold order to denature or destroy such food or to bring it into compliance with the provisions of this ordinance: *Provided, That* such order of the health authority to denature or destroy such food or bring it into compliance with the provisions of this ordinance shall be stayed if the order is appealed to a court of competent jurisdiction within 3 days.

4. FOOD-SERVICE ESTABLISHMENTS OUTSIDE JURISDICTION OF THE HEALTH AUTHORITY: Food from food-service establishments outside the jurisdiction of the health authority of the municipality of _____ may be sold within the municipality of _____ if such food-service establishments conform to the provisions of this ordinance or to substantially equivalent provisions. To determine the extent of compliance with such provisions, the health authority may accept reports from responsible authorities in other jurisdictions where such food-service establishments are located.

5. PLAN REVIEW OF FUTURE CONSTRUCTION: When a food-service establishment is hereafter constructed or extensively remodeled, or when an existing structure is converted for use as a food-service establishment, properly prepared plans and specifications for such construction, remodeling, or alteration, showing layout, arrangement, and construction materials of work areas, and the location, size, and type of fixed equipment and facilities, shall be submitted to the health authority for approval before such work is begun.

6. PROCEDURE WHEN INFECTION IS SUSPECTED: When the health authority has reasonable cause to suspect possibility of disease transmission from any food-service establishment employee, the health authority shall secure a morbidity history of the suspected employee, or make such other investigation as may be indicated, and take appropriate action. The health authority may require any or all of the following measures: (a) the immediate exclusion of the employee from all food-service establishments; (b) the immediate closure of the food-service establishment concerned until, in the opinion of the health authority, no further danger of disease out-

break exists; (c) restriction of the employee's services to some area of the establishment where there would be no danger of transmitting disease; and (d) adequate medical and laboratory examinations of the employee, of other employees, and of his and their body discharges.

7. ENFORCEMENT INTERPRETATION: This ordinance shall be enforced by the health authority in accordance with the interpretations thereof contained in the compliance provisions of the 1962 Edition of the "United States Public Health Service Food-Service Sanitation Ordinance and Code," three certified copies of which shall be on file in the municipal clerk's office.

8. PENALTIES: Any person who shall violate any of the provisions of this ordinance shall be guilty of a misdemeanor and upon conviction thereof, shall be punished by a fine of not more than _____. In addition thereto, such persons may be enjoined from continuing such violations. Each day upon which such a violation occurs shall constitute a separate violation.

9. REPEAL AND DATE OF EFFECT: This ordinance shall be in full force and effect 12 months after its adoption and publication as provided by law; and, at that time, all ordinances and parts of ordinances in conflict with this ordinance are hereby repealed.

10. UNCONSTITUTIONALITY CLAUSE: Should any section, paragraph, sentence, clause, or phrase of this ordinance be declared unconstitutional or invalid for any reason, the remainder of said ordinance shall not be affected thereby.

FOOD HANDLING AND PERSONAL HYGIENE

The next consideration of an operator, and perhaps one of the most important to success, is food handling and personal hygiene.

Personal hygiene refers to those qualities needed to give patrons the feeling of being attended by a clean, healthy worker. Employees will exhibit good personal hygiene by following the pointers below:

1. Stay well and have a healthy appearance.
2. Have clean work habits.
3. Keep your body clean and fresh; understand the use of deodorants.
4. Wear clean, ironed clothing and polished shoes.
5. Stand and walk with good bearing.
6. Wear your hair close to the head.

7. Brush your teeth after meals.
8. Do not wear jewelry on your hands.
9. Keep your hands clean; hands must be washed after each visit to the toilet.
10. Have good posture; eventually it will become a part of you.
11. Use a nail file to clean under your nails; they must be clean.
12. Get a chest X-ray once a year.

chapter 12

housekeeping

A clean and orderly establishment attracts and retains customers. Housekeeping refers to the cleanliness and orderliness of floors, walls, ceilings, tables, chairs, linens, utensils, china, glassware, and equipment as well as to their proper use and orderly appearance both in the front and back of the house. Good housekeeping practices can be detected upon entering an establishment. It's in the air and it reflects itself in the employees of the house. Like attracts like. A house that has good housekeeping practices will have clean employees and, likewise, a better clientele.

TIPS ON GOOD HOUSEKEEPING

1. Store eating utensils properly.
   a. Use easily cleanable shelf surfaces without paper covering or paint.
   b. Shelves should be at least eight inches from the floor.
   c. Store silver so that it will be removed by the handle.
   d. Invert cups and glasses.
   e. Storage areas should be away from heavy traffic, splash from sinks, etc.
2. Use good kitchen utensils and store them properly.
   a. Utensils must be made of smooth, easily cleanable materials.
   b. Never use empty tin cans as utensils.
   c. Utensils must fit in the sink for washing.
   d. Wash them promptly and thoroughly.
   e. Store them away from heavy traffic areas.

3. Clean equipment regularly and thoroughly.
    a. If necessary, take equipment apart for cleaning.
    b. Disconnect electric equipment before cleaning.
    c. Clean all work surfaces before placing food on them.*
    d. Never pick anything up from the floor and set it on a working surface.
4. Good planning and layout make good housekeeping easier.
    a. Arrange the flow of food in a continuous line from the receiving platform to the customer.
    b. Plan the food service so that it does not cross the path of dirty dish removal.
    c. Place pipes, drains, and wires so they do not interfere with floor and wall cleaning.
    d. All restaurant equipment should comply with National Sanitation Foundation standards.
5. Keep floors and rest rooms clean.
    a. Clean floors often and keep drains clean.
    b. Wipe up spills immediately.
    c. Using a dust-free method, sweep often between scrubbing.
    d. Have single service towels in rest rooms.
    e. Provide ample, easily cleaned waste containers and empty them often.
    f. Keep soap containers filled and operating.
    g. Keep fixtures clean and free from stains.

A regular schedule for cleaning is a must—write it out and post it. Good housekeeping is good business—good housekeeping prevents accidents.

These housekeeping tips are what the public wants in an eating establishment. The public also makes certain demands of the workers.

1. Your customers want you to:
    a. look clean and healthy
    b. give efficient and proper service
    c. serve good clean food
    d. take a courteous interest in them
2. Your employer wants you to:
    a. please customers
    b. be loyal, cooperative, and dependable

---

* If table tops or the tops of other pieces of equipment have aprons or turndowns, be certain to clean their inner and under surfaces.

3. Your fellow workers want you to:
    be cheerful, tolerant, and helpful

VERMIN

No establishment open to public patronage can tolerate vermin. The services of a good exterminator are a must. Their costs are usually reasonable. The cooperation of every employee in reporting the presence of vermin of any kind is an essential part of his or her duties.

Insect and Rodent Control

How can we control rats and mice if we do not employ a pest control contractor?

1. Get rid of their nesting places. Clean up all rubbish piles inside and outside the premises.
2. Build them out. Block all possible rat entrances. Rat-proof the building's foundations.
3. Starve them out. Protect food at night. Keep garbage containers closed. Do a thorough cleanup job.
4. Kill them. Use traps for temporary control.

How can we control flies?

1. Get rid of their breeding places. Control the sources.
2. Keep them out. Screen doors and windows properly. See that all doors open out and are self-closing.
3. Do a good job of housekeeping. Keep foods covered. Keep garbage containers tightly covered. Promptly remove accumulations of food.
4. Kill them. Use insect sprays, baits, traps, swatters, and flypapers. Caution: Never use sprays when any food is exposed in the room.

How can we control cockroaches, mites, and other insects?

1. Be alert to the first signs of infestation. Destroy infested foods.
2. Do a good job of housekeeping and storage.
3. Use the proper insecticides, but use them carefully.

PREVENTIVE MEASURES

Preventive sanitation measures should constantly be practiced. Good food-handling practices should be followed at all times to ensure the safekeeping of foods. Various foods and the methods for keeping them safe for human consumption are listed below:

FOWL. Cooked or uncooked chickens, turkeys, and other fowl should not be left out at temperatures above 40 degrees F. It should be used immediately or refrigerated until used.

SANDWICH FILLINGS. Sandwich fillings must not be combined in batches that are too large to be used immediately. Meat and other ingredients may be chopped but they should be kept separate from binding agents, such as mayonnaise, until just prior to use. Then they should be served immediately. No food of this type

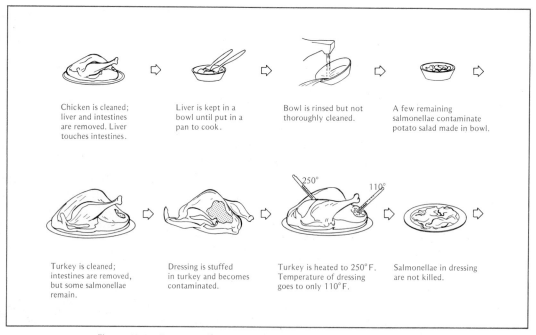

Chicken is cleaned; liver and intestines are removed. Liver touches intestines.

Liver is kept in a bowl until put in a pan to cook.

Bowl is rinsed but not thoroughly cleaned.

A few remaining salmonellae contaminate potato salad made in bowl.

Turkey is cleaned; intestines are removed, but some salmonellae remain.

Dressing is stuffed in turkey and becomes contaminated.

Turkey is heated to 250°F. Temperature of dressing goes to only 110°F.

Salmonellae in dressing are not killed.

Figure 12-1. Two typical ways in which salmonellae thrive.

should be premade and kept for several days. Enough should be made to last through a particular meal, but no more. Great care should be exercised in the use of mayonnaise and salad dressings with these foods.

COOKED HAM. Cooked ham should not be exposed to room temperature for any length of time. If ham is cooked and kept warm during a serving period, it must be kept above 130 degrees F. If the ham is to be used cold, it should be refrigerated as soon as it has cooled. Ham that is cooled and cooked should not be left outside the refrigerator for any length of time. The only exception is when it is being served. When that has been completed the ham should immediately be returned to the refrigerator.

DEHYDRATED FOODS. All dehydrated foods absorb moisture very easily when exposed to the air in an unsealed container, so they

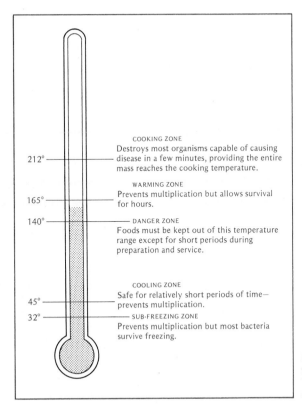

212° — COOKING ZONE
Destroys most organisms capable of causing disease in a few minutes, providing the entire mass reaches the cooking temperature.

165° — WARMING ZONE
Prevents multiplication but allows survival for hours.

140° — DANGER ZONE
Foods must be kept out of this temperature range except for short periods during preparation and service.

45° — COOLING ZONE
Safe for relatively short periods of time—prevents multiplication.

32° — SUB-FREEZING ZONE
Prevents multiplication but most bacteria survive freezing.

Figure 12-2. Thermometer for the control of bacteria (Source: *The Yearbook of Agriculture*—1966).

must be kept sealed until they are used. When water is added to dehydrated foods to return them to their original form the growth of bacteria may begin. After dehydrated foods have been reconstituted they should either be refrigerated below 50 degrees F or heated above 130 degrees F until they are ready to be used.

LEFTOVERS. Great care should be exercised in the usage of leftover items. Leftovers should be consumed within a twenty-four-hour period. Leftover meat, vegetables, and gravies should not be allowed to stand at room temperatures. These items should be kept under refrigeration at all times. Reheat leftover meat so that it reaches 165 degrees F throughout.

FROZEN FOODS. Frozen foods can be stored at temperatures of 0 degrees F. They may also be stored at −15 degrees F or lower. Some frozen foods can be cooked without any thawing period. Others, because of their size or the way in which they are to be used, do have a thawing period. Thawing, which should be done with large pieces of meat, fish, and poultry, is done under refrigeration.

CUSTARDS AND PUDDINGS. Custards and puddings should always be refrigerated as soon as possible following their cooking and cooling, and kept there until serving time. They should not be prepared more than three to four hours before serving.

MILK AND CREAM. Liquid whole milk and cream should be delivered at a temperature below 44 degrees F, refrigerated at once, and kept under refrigeration at all times. Milk should not be left outside the refrigerator. It should be returned to the refrigerator as soon as possible after each use.

Evaporated milk can be handled the same as any canned foodstuff until the can is opened. Then it must be given the same care that is given to liquid whole milk. It must be stored in a refrigerator at all times. This milk can be refrigerated in its original can without fear of contamination.

CLEANING MATERIALS AND SANITIZERS

Cleaning utensils, equipment, and facilities is of paramount importance to food service establishments. Floors, ceilings, walls, tools, equipment, etc., must be thoroughly and regularly cleaned. There are many types of cleaning materials on the market. Each is designed to do a specific job.

Vermin

There must be no vermin in the house. An establishment that prides itself on cleanliness and has an appreciation for health regulations cannot afford to have vermin of any kind. Vermin are unpleasant to see, are carriers of germs, and produce an unpleasant odor. Once any trace of them can be seen, steps should be taken to correct this problem. A good professional firm that is hired on a contract basis is by far the best approach to eliminating this condition. By having a good contract firm, the vermin problem is being checked before it starts. Antivermin preparations of breathing, eating, and contact poisons are available to aid the exterminator with his job. The best protection from vermin is a clean house where everything is in its place. Particular attention should be given to all work areas but first and foremost to receiving and storage rooms. Most infestations start with vermin delivered to operators in cartons, cases, and other containers which carry supplies from purveyors.

Floors

Kitchen floors, when possible, should be made of a water-resistant material such as tile or terrazzo. Nonslip materials should be incorporated where these hard surface materials are used. Abrasive strips are available for protection against falls and slipping. Rubber runners can also be used in hazardous footing areas. These are usually installed later and may be removable for cleaning purposes.

Protective strips can be laid between ranges, steam tables, the space in back of ranges, and the space in front of stock pots and other kettles. Removable hardwood racks are also used for this purpose. The racks can be taken apart and run through the dishwasher daily for cleaning.

All kitchen work areas need adequate and easily cleaned floor drains. When floor drains are adequate, hose cocks with an abundant supply of hot water add greatly to the required cleanliness of all kitchen floors.

Walls

Tile walls are excellent but most expensive. Prefinished tileboard is not as costly and is available in many colors. A heavy plaster finish under a high gloss enamel is also a good washable material.

Ceilings

Sound-absorbing materials are most desirable because they keep down work noise.

Lighting

Fluorescent lights are ideal and cheaper to operate in the long run.

Ventilation

Dishwashing machines continually exhaust hot moist air. All the other cooking processes also contribute their share. Proper ventilation produces better workers and a better finished product.

Modern engineering has finally removed a taboo that previously existed against mechanical ventilation of kitchens. In newer installations it is possible to air condition kitchen production areas.

Cleaning Compounds

There is a variety of establishments in the food service industry and they have many types of surfaces that require cleaning. Cleanliness is most important to catering establishments. Everything must be meticulously clean wherever the guest looks. Hallways, dining rooms, rest rooms, equipment, china, utensils, etc. — all are expected to be cleaned to perfection for visiting guests.

Because there are many types of materials and surfaces to clean, many types of cleaners have been developed to remove dirt in whatever form it may be found.

Types of Cleaning Products

Abrasive or scouring cleaners come in liquid or powder form. The word "abrade" means to wear down. This type of cleaner cleans by lightly removing the surface on which it is used. The degree of cleaning that an abrasive material will do depends on what is used. The harder the abrasive agent the faster the results in cleaning. This is because the harder agents wear down more of the surface being cleaned. Quartz is one of the hardest minerals. The size to which the mineral is ground also determines the abrasive quality. The quality of an abrasive cleaner that is used on pots and pans would cause no concern. However, when it is used on plastic tile or silver a coarse abrasive might produce scratching and other undesirable results.

Removing dirt with an abrasive-type cleaner depends a great deal on mechanical action, even though good scouring powders also contain chemical substances. These cleaners are particularly good for surfaces that are very dirty and stained.

Abrasive powders are partially soluble and require good rinsing so that small particles do not remain. The abrasive cleaners on the market range from a mild to a very strong abrasive action.

Detergents as a cleansing agent may be any of numerous synthetic water-soluble or liquid organic preparations. They all have the ability to emulsify oils and hold dirt in suspension. Detergents are mainly sold for hand or machine washing and for cleaning grease from a surface. These products are most effective when they are used in hot water.

Detergents are completely soluble. They are prepared to eliminate or compensate for unfavorable conditions in the water. Some detergents are combined with a germicide that keeps the bacteria count low and thus produces a utensil that is sanitized as well as cleaned.

A sanitizer or germicide has to be registered with the U.S. Environmental Protection Agency. When a sanitizer is combined with a detergent it may be called a "detergent-sanitizer." Sanitizers are used on many utensils and work surfaces.

Uses for Sanitizers:

1. in the third sink for rinsing pots and pans
2. on worktable and equipment surfaces
3. for cleaning tabletops in the dining area
4. on shelving in the refrigerator and storage areas
5. in cleaning rags, sponges, and brushes

Points to Remember in Using Sanitizers:

1. in most instances it takes very little to do the job
2. using too much is wasteful
3. use it in the third sink for rinsing dishes

Floor Cleaners

When washing a floor no more water should be used than necessary. Water should not be allowed to remain on floor after scrubbing. It should be picked up as soon as possible. A scouring or abrasive powder can be used on heavily stained areas. As a general rule, most synthetic detergents are less harmful to rubber and asphalt tile than are soap products. Synthetic detergents are also preferred on terrazzo and concrete floors because they will not leave the film deposit that soaps will.

Floor Polish

Floor polish is a mixture of waxlike materials and turpentine. It is used on linoleum, rubber, wood, composition, and stone floors. Some polish requires rubbing to obtain the characteristic high luster of a waxed surface. Other types, that provide a long-wearing self-polishing finish, are available for practically every type of floor.

Metal Cleaners and Polishes

There are many cleaning and polishing powders, liquids, creams, etc., that are designed for use on specific types of metals. Cleaning and polishing is achieved by the chemical reaction of properties in the cleaner in conjunction with the mechanical action of brisk hand rubbing. A good metal cleaner that provides a high luster also has an abrasive agent that wears down the surface slightly. This wearing action is so minute that it is visible only in microscopic closeup. If a cleaner is used that has either no abrasive or a soft abrasive, there will be a poor luster when the cleaning is finished.

The cleaning agents in the polish may be soap, inflammable spirits, or others that are good dirt solvents.

Silver Cleaners and Polishes

Silver cleaners and polishes are intended to remove tarnish, which is the result of the chemical reaction of silver with air or some foodstuffs. Tarnish takes the luster off silver. It can be removed with polish or by placing the silver in a simple detarnish bath.

A polish may be a liquid or a paste. Silver polish contains a mild abrasive agent and detergent. The abrasive in the polish removes a very small amount of silver along with the tarnish. Since silver is a soft metal, the abrasive cannot be too hard and must be very fine in grade.

Specially treated cloths are available for polishing silver.

A detarnish bath is easy to prepare and a good practice to follow in the daily washing of flatware. For a short period of time, the silverware is dipped into an aluminum pot that contains the solution in hot water. This removes the tarnish. The bath should be used prior to washing the silverware as described in the section on dishwashing. Care should be taken that stainless steel knives with silver handles are not dipped in a detarnish bath. It may result in stains on the surface of the stainless utensil.

Burnishing machines are widely used in large establishments to routinely clean and polish silver. The burnishing action improves the silver plating by rolling scratches and tightening the pores.

chapter 13

dishwashing

Whatever method is prescribed by the house, the handling of dishes is of extreme concern. The proper procedure of sorting, scraping, washing, rinsing, and storing is very important, as is the use of a good chemical. The cleanliness of the sink or machine is another necessary factor if clean dishes are to be provided. An abundant supply of hot water at 180 degrees F for the final rinse and a clean conscientious worker are also basic to the ideal handling of this very vital function. Figure 13-1 outlines a typical dishwashing station. Figure 13-2 shows a dishwashing room.

DISHWASHERS

There are many dishwashing machines on the market. No two kitchens are exactly alike but there is a model available to suit almost every need, regardless of how large or small an establishment may be or how many pieces are to be washed. Whatever the demands, the fundamental steps in cleaning dishes remain the same. However, each establishment modifies this procedure to suit its requirements. The entire job of washing dishes involves scraping, washing, and rinsing.

1. Scraping—If dishes are scraped manually, particles of food are removed with a hand spray of cool water. The removal of food can also be done by machine with fresh prewash water that is pumped and recirculated. Machines can be purchased either way. The water used in this phase should not be too hot. The recommended temperature is between 110 and 120 degrees F.
2. Washing—Dishes are subjected to pumped wash water. The number

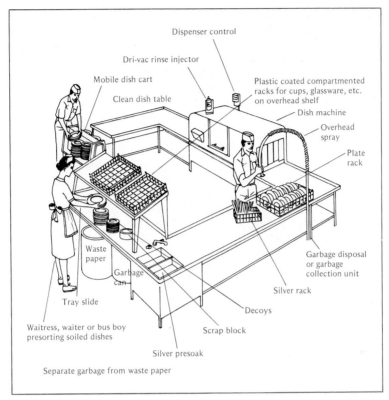

Figure 13-1. A typical dishwashing station.

of wash arms and spray heads depends on the size of the machine. The number and size of pumps and tanks also depend on the size of the machine. A water temperature of between 140 and 160 degrees F is maintained in the wash tank.

3. Rinsing—Dishwashing machines have a final fresh-water rinse at 180 degrees F or over. Some also have a prerinse. In this case a hot-water rinse precedes the final fresh-water rinse. This water is held in a reservoir and is pumped over the dishes. Varying qualities are available in different models, subject to what an establishment's space and funds permit. The hot-water rinse or power-rinse water should be 170 degrees F. A final fresh-water rinse is 180 degrees or over.

Remember: The bigger, better, more costly machines cannot do more than anything already described. What they can do is handle a bigger volume in a shorter period of time. Some very large machines

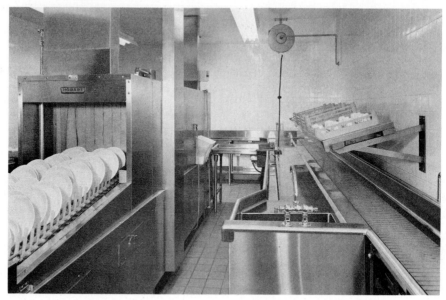

Figure 13-2.   Dishwashing room in a large cafeteria.

have a drying chamber that permits even more speed in handling dishes.

The selection of the proper dishwashing machine is extremely important. The time an owner and her or his designer, architect, and fixture-house representative give to projecting how many pieces of china, glassware, and silver will be handled per hour is time well spent. It is only by giving careful consideration to these factors that a proper selection can be made. It is a good idea to get a dishwasher that is as large as the budget permits. Then an unexpected growth in volume will not bring the unwanted stress or pressure that results from a backlog of china, glassware, and silver remaining to be processed.

Figure 13-3 shows a representative sample of the many types of dishwashers available. The fountain or counter unit (a) is mounted under a counter or left free standing. It is for smaller operations. The wash and rinse cycles are automatically timed. The hood type (b) is available with automatic or manual controls. In a smaller operation, it would be used for all dishes; in a larger one, for glasses only. Dishes are placed in a rack and enter from either direction. The door type (c) is slightly larger than the hood type. It is controlled either manually or semi-automatically. As in the hood type, dishes are placed in racks. Open-end rack machines (d) come in a variety of sizes. The one shown is a single tank

Figure 13-3. Various dishwashing units.

and features a power wash and a fresh water final rinse. Open-end rack machines can have other tanks with the ability to scrape or pre-wash dishes. Two conveyor or continuous racking machines (e) and (f) are

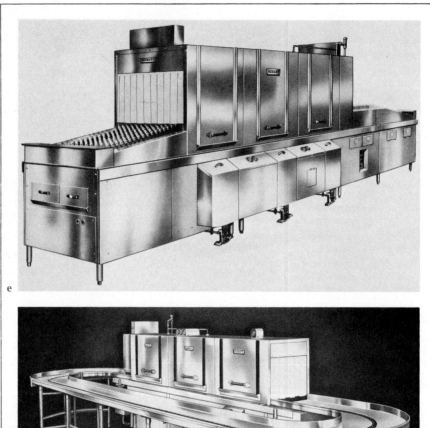

Figure 13-3. (*Continued.*)

shown. The machine shown in (e) does not require that dishes be racked; the other machine (f) automatically sends the racks of dishes through the various cycles of the machines.

Figure 13-4 shows the racks and conveyor links on which dishes are loaded. Item (a) is a tilt cup rack, (b) is a multi-purpose rack, and (c) is a series of conveyor links used in machines such as the one shown in Figure 13-3 (e).

The best investment in dish tables are those of heavy-duty stainless steel. The dish tables for soiled and clean dishes should be large enough to handle the loads that are produced during the heaviest meals. These tables should be planned so that any excess piling of dishes will be avoided and so that there will be an even work flow into and out of the dishwashing machine.

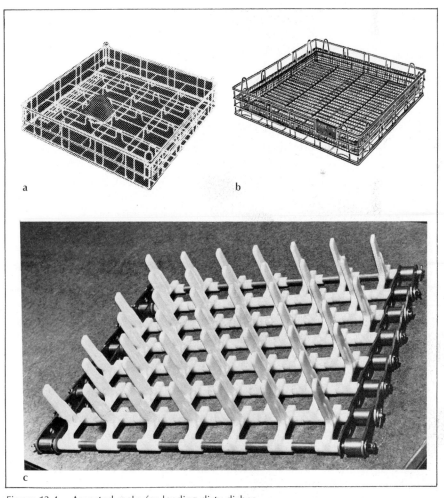

Figure 13-4.   Assorted racks for loading dirty dishes.

DISHWASHING

The dish pantry is one of those areas that too frequently receives no more than a passing glance from management. Not enough can be said of the importance of this area. As much thought should be given to the layout and sequences of work flow in this department as to that of any other department. This is the place where all the china, glassware, and utensils from various dining places in the establishment are brought together again and again. So many individual pieces are hurriedly accumulated here and so much is done to them in such a short period of time. This is the area of highest breakage if not enough thought has been given to its design. Managers must make it a point to understand this department and not permit other matters to seem more urgent. A poorly planned dish pantry can be very costly in labor and replacement costs, so it is good business to have adequate supervision of the dishwashing procedures. This principle should be followed as the rule, not as the exception.

The glass and dishwashing departments should be located as close as possible to an exit from the serving areas. If at all feasible, that should be a one-way exit. In any new or remodeled construction, include conveyor belts from the dining area to the glass and dishwashing areas in kitchens if the physical conditions permit. They should pay for their cost in reduction of breakage and noise.

Spray-Type Dishwashing Machine

PROCEDURE TO START MACHINE

1. Check to see that scrap trays are clean and in their proper place. See that the overflow pipe is free and in the correct position.
2. Check to see that the curtains are clean and hanging in position.
3. Check the wash and rinse arms and the spray jets. Make certain they are clean and in working order.
4. Close the tank drain valves.
5. Open the water valves to fill the tanks. Close the valves when the water reaches the top rim of the tank or overflow.
6. Turn on the tank heaters.
7. Check to see if enough detergent is in the reservoir and make certain the hand-fill dispenser is operating.
8. If an electric detergent dispenser is used, make certain it is operating.
9. Check to see that rinse reservoir is filled and that injector is working.

10.   Turn on the machine, making certain that the temperatures for wash and rinse are correct.

TO CLEAN THE MACHINE:

1.   Open the drain valves so that water can run out of the tanks.
2.   Remove the curtains, scrub them with soap and water, and permit them to dry.
3.   Remove the wash arms, poke out any soil clogged in the jets, and rinse the arms and jets.
4.   Remove and empty the scrap trays. Clean them with a brush, soap, and water. Rinse them with the spray hose.
5.   Use a hose to wash down the inside of the machine. Check to see that pieces of equipment have not fallen into the tank. Check to see that the pump filters are free of any clogging soil or other items.
6.   Check the sides of the machine for lime deposits and use a solution to remove them.
7.   Clean the top and sides of the machine, scrub all dishtable areas, and rinse everything down with the hose.
8.   Rinse down the walls and the floor.
9.   Inspect the inside for proper reassembling and cleanliness.

Surge-Type Dishwashing Machine

This type of machine is simple to operate and cheap to run. It is intended only for smaller operations. The unit is slightly higher than a table and consists basically of two open-top rectangular tanks into which baskets of dishes are lowered. They go into the wash first and then into the rinse solution. The wash action is provided by means of a motor-driven centrifugal pump that is mounted on the end of the machine. This pump creates a tumbling, boiling action in the wash water, drawing and throwing water across and around the dishes. There is no action in the rinse water; the basket is lowered in this tank to rinse the dishes. Each tank has its own controls and heaters. The water temperatures are the same as those in the spray machines: 140 to 160 degrees F for the wash and 180 degrees F for the final rinse. The rinse tank should have an overflow, and the faucet should be open to bring in fresh water when the unit is in operation.

It is essential that dishes be thoroughly scraped before they are racked and washed. Dishes should be placed in the racks very carefully so as not to overcrowd.

Hand Washing of Dishes

This might be the procedure used in small establishments. Where hand washing is the practice, a three-compartment sink is set up similarly to the pot and pan sink. A work area is needed so that dishes can be scraped. The dishes are washed in one sink, then given a fresh-water rinse, and finally a very hot rinse or a cooler germicidal solution rinse. The dishes can be racked in special dip baskets so that they can be handled in very hot water. If dishes are washed by hand it is best to air dry them for sanitary reasons.

Handling of Dishes

Procedures for handling dishes in dishwashing stations or rooms (see Figure 13-1) are as follows:

TO WASH:

1. Place glasses, cups, and bowls in the overhead compartment racks. These items are put in the racks upside down.
2. Remove heavy food particles from the dishes before they are racked or placed on a conveyor dishwashing machine.
3. Rack dishes that are all of one kind together. Then rinse them with the overhead spray to remove any remaining heavy food soil.*
4. Set up a silver presoak pan on the table that is used for soiled dishes.
5. Set out decoy dishes on the table so that bus personnel can stack the dishes as the bus boxes are unloaded.
6. Mix and rack the silver with their eating ends up.

TO STORE:

1. Bring the clean-dish cart or Lowerator cart to the clean end of the dish machine and load the clean dry dishes as they come out of the machine.
2. Glasses, cups, and bowls are left in the stacking racks as they come out of the machine. The stacking racks are then placed on four-wheel carriers and stored until the contents are needed once again.

* Overhead spray is used only where the prewash operation is not a part of the dish-washing machine.

POT AND PAN
WASHING

Pots and pans need the same attention and cleanliness as utensils and fine pieces of china. A clean pot or pan will guarantee that the foods prepared in it will taste just as the preparer wants them to taste. A greasy film or a small particle of food left in the pan will change the flavor of almost any dish.

Three sinks are most desirable for washing pots and pans. In the first sink the pots and pans are placed to soak after having been scraped of fats or burned-on foods. The pots are also scrubbed clean in this sink. The second sink is a fresh-water rinse. There should be a small trickle of fresh water flowing continuously. The sink should also be equipped with an overflow outlet so that grease can be floated off as the water is freshened. The third sink is either a hot-water rinse or a germicide rinse. If hot water is used, a burner unit can be mounted on the sink to maintain the rinse temperature. An overflow outlet is also needed in this sink to keep the water fresh. A booster heating unit is not needed if a germicide solution is used.

When filling the wash sink the detergent compound should be dissolved in cool or lukewarm water in the bottom of the sink before

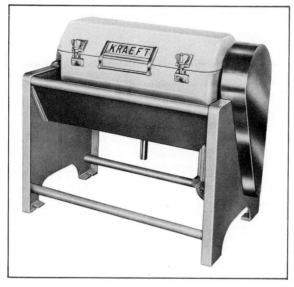

Figure 13-5.   A burnishing machine, a special unit for the polishing of flatware and holloware silver.

filling it with fresh water. This eliminates the formation of insoluble "soap balls" that are seen so often in sinks.

In recent years a new approach to pot and pan washing has been developed. Washing units can be mounted on a pot sink, cut into the side of the sink, or be added as a completely new unit. As pots are placed in the sink to soak, a "live-water torrent" swirls throughout the sink, keeping the water constantly in motion. No time is wasted in scouring. The pots and pans are simply placed in the surging water and left there. A 400-gallon-per-minute pump action pulverizes food particles in the water so that everything disappears down the drain when sink is emptied. When a pan is needed for use it is taken from the sink, the detergent is quickly rinsed off, and the pot is ready.

WAREWASHING

Silverware

1. Soiled silverware should be gathered at the soiled-dish table by workers or service personnel and left to soak in a sink or container. A detarnish solution* may be added to the soaking silver.
2. The silver is next removed from the presoak sink and placed into the compartments of the silver racks. The eating ends are up. The knives, forks, etc., should be mixed for better washing.
3. The silverware is run through machine and allowed to stand for a few minutes to air dry.
4. The silverware is then placed on a sorting table over a clean dry dishcloth.**
5. The silverware is picked up by the handle and inspected.
6. Finally, the silverware is placed into holders with its handles up so that service personnel can easily carry it into the work areas.

---

* The detarnish bath is a simple process that removes the tarnish on silver. All that is needed is a pot container large enough to hold a large amount of silver and flatware.

The pot in which everything is soaked should be made of aluminum. If it is made of some other material, a piece of aluminum foil should be placed on the bottom. The container should be half filled with hot water and one of several different detarnishing agents can be added. The silver items should be submerged so that they are in contact with the aluminum or with other silverware that is touching the aluminum. A few minutes of this is sufficient to remove normal tarnish. Care must be taken not to employ any detarnishing materials that might produce a toxic residue.

** Steps 4 and 5 can be eliminated by making a grouping and an inspection in step 3 and then inverting the silverware in the special holder that is described in step 6.

Glass Washing

Clean, sparkling glassware is an essential standard in all establishments. Food, fingerprints, lip marks, water spots, and other common soils must be removed from top to bottom, inside and outside.

There are several procedures that can be followed when washing glasses. Glassware, because it is transparent, requires careful handling. When glasses are washed at a sink, a sink with three compartments is most desirable. The first sink is the wash sink and requires a brush and a good compound. Water should be kept at 110 to 115 degrees F. Small heating elements are available to do this. The second sink is a fresh-water rinse. This should be fitted with a stand pipe or an overflow. The faucet can be left slightly open to permit fresh warm water to come into the sink. The third sink is also a rinse sink. This sink should be charged with germicide in order to sanitize the glasses.

Glasses can also be washed by machine. A special glass-washing machine can be used as well as the conventional dishwashing machine. If the dishwashing machine is used, care should be taken to see that fresh water is in the machine when washing glasses. Glasses that are to be washed in a conventional machine are run through the tanks with fresh water after all the other items are finished and water has been changed in the machine. Glasses should never be mixed with dishes.

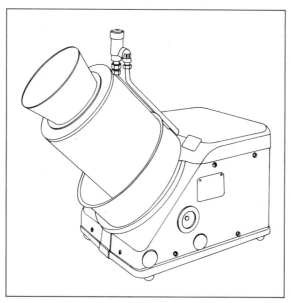

Figure 13-6. An individual glass washer.

Various types of machines and washing applications are available for washing glasses. In one glass-washing machine the individual glasses are hand placed on revolving nylon brushes that scrub the glasses clean. The glasses are racked as they are washed. When the rack is filled, it is placed in the rinse compartment. After closing the sliding top, the switch is turned on. This activates the timed rinse. For a full fifteen seconds two revolving rinse arms send swirling streams of fresh water into and around the glasses, rinsing them to sparkling cleanliness. The water in the washing compartment is held in a sink well that is equipped with a strainer and a strainer pan. A model of this sort is of table height and has a rinse compartment fitted with a sliding top that serves as a cover and as a convenient workboard. In this machine the glasses are scrubbed inside and out by the combined action of the brushes and the forced circulation of the water.

part VI

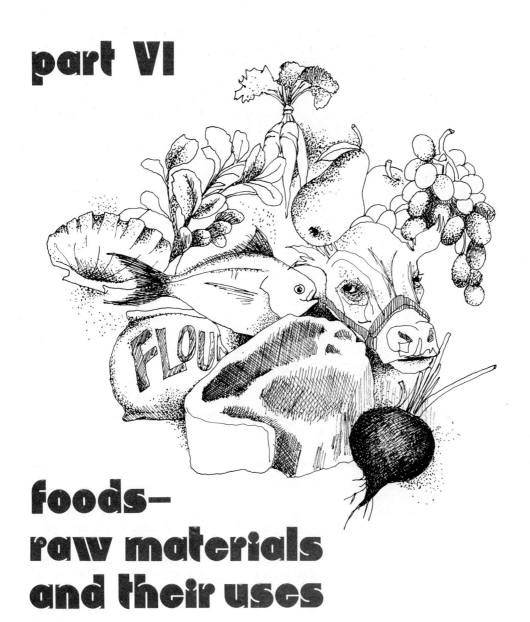

foods--
raw materials
and their uses

chapter 14

marketing, distributing, and storing food

MARKET STRUCTURE

A good market structure means more than just getting a product to market. If the foodstuff is fresh, it also includes protecting a living organism from heat, cold, moisture, dryness, and improper handling while moving it to a distant point.

As produce is picked from the field, trucks ship it to neighboring states and provinces. Long-distance hauling requires refrigerated freight cars packed with ice not only to keep fruit and other products fresh but also to preserve nutritive values as they travel to other points. Some fresh produce is shipped overseas. These shipments require refrigeration compartments for the journey.

Grain products are first sent to country elevators. From there they go to terminal elevators where some processing may take place prior to shipment to a mill for grinding. Special rail cars are designed for long-distance transport of grains. Specially covered cars ensure cleanliness.

The trucking industry provides different types of carriers with varying degrees of insulation and numerous types of mechanical refrigeration equipment. Some are designed in such a way that, by installing dividers, separate loads requiring different temperatures can be carried at the same time.

Standardization has made it possible for carriers to interchange trailers and permit the "piggyback" technique. The trailer is loaded with a product that may or may not require specific temperature control and it pulls this to a railway. At the railway the trailer is placed on a flat car.

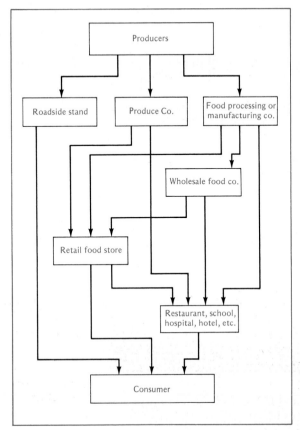

Figure 14-1. The principal supply routes by which foods get to the consumer.

The railroad then hauls the trailer to the specified city. At this point the trailer is coupled to a tractor and delivered to its final destination.

The same thing is done in hauling a trailer on board a ship. The trailer is pulled by tractor or shipped by rail to a port. On arrival, the trailer is coupled to another tractor and hauled to its final shipping point.

Transportation is an important part of the story of getting fresh foods and other food products to market, but it is not all of the story. Producers, roadside stands, cooperatives, manufacturers, produce companies, jobbers, brokers, salespeople, advertising people, merchandisers, and wholesalers, all working together, form a communication web with the most elaborate equipment available.

The complex system of marketing demands excellence in both communications and transport. Both require a large number of people with diversified skills.

The food cooperatives are highly specialized and efficient. They have a lot to do with the quality of a food product and also influence its marketing pattern.

Food cooperatives may be large or small. A cooperative sets quality standards that each individual member must meet before the cooperative accepts his or her product for marketing.

The cooperative meets the specifications of the large buyer by consistently selecting products in large batches of similar quality. This results in the farmer being able to get better prices for the product and the processor and consumer handling a quality-controlled product.

The Sunkist brand represents one of the more famous cooperatives. The Sunkist organization is a cooperative of citrus growers that banded together prior to the turn of the century to produce citrus products.

THE DISTRIBUTION OF FOODS

Moving the wide variety of foods to markets where consumers are located is a complex affair. The food must be delivered at all times of the year in quantities consumers want to buy. This involves a number of different agencies, each of which has a separate marketing and distribution function. The complete job involves warehousing goods after processing, financing the product while it is in the course of distribution, advertising and sales promotion, transportation from point of production to point of consumption, breaking down large units of goods into smaller lots, and finally selling to the commercial or institutional buyer.

Various channels are used to market foods from the producer or canner to the buyer. Most producers and canners do not employ their own field sales force. Instead, they arrange to have food brokers sell their products for them.

Food brokers act as selling agents by finding markets of food consumption. They do not take title or possession of the canned foods or food products. They only arrange for sales to wholesalers and chain organizations within their territories, subject to the producers' approval of quantity and price. The brokerage commission is generally paid by the seller rather than the buyer. Brokers handle noncompetitive lines and thus often represent packaged, frozen, and canned foods at the same time, including nationally advertised brands.

Marketing Costs

The services of distribution are essential in bringing the product to the buyer. These services cost money, regardless of the agency that performs them. Shortcuts can be devised to eliminate one or more of the agencies, but no shortcut can eliminate the service itself.

The buyer has to realize that the price paid for any product includes not only the cost of the food itself but also the cost of bringing the product where it is wanted, when it is wanted, and in the proper form and quantity. One of the important factors in the distribution system is financing. By the time an establishment pays the wholesaler for a food item, many weeks or months may have elapsed since the food was processed or canned. The farmer, the processer, the broker, the wholesaler, the transportation facilities, and the advertising agencies could not wait all this time to be paid for their services. Money must be provided for purchases and payrolls, taxes and insurance, maintenance, repairs, the equipment of warehouses and stores, and other such business necessities.

The cost of marketing a product between the time it is ready for market and purchase by the consumer amounts to a large part of the retail price. Current statistics are that the farmer receives approximately 38% of the retail price and that the remaining 62% goes for processing, handling, and marketing.

STORAGE OF FOODS

Foodstuffs are perishable. They lose their quality after varying lengths of time. Some foods require refrigeration and others require only protection from sunlight, heat, dampness, dirt, and vermin.

In a commercial establishment both refrigerated and nonrefrigerated items are commonly stored in the same walk-in fruit and vegetable box. This box has a temperature range of 36 to 45 degrees F with a relative humidity of 85 to 95 percent. It would be impractical to store every item at its own ideal temperature because of the many temperatures that would be required. Most items in a commercial operation are held for a relatively short period of time. The ideal conditions for nonrefrigerated storage are a storeroom with good ventilation, a relative humidity of 50 to 60 percent, and a temperature of 50 to 60 degrees F.

Refrigerated Storage

There are different storage, temperature, and humidity factors that are ideal for each food item. However, ideal conditions for every kind of food are impractical in a commercial operation because they vary so widely. For example a head of lettuce is best preserved at 32 degrees F with a relative humidity of 90 to 95 percent but lemons are best preserved at a temperature of 55 to 58 degrees F with a relative humidity of 85 to 90 percent. These ideal figures were determined after careful study under laboratory conditions. Foods that are preserved by refrigeration require ideal temperatures that range as much as 45 degrees.

Table 14-1 is intended as a guide for temporary storage. A slightly colder temperature is necessary for longer periods of storage.

Some fruit and vegetables need only to be stored at room temperature or a few degrees cooler. Foods stored in this fashion require a

Figure 14-2. A walk-in refrigerated unit.

Figure 14-3. A large refrigeration unit showing (a) a walk-in door and (b) reach-in doors.

TABLE 14-1. A GUIDE TO BOX REFRIGERATION AND HUMIDITY

BOX	TEMPERATURE	RELATIVE HUMIDITY
Fresh Fruit and Vegetables	36–45	85–95
Meat	32–36	75–85
Dairy	35–40	75–85
Fish*	30–34	75–85
Frozen	−10	

* Fresh fish is packed in ice at this temperature.

dry, well-ventilated room with temperatures ranging from 55 to 60 degrees F. Foods that may be stored in this fashion include green tomatoes, sweet potatoes, winter squash, bananas, and dry onions. It is best to store potatoes in a dark room.

FOODS ABSORB ODORS. Fruits and vegetables may impart odors and absorb odors from one another. For this reason extra care is taken to avoid storing certain foods together and to provide extra protection for those foods that have odor-absorbing qualities.

TABLE 14-2. FOODS THAT GIVE OFF AND ABSORB ODORS

FOOD	GIVES OFF ODORS	ABSORBS ODORS
Apple (fresh)	yes	yes
Butter	no	yes
Cabbage	yes	no
Eggs (shell)	no	yes
Milk	no	yes
Onions	yes	no
Peaches (fresh)	yes	no
Potatoes	yes	no
Turnips	yes	no

chapter 15

fruits and vegetables

FRUIT

A fruit can be defined as the edible reproductive body of a seed plant. Fruits come in various shapes and forms. Many kinds consist of more than 80 percent water.

Food Value

The calorie content of the more popular fruits is low. However, they are very rich in needed minerals as well as essential vitamins.

Buying and Storing

Fruit items are purchased fresh as needed. In many establishments it is a daily routine. In a resort establishment this might not always be possible because of distance from a purveyor.

Low temperatures are essential in the storing of fruit. A range of 36 to 45 degrees F is desirable. If the air in the storage room is too dry, the moisture passes from the fruit into the air. This causes the fruit to shrink prematurely. The floor can be sprayed or materials used to hold a certain amount of humidity in the air. If there is too much humidity a mold will rapidly develop and decay the fruit. Fruits in general require careful handling and storage to avoid destruction and loss.

Experience is needed to determine when a fruit's eating quality is at its peak. Today's crops are generally marketed by growers at or near that peak. Most of the storage needed to bring the products to the stage of marketability takes place en route between the producer and the market of final purchase.

Prevention of Darkening

Some fruit may darken quickly when cut edges are exposed to air. If possible, these fruits should be used as soon as they are cut. If this cannot be done, spreading a little lemon juice or other tart fruit juice over the cut edge will assist in keeping the natural color. These fruits should also be covered and refrigerated to avoid exposure to air. Examples of some of these fruits are apples, peaches, and bananas.

Fresh Fruit

Most of the fruit that is used in the catering trades has undergone some degree of processing. This is because it is easier to store processed fruit. It is also more readily available as the need arises. Preservation has made the idea of a season for fruits less meaningful than it once was. Today most fruits are available almost year round in some preserved state or another. However this does not mean that an astute operator does not take advantage of the fruits locally in-season at a particular time. By doing so, an establishment will profit both by low cost and by providing a boost in the variety of foods available to a patron. Fresh fruit is purchased daily or weekly for the most part.

Fruit Products

Fruit juice is the liquid form of fruit. Fruit juice contains the same valuable substances as the natural product and is in a form agreeable to most people as well as to the human body. Juices that are properly labeled contain no added water. They are solely juice and fine-cut pulp. Nectars are mostly mixtures of juice and pulp, water, and in some instances sweetening agents. Artificial flavors that are not natural food products are also on the market. Concentrated fruit juice is the extract of a fruit reduced, in a low temperature vacuum, to approximately 20 percent of its original bulk.

Vinegar

Many fruit juices are now bottled and sold as beverages. Apple juice is also used to make vinegar. Wine vinegar is another fruit product. It is made from wine that was in turn made from fruit. Both wine and apple vinegar are used in the food service industry. Some are seasoned by addition of herbs such as tarragon.

Dried Fruits

Dried fruits contain from 15 to 25 percent moisture and a high percentage of sugar. A low storage temperature is required for the preservation of the quality of dried fruit. The fruit may be dried naturally, as is the walnut and the almond, or it may be artificially dried. In either case, the water has been removed from the fruit. Some popular dried fruits are apples, peaches, prunes, apricots, currants, raisins, dates, and figs. The fruit may be dried in any of the following ways:

1. by exposure to the sun in the open air
2. by placing the food in heated units and removing the water by evaporation
3. by the combined use of controlled heat and circulated air

Fruit Uses

The many types of fruit available and the many ways in which to prepare them make fruit an ideal food to serve. Fruit and fruit products have a variety of uses on many popular menus. Fruit can be consumed in its natural state with little preparation or it can be combined with other foods served either fresh or cooked. An example of this would be a Waldorf salad or a mincemeat pie. Fruit can be used on a daily menu in the following ways:

1. As an *appetizer.* Fruit can be served fresh by itself on a plate or in a supreme dish. A fruit product in the form of a juice or in combination with other foods is also a good appetizer.
2. As an *entree.* Fruit, served in combination with other products, constitutes a nourishing and eye-appealing main course. An attractive example is fresh fruit salad with sliced chicken.
3. As a *dessert.* Again, a fruit can be used in its natural form, it can be cooked, or it can be combined, cooked or uncooked, with other foods to compliment the finest meal.

The palatability of fresh fruits or vegetables is judged first by its appearance. There should be no defects visible. When possible, taste test fruit for flavor and texture. With certain fruits, melons and berries for example, a bouquet is also present. These qualities depend upon soil type and climate conditions during growth, the stage of maturity at harvest, and how the product was held and stored after harvest. In wholesale transactions there is a voluntary method for defining size and grade of fruits and vegetables. However, the size of the item does not relate to the qualities that are most important, flavor and texture.

Storage

When storing fresh fruit, care should be taken that there is no transfer of odors from foods that give off smells to foods that absorb them. Fresh fruits store well with fresh vegetables that require refrigeration. Stored fruit continues to breathe in storage and some moisture is passed into the air. The air in the box should not be dry or it will draw the moisture more quickly from the fresh fruit. The recommended relative humidity for storing fruit is 85 to 95 percent. The recommended temperature of the box is 36 to 45 degrees F. The temperature of the air also has a lot to do with the amount of moisture that leaves the fresh fruit. Remember: If the moisture in the air and temperature level are as they should be, your fresh fruit will not be shrunken and wilted.

Canned Fruits

Most of the popular fruits are available in canned form and come in containers of various sizes to meet the needs of the industry. A large portion of the fruits used in the industry are purchased this way. Canned fruits are available in a mixture, sliced, cubed, halved, or whole. Some are also available in the form of a nectar, a sauce, a juice, or a concentrate. They can be purchased packed in their cooking water or in light or heavy syrup. Others are spiced or brandied.

The method of canning that will be described in the section on vegetables is generally the same followed for the canning of fresh fruit. The time of picking and the speed of canning are of the utmost importance. Canned items can be ordered as needed, but a yearly contract at harvest time may result in a better price.

Fresh fruits are also frozen in a very quick freeze method as soon as possible after picking. That method will be described in the section that deals with the use of vegetables. Fruits can be frozen either sweetened or unsweetened. They are available whole, as juices, and as concentrates. More of the natural flavor is preserved in the freezing process than in other methods of fruit preserving. However, special freezer storage equipment is needed to ensure the proper keeping qualities of frozen foods. Frozen juices need not be thawed. Frozen fruit should be thawed in a refrigerator or under running water. Frozen fruit will lose its quality quickly if the temperature increases. Once damage occurs to frozen fruit because of an increase in temperature it cannot be corrected by refreezing. The damage will stay with the food. Frozen fruits can be held at −10 degrees F for a period of six to twelve months. They can be purchased as needed or a yearly contract can be developed with a right of withdrawal at harvest time. Remember: It is important to have a loyal purveyor. An unscrupulous dealer who quotes a low price may result in a very temporary saving.

Tips on Uses of Some Fresh Fruit

APPLES (Some). The best eating apples are Jonathon, Delicious, McIntosh, and Yellow Newton. The best baking apple is the Rome Beauty. It retains its form. The best cooking apples are the Winesap, Jonathon, and Rhode Island Greening, which is a tart-tasting apple.

AVOCADOS. When ripe an avocado's texture is as firm as butter. To ripen it, store it in a warm room for three to four days. To stop ripening, store it in a cool dry place.

BANANAS. Bananas that are used for cooking should be light yellow in color. The tips may be green. These will hold their shape best.

GRAPEFRUITS. When grapefruits are good they are heavy, firm and have a thin skin. Since the juice is the most important quality to a guest, the heavier fruits are the most desirable.

MELONS (also Called "muskmelons"*). Melons belong to the gourd family which includes pumpkins, squash, and cucumbers. The netted varieties of melon are commonly called "cantaloupes."** A sweet melon is matured on the vine. The more fragrant the melon the sweeter the melon. Melons grown in the United States may be categorized into the following groups:

1. Netted and ribbed rind: These netted melons are covered with a green or yellow-green rind. The rind is divided by riblike sections and the surface is covered by a netlike covering of ridges. The flesh

---

* This is because of the fragrance of ripe fruit. The word "musk" stems from a substance used as a perfume fixative.

* This derives its name from the sixteenth-century papal villa in Cantalupo, Italy, where it was first grown.

is reddish orange to peach in color. The popular commercial types of these cantaloupes are the Bender, Rocky Ford, and Hales Best.
2. Netted or smooth rind (no ribs): These are winter melons. The popular commercial types are the Persian (orange meat), the Casaba (white meat), the Honeydew (smooth rind, green meat), and the crenshaw (smooth rind, peach-color meat).
3. Watermelons: These melons vary in size, shape, and color. The rind color may be a light or dark green. The rind may be solid in color, spotted, striped, or marbled. The flesh may vary from a white to yellow to a red color. Unlike other melons, it has no center cavity. Its name is derived from its abundance of watery juice. The seeds can be roasted and served as an appetizer.

The rind of some melons can be pickled or spiced and then used as relish or as an accompaniment to entrees.

ORANGES. The *navel* is round, has an orange color, has no seeds, and is easy to peel and separate. It has a navel-like pit at the narrow end where a small secondary fruit is enclosed. The Valencia is a juice orange. It has a thin skin, seeds, and a touch of green in its color. Oranges are sold by the count. They come 100, 150, 200, etc., to a crate.

PAPAYAS. Papaya is a melon-shaped fruit of a palm-type tropical tree.

PEACHES. There are two types of peaches. Freestone is the type whose pit pulls away from the flesh easily. It may be either white or yellow in color. The pit of the clingstone clings to the flesh, which may also be either white or yellow in color.

MANDARINS. These are the small orange-colored fruits that are similar to tangerines and used so much nowadays either canned or fresh in fruit sundaes, salads, etc.

PEARS. Fresh pears of several varieties are available year-round. The peak for the harvesting of pears is mid-August to late October. Various types of pears are available at different times of the year. A ripe pear for eating purposes is soft to the touch on the stem end. Unripe pears that are kept at room temperature will ripen to the desired taste. Ripe pears should be refrigerated. Pears should be firm when purchased and free of spots or bruises. Pears are best when they are picked green and ripened in storage until they are soft enough for eating. A dry cool storage is best for ripening pears.

The best pear for eating has soft juicy flesh that is covered with a thin smooth skin of a greenish-yellow to a yellow-reddish color. These pears are the Bartlett, Anjou, Comice, and Bosc. The Bartlett has a bell shape and a light-yellow color. It does not keep well. It is a late-summer pear. The Anjou is a spicy pear with green skin and a fine grain. It is in season from late fall through the winter. The Comice has green skin, a superior quality, and great beauty. It is in season from the late fall through the winter. The Bosc has a long neck and russet skin. It is a late-fall to midwinter pear.

The best pears for spiced pickling or cooking are the solid or firm pears. Their skin is coarse and the flesh is not fine grained. These pears may be rounder in shape and range in color from yellow to a reddish brown. The taste of this pear is more spicy. Pears that fit this description are the Kieffer and Seckel. The Kieffer is round in shape and yellow to reddish-brown in color. It is a winter pear with a spicy taste. The Seckel is a small, sweet, juicy fruit that is also used as a dessert. It is an early summer pear.

PINEAPPLES. Pineapples are ripe when they are soft but firm and have a fragrant smell, and the leaves pull easily from center.

PRICKLY PEARS. Prickly pears are the fruit of a species of cactus. They are eaten raw or used in salads.

TANGERINES. Tangerines belong to the citrus family and look much like a small flat orange. They peel easily and the sections pull apart easily.

WATER PACK. This refers to canned fruit that is packed in water with no sugar added.

SYRUPS (in Canned Fruit). This refers to the sugar content in the syrup used in canned fruit. It can be extra heavy, medium, light, etc.

VEGETABLES

More vegetables are being consumed annually in the United States than ever before. Many fresh vegetables are available throughout the year. This is made possible by a very good transportation system, a wide range of climate conditions throughout the country, and the expanded use of refrigeration. Figure 15-1 shows some common vegetables. Vegetables can be divided into the groupings shown on page 200.

CUCUMBERS

TURNIPS

MUSKMELONS

RADISHES

ONIONS

BEETS

Figure 15-1. Some common vegetables.

PUMPKIN

WATERMELONS

GARLIC

SWEET POTATOES

CARROTS

STRING BEANS

Figure 15-1. (*Continued*).

TOMATOES

PEAS

POTATOES (MORLAND)

SWEET OR BELL PEPPERS

CABBAGE

KALE

Figure 15-1. (*Continued*).

KOHLRABI

EGGPLANT

LEAF LETTUCE

CORN

Figure 15-1 (*Continued*).

1. *ROOT AND TUBER VEGETABLES.*   These are the edible underground parts of different plants. Some root and tuber vegetables are radishes, turnips, carrots, beetroot, and potatoes.

2. *FLOWER VEGETABLES.*   Cauliflower, artichokes, and broccoli are examples of this type of vegetable. Although they are thought of as flower vegetables, they may have stalks and leaves as well as flower buds, etc.

3. *LEAF AND STALK VEGETABLES.*   The leaf and stalk vegetables are the most widely used fresh vegetables. They include items such as lettuce, endive, cress, dandelion, varieties of cabbage, brussel sprouts, asparagus, rhubarb, and celery.

4. *SEED AND POD VEGETABLES.*   These vegetables include peas, peppers, beans, lentils, okra, etc. These vegetables may be the seed or the seed case of the plant. These vegetables can be eaten fresh, or they may be dried and ground or cooked in various ways. Some seeds are eaten ripe. Corn cereals are an example of this. Others, such as green peas and green corn, are eaten before they fully ripen.

5. *BULB VEGETABLES.*   These vegetables are actually the roots of some vegetables growing in the soil. Onions, leeks, shallots (also called eschalottes), and chives are of this type.

6. *FRUIT VEGETABLES.*   These are the edible yields of a plant, as opposed to the edible plant in itself. Some fruit vegetables are tomatoes, squash, cucumbers, pumpkins, eggplant, etc. Many varieties of these are grown for different uses. They can be used raw or cooked, by themselves or combined with other foods. These items are the fruits of the plant but, in popular usage, they are referred to as vegetables.

Preparation of Vegetables

Vegetables require special care in selection, cleaning, storage, and handling. Many, such as relishes and salads, are eaten raw, so special attention should be given to how they are washed. Washing, sorting, and inspecting are necessary to ensure that nothing that would be harmful if consumed, such as chemical spray or any tiny living thing, is left on the plant.

Vegetables have an endless variety of uses and provide a rich range of flavors. In some vegetables one part of the plant is eaten, such as the leaf, while with others this part is discarded and another part is eaten. Vegetables play an important part in the cooking practices of all people. Their consumption is essential to a balanced diet in most parts of the world. Even the quality of the meat we eat is dependent on products of the vegetable kingdom that are eaten by the animals.

Care must be used in the preparation of vegetables so as not to destroy their nutritive value. Vegetables should not be overcooked. Much of their value to the human body is left in the water in which they were cooked, so the water should also be used.* When vegetables are cooked with other nutritively rich foods, they have the ability to absorb such substances and pass them on.

Vegetables that are delivered daily are the ones that have the best flavor and quality. These are brought directly from the farm, city market, or wholesaler where they were freshly cut or kept moist and crisp by refrigeration or, possibly, ice pack. Present growing and marketing conditions provide an abundance of fresh vegetables available twelve months of the year. No longer is the seasonal aspect a concern of the quantity vegetable buyer employed by today's commercial kitchens.

Vegetables should be prepared by people who have been thoroughly trained in the proper handling and various preparation methods of vegetable cookery. In a large operation these people are known as vegetable cooks. In a smaller operation this responsibility may be combined with another job. The job can be handled by a man or woman. The nature of the work done and skills developed by these workers are varied. They must know how each vegetable is received, cleaned, stored, and cooked. They have to understand the nutritive value of the different vegetables and how this can be preserved in cooking. They need to know how vegetables are served, either plain or in a sauce, and which way is more complimentary to specific entrees. They must know how to cook the large variety of vegetable dishes that appear on daily menus and party menus. They must be able to requisition vegetables from the storeroom as needed. They may also serve vegetables during meal hours.

A large operation would also have vegetable preparation workers who would assist the vegetable cook. These people inspect the kitchen ice box every morning to determine what leftovers there are and discuss with either the vegetable cook or the chef how this food should be used. They also receive and inspect vegetables as they are delivered

---

* Many establishments add it to their stock pots. Others use it to enhance the flavor of boiled meats and other meat entreés.

from the storeroom. They wash, trim, and peel the vegetables, as each requires, and store them under refrigeration. Some vegetables may require storage in water. Others simply have to be covered. The vegetable preparation workers cut potatoes or wrap them in foil, as the menus require, and may also cut standard vegetables that are used in quantity. They change water and in general care for vegetables until they are used. They distribute vegetables that are ready for cooking to various departments. This work is done in the vegetable preparation area which has the needed refrigeration tools, sinks, and equipment.

Receiving

A check has to be made of all vegetable purchases as they are received. This will ensure that the quality received is the quality that was ordered. Receiving persons may do nothing but handle all the receiving and issuing of foodstuffs, but they may also have another job. In either case they must be trained to recognize deviations from specifications. Here, at the point of receiving, is where the correction of errors should take place.

Storage of Vegetables

As a rule, fresh vegetables are purchased on a day-to-day basis. Fresh vegetables are delicate. Even under ideal refrigeration conditions, fresh vegetables that are kept too long acquire a limp feeling and change from their natural color. When this happens the taste is not the same and the nutritive value to the human body also drops. A vegetable that is ripe and firm to the touch is the best vegetable to buy, but it must be bought with the thought of quick usage. Do not depend on refrigeration for preservation. It should be thought of as a short-term holding action with a very natural process of maturity. A damp coolness is best for the vegetable storage box. The ideal temperature is 36 to 45 degrees F and with a relative humidity of 85 to 95 percent. Some vegetables, such as dry onions, squash, unripe avocado, and sweet potato, can be stored at room temperature. Potatoes should be stored in a dry, dark, well-ventilated room with a temperatures of 55 to 60 degrees F.

Quality Standards

FRESH FRUITS AND VEGETABLES. Close to the turn of the century, new and expanded areas of production opened in various parts of the country. In most cases these were distant from the major market areas. This long distance in trading quickly developed a need for a common denominator in language and product identification. To meet this need and demand the U.S. Department of Agriculture began work on developing grade standards. The first standards were provided in 1917. They were for the grading of potatoes. From that beginning, standards were developed for nearly all fresh fruits and vegetables. A large number are now in effect covering almost all products. The standards were developed with the cooperation of the industry and every effort is made to have them reflect both good commercial practice and the needs of growers, processors, sellers, buyers, and consumers.

Most fresh fruits and vegetables are packed and sold on the wholesale market on the basis of U.S. grades. There are standards for seventy-two different kinds. There are also thirteen consumer standards that were developed for use at the retail level.

GRADE NAMES. The typical range of wholesale grades for fresh fruits and vegetables includes U.S. Fancy, U.S. No. 1, and U.S. No. 2. There are sometimes grades above and below that range. For example, grades for apples are U.S. Extra Fancy, U.S. Fancy, U.S. No. 1, and U.S. Utility. The consumer grades are, generally, U.S. grades A, B, and C.

The grades assigned to fresh fruits and vegetables are determined on the basis of the product's color, size, shape, degree of maturity, and freedom from defects. Defects are those caused by dirt, freezing, disease, insects, and mechanical injury.

Frozen Vegetables

Fresh frozen vegetables are very much like fresh vegetables in appearance, color, and flavor. The preparation and cleaning that are necessary with fresh vegetables are not necessary with frozen vegetables. The cost of using frozen vegetables is higher, however, and the taste is not always quite the same as garden-fresh vegetables. Frozen vegetables must be stored in temperatures below zero. If the temperature rises above this, they will have a quality loss shown in color change and then loss of flavor. Studies conducted in various parts of the country show that frozen vegetables maintain their quality for a year when stored at temperatures below zero. An even lower temperature will retain quality for a longer period, but quick turnovers are still the best practice for most operations. Frozen vegetables, unlike other frozen foods, do not require thawing prior to cooking. The only exception to this is corn on the cob.

Shortly after vegetables and fruits are harvested, their color, texture, and flavor begin to change. This is nature's way of returning to the earth what was taken from it. People's concern through the ages has been to slow down or stop this action. Preservation is the protection of foods against spoilage. People have always sought ways to preserve food in time of plenty so that it can be used in the nonharvest time of the year. Across the ages it has been discovered that food could be preserved by drying, smoking, salting, pickling, canning or preserving, and now by quick freezing. While these methods are good, they are not perfect. People are still looking for a way to preserve the food with little change in its original flavor, texture, and color.

A Gloucester, Massachusetts explorer, scientist, and inventor by the name of Clarence Birdseye was the discoverer of the quick freeze method. Food is frozen so rapidly that the original qualities remain unchanged. This discovery solved the problem of preserving food in its natural state and gave birth to a line of frozen foods that still bears the founder's name. Foods were frozen, prior to this, but it was a time-consuming process. Foods were held in refrigerated rooms until they were frozen solid. In the slow freezing process large ice crystals form and ultimately, in the thawing process, these crystals break down the fragile construction of the food cells. The faster the food can be frozen the

Figure 15-2. An immersion freezer.

smaller the ice crystals. With quick freezing no change in the original structure of the food occurs when it is thawed.

Multiplate freezing is the most successful method of quick freezing. This process places cartons of food between metal plates so that the plates come in direct contact with the packages. The plates are mounted in the freezing cabinets where the foods are sandwiched in place. These multiplate freezers are made in portable sizes so they can be transported from point to point and follow the crops. This means the crops can be packaged as soon as possible.

The original cost of frozen foods may be slightly higher than canned foods, but this is offset by savings in waste and labor costs due to less preparation. There is no waste in a frozen product and no added labor. Frozen vegetables are cooked in much the same way as fresh. The only difference is the time needed to complete the cooking. Small packages of frozen food can be placed directly into boiling water.

A frozen item must be kept at a low temperature to avoid any adverse changes in the product. As is true in canning, it is most important that the time between harvesting and quick freezing be as short as possible to ensure the food's preservation at the point of perfect maturity.

Canned Vegetables

Canned vegetables are popular in the industry because they can be handled or stored with relative ease and because, as with frozen vegetables, the steps of cleaning, etc., have already been completed. The cost of canned vegetables may be less than frozen and, at most times of the year, may be less than fresh vegetables. Canned vegetables may have a slight flavor change. This is partially due to the sterilizing step in the canning process.

BIRTH OF CANNED FOODS. A previously unknown Parisian confectioner by the name of Nicolas Appert began the development of canned food. Through his experiments in 1809 he won the coveted prize offered by Napoleon to the person who could find a new way to preserve foods to feed his large army all year around. This was important because an army truly travels on its stomach. In the middle of the nineteenth century Louis Pasteur discovered the cause of food spoilage. Thus began the scientific application of heat in preserving food.

Commercial canning began in this country in the early nineteenth century. It grew rapidly along with the historic expansion of a new and growing country. Canned foods followed the pioneers then as well as the explorers, liberators, hunters, and others in our modern twentieth-century society too numerous to mention.

Cans or jars of identical size may show a different net weight on the label. This is due to the difference in the density of the foods. Figure 15-3 shows some common can sizes.

Fruits and vegetables used by the majority of canners are mostly grown by farmers under contract. This arrangement permits the canner

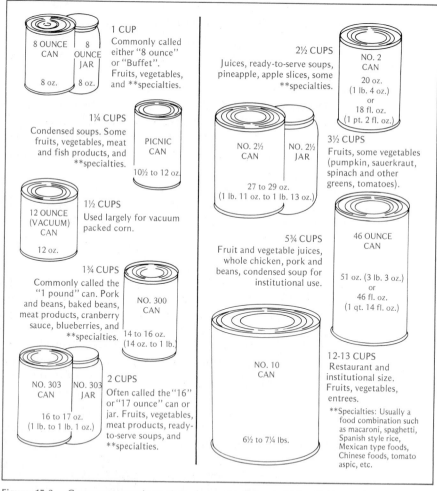

1 CUP
Commonly called either "8 ounce" or "Buffet". Fruits, vegetables, and **specialties.

8 OUNCE CAN — 8 oz.
8 OUNCE JAR — 8 oz.

1¼ CUPS
Condensed soups. Some fruits, vegetables, meat and fish products, and **specialties.

PICNIC CAN
10½ to 12 oz.

1½ CUPS
Used largely for vacuum packed corn.

12 OUNCE (VACUUM) CAN
12 oz.

1¾ CUPS
Commonly called the "1 pound" can. Pork and beans, baked beans, meat products, cranberry sauce, blueberries, and **specialties.

NO. 300 CAN
14 to 16 oz.
(14 oz. to 1 lb.)

NO. 303 CAN
NO. 303 JAR
16 to 17 oz.
(1 lb. to 1 lb. 1 oz.)

2 CUPS
Often called the "16" or "17 ounce" can or jar. Fruits, vegetables, meat products, ready-to-serve soups, and **specialties.

2½ CUPS
Juices, ready-to-serve soups, pineapple, apple slices, some **specialties.

NO. 2 CAN
20 oz.
(1 lb. 4 oz.)
or
18 fl. oz.
(1 pt. 2 fl. oz.)

NO. 2½ CAN
NO. 2½ JAR
27 to 29 oz.
(1 lb. 11 oz. to 1 lb. 13 oz.)

3½ CUPS
Fruits, some vegetables (pumpkin, sauerkraut, spinach and other greens, tomatoes).

5¾ CUPS
Fruit and vegetable juices, whole chicken, pork and beans, condensed soup for institutional use.

46 OUNCE CAN
51 oz. (3 lb. 3 oz.)
or
46 fl. oz.
(1 qt. 14 fl. oz.)

NO. 10 CAN
6½ to 7¼ lbs.

12-13 CUPS
Restaurant and institutional size. Fruits, vegetables, entrees.

**Specialties: Usually a food combination such as macaroni, spaghetti, Spanish style rice, Mexican type foods, Chinese foods, tomato aspic, etc.

Figure 15-3. Common container sizes for canned food. **Specialties* indicates a food combination such as macaroni, spaghetti, Spanish rice, etc.

to supply special seed to ensure getting the most suitable variety as well as to permit the supervision by the canner's trained field people of the growing and harvesting of the crops.

The canning process is one of the most effective methods of preserving fruits and vegetables. Changes may take place in color, texture, and taste after the product is canned. These changes are accelerated at a higher temperature. The lower the storage temperature the better. Storage at 45 to 60 degrees F is good. Spoilage of canned foods can be detected by the following signs:

1. Bulging ends of tin cans
2. A soft or mushy state of the contents
3. Gas bubbles on the top of a container where contents are visible
4. Liquid gushing out an opening in the top of the container
5. A sour odor

When any of these factors are evident, the best policy is to discard the contents. Particular care should be exercised at harvest time to ensure the proper stage of ripeness. The fresh items must reach the factory as fast as possible so that they are processed in the shortest time possible.

BASIC PROCEDURES IN COMMERCIAL CANNING. The procedures of receiving, cutting, pitting, peeling, sorting, grading, and slicing vary with the nature of the product that is canned. There are important canning operations common to all products.

THE CLEANSING OPERATIONS. This is one of the most important steps in the canning process. Cleaning lowers the amount of bacteria that is found in raw foods. This step reduces the burden of the heating process by destroying pathogenic organisms. Different methods of washing can be used, depending on the product. Some products receive an air blast while on a moving belt or screen before the actual washing cycle.

THE BLANCH. Another important and basic operation in canning procedures for many vegetables and some fruit is known as the "blanch." The raw food is placed in warm or hot water or treated with live steam. Equipment is specially designed to handle individual products and may be capable of being adjusted so specific raw materials are held at the proper temperature for specific period of time. Blanching accomplishes several desired effects:

1. It softens fibrous plant tissue.
2. It serves as an added cleansing measure.
3. It releases gases in the plant cells, thereby avoiding stress in the can during the heating process.
4. It fixes the color of the product. No further changes take place in the can.
5. It controls organisms that cause spoilage. In some cases it removes disagreeable odors or flavors.

THE EXHAUSTING.   During this operation, the open can that is holding the raw food is passed through an exhaust box where hot water or steam is used to expand the food by heating it. This forces air and gases to escape through the top of the can. The length of time and the temperature used in this operation vary with the nature of the product. The exhausting can also be accomplished by heating the food, filling the can while it is still hot, and then sealing it; by adding boiling water or brine to the food in the can; or by withdrawing air and other gases from the can with special vacuum machines and sealing the can at the same time. This last process is called "vacuum pack."

SEALING THE TIN.   This is also a very important process. The heat applied prior to the sealing of the tin destroys the spoilage organisms on the raw food material. A proper seal on the container prevents reinfection of the food. A permanent airtight seal is of paramount importance to the maintenance of quality within the tin.

HEAT PROCESSING.   In this operation the sealed container is exposed to boiling-hot water or to steam that has been under pressure for a specific period of time. This destroys spoilage organisms that are present in the raw material. The sealed can prevents any reinfection. Adequate heat processing varies by product. In general acid foods, including the common fruits and some vegetables or vegetable products, are easily heat processed. Sealed containers of these foods ordinarily only need to be heated long enough to permit them to reach the desired temperature in the center of the can. This is usually 200 degrees F or slightly less. Some acid foods can be processed by filling the cans while the food is sufficiently hot, sealing and inverting the cans, and cooling them. Nonacid foods require a temperature of approximately 240 degrees F for adequate heat processing. These foods are processed under steam pressure. Machinery and accessory instruments are available to permit precise scientific control of commercial processing operations.

COOLING THE TIN. As soon as the objective of the heat treatment has been achieved, it is important to check the action of the heat. This prevents undue softening of the texture or change in the color of the food. Two modern practices are used in the cooling process. Air cooling can be used for the cooling of smaller units or when a slower cooling process is desired for the best final results. The other practice is water cooling which can be carried out by flowing water into the cooker under air pressure, by conveying the containers from the cooker to a tank of cold water, or by placing them under a cold-water spray. When cans are pressure cooled, the pressure is maintained in the retort during the cooling of the cans to counterbalance the pressure that is produced within the can at the same time.

During the canning process the cans are marked or stamped with a code to identify the product prior to labeling and also to identify the worker who canned the product.

Canneries may hold items for a short period following the canning process. Any defects in the process should appear within this time. A buyer who receives a defective can may simply return the item and it will be immediately replaced by the purveyor.

The canning process may vary with the item or the type of container to be used. For instance, some fruit juices can be sterilized and passed directly into a sterilized bottle. Canning factories today require a great deal of machinery to do the various jobs efficiently. Some canneries place much importance on the type of raw material grown and assist in growing crops. Others grow some of their own raw materials.

In canning, it is very important that the product be taken from the field and put into the can in the shortest possible time. Once the proper stage of maturity has been reached, quick procedures are brought into action. Canneries may work through the night during the harvest season in order to complete the work quickly.

A good growing season will produce a good harvest which in turn produces a large "pack." The carryover from last year's pack plus the size of the new pack are the two most important factors in establishing the price level. Canned items are usually cheaper than frozen items.

LABELING. The Federal Food, Drug and Cosmetic Act specifies a list of facts that must be included on the label of a product if it is to be legal for interstate commerce. These facts were determined in a joint study by the government and the National Canners Association, which represents the canning industry. The National Canners Association, of course, reflects the attitude of its hundreds of members. The law provides that every label must state the following facts:

1. The product name.
2. The name and address of the manufacturer, packer, or distributor.
3. The net contents of the container by weight or liquid measure.
4. The variety, style, and packing medium. For example, light syrup, heavy syrup, diced, etc.
5. Dietary properties.
6. If the quality or filling standards meet or fall below those set by the Food and Drug Administration. For example, pieces, uneven cuts, etc.
7. If no standard of identity has been set by the government for a product, then the ingredients should be listed on the label.

These are the minimum points that the canner must meet. Under a voluntary program of descriptive labeling instituted by the canning industry a number of years ago, canned food labels bear additional information, not required by law, but designed to aid the buyer in selecting a canned food. Some packers may want to give consumers more information such as color, size, recipes, or a picture of the product.

Dried Vegetables

These are generally not as widely used as are the fresh, frozen, or canned vegetables. Dried vegetables are used more often when making soups or when the vegetables are combined with other foods. In reducing the water, the original appearance is changed. One of the more recent dehydrated vegetables that has become popular in the trade is instant potatoes. This has great appeal where the cost of labor is an important factor. Dried foods should be stored in tightly covered containers and kept in a cool, dry place. Dried vegetables have 8 percent moisture or less and have a low sugar content.

Buying Vegetables

It is unsound to think of buying vegetables by price alone. Low cost does not make up for poor quality. The best approach to buying vegetables lies in picking a quality product at a fair price. Fresh vegetables should not be bought too long before they are used.

There are indicators that are valuable for recognizing the condition or quality of items purchased. Color, size, shape, odor, and degree of firmness show the food's condition, maturity, or ripeness. These factors affect the flavor, texture, and the presentability of the vegetable.

Footnotes on Vegetables

CABBAGE. For our purposes we will concern ourselves with three types: the common cabbage that varies from green to light green and has a solid head; the red cabbage with reddish-purple leaves and a somewhat stronger flavor than common cabbage; and the curly cabbage with looser leaves that are generally darker in color.

CHIVE. This is a small onionlike plant that grows in clusters. Its leaves are hollow. It belongs to the onion family.

CRESS. Watercress is a leafy green plant that grows in shallow streams with sandy bottoms. It is used as a garnish and in sandwiches.

ONION. The Bermuda onion has a flat shape and mild flavor. It is eaten cooked or raw. The Spanish onion is a sweet mild onion. It is large and round or oval in shape. The American types include both Bermuda and Spanish onions in red, yellow, or white.

SWEET POTATO. There are two types of sweet potatoes, those that have a dry heavy texture when cooked and those that after cooking are soft and moist. The dry type is yellowish inside when cooked. The moist type is reddish in color. The moist potato is often referred to as a yam.

WHITE POTATO (or Irish Potato). The Idaho potato is preferred for baking, french frying, stuffing, and mashing. Ohio or russets are preferred for boiling, steaming, or using in casserole dishes.

SQUASH. There are two types of squash: summer squash and winter squash. Summer squash has a soft exterior and keeps for a relatively short period of time. Winter squash has a hard exterior and keeps very well.

SHALLOT. This is a bulbous green onion that is used as a seasoning. It is sometimes called "eschallotte." The shallot is used in most European cookery and by foreign-born or foreign-trained chefs.

QUALITY STANDARDS

Processed Fruits and Vegetables and Related Products

KINDS GRADED. A large number of grades have been developed for a great variety of processed fruits and vegetables, whether canned, dried, or frozen, as well as for a number of related products such as olives, pickles, jellies, and jams. The U.S. Department of Agriculture has also established standards of quality that may be used by manufacturers in the packaging of their items. If these marks are used, the can content must come up to the established standard. The letters "U.S." appearing before the mark of standard mean that the item was packaged under government supervision (see Figure 15-4).

Figure 15-4.   A grade mark used on canned, frozen, or dried fruits and vegetables.

GRADE NAMES.   These are usually U.S. Grade A (Fancy); U.S. Grade B (Choice or Extra Standard); and U.S. Grade C (Standard). There are very few exceptions to this pattern.

WHAT THE GRADES MEAN.   U.S. Grade A (or Fancy) means that the processed fruits or vegetables are of excellent quality. There are no defects, the product has a good color, it is uniform in size, and it has reached the proper state of maturity or tenderness. U.S. Grade B is good quality, but not uniform in size, color, or texture. U.S. Grade C indicates not as good a quality although it may be as nutritious.

Operators in the food industry will not find all foods identified by grade, although most of the trading in food, prior to the operator level, is done on the basis of U.S. Department of Agriculture (USDA) grades.

Not many products carry the U.S. grade marks. The ones you will most likely see are on frozen vegetables, frozen orange juice, and jam. However, if the label has one of the grade names without "U.S.," it must measure up to that quality even though it has not been officially graded.

chapter 16

milk and milk products

Dairy products, of which milk is basic, are essential in our industry because they rate high in nutritive values. The use of milk, cream, butter, and cheese in cookery falls into two categories:

1. as a part of the cooking ingredients of various dishes
2. as an entrée by itself or combined with other basic foods

In America the word "milk" is understood to mean cow's milk. Other milks are specifically referred to as sheep's milk, goat's milk, etc. This same designation is made for milk products. The large variety and uses of milk products make it necessary for people in the trade to have an appreciation of the product.

MILK

Fresh milk is milk just as it comes from cows that are properly fed and regularly milked. It is not changed in any way. This whole milk consists of approximately 13 percent dry ingredients and 87 percent water. The proportions are variable. They are especially affected by the milk fat. Under good conditions milk may have as much as 4 percent or more of milk fat. The variance may be the result of inherent factors of breeding, time of milking, season, soil, and feed.

Milk Grades

The local health offices of each community are responsible for the care and sanitary condition of milk that is handled in their community. There is a uniform standard governing milk production and distribution among the states. However, most states have regulating agencies with their own sanitary marketing agreement. Only Grade A milk is shipped out of one state into another.

To foster high standards of measure, the United States Department of Agriculture and the United States Public Health Service have developed the Milk Ordinance and Code as a guide for standards. They recommend the use of this code by those engaged in milk production.

The Milk Ordinance and Code can be adopted as the standard by any state or local community. It governs conditions relating to:

1. the health of cows
2. the health of milk workers
3. the sanitary condition of barns, milk-handling equipment, and storage
4. pasteurization

Milk produced according to these guidelines is referred to as "Grade A" milk. When milk does not reach these high standards, it is referred to as "Grade B" milk. The grade is marked on the bottle top or on the side of the carton in which the milk is bought.

Grade of milk refers only to the sanitary conditions under which it was produced and the bacteria count that the finished product contains.

Pasteurized Milk

This is milk that has been heated to a temperature of 185 degrees F in order to destroy any bacteria. It is done without any noticeable change in the product.

Homogenized Milk

This is pasteurized milk that has been processed through a homogenizing machine. The homogenizing machine breaks the fat globules of milk into very fine particles, thus mixing it thoroughly with the milk so that no layer of cream will develop.

Vitamin D Milk

This is a pasteurized and homogenized milk that has had its vitamin D content increased.

Skim Milk

Skim milk is a pasteurized milk that has had almost all the fat removed.

Acid Milk

Sour milk is milk containing lactic acid bacteria. Buttermilk is the liquid that remains in the container after the making of butter. Yogurt is made from milk combined with special types of lactic acids.

Cream

Cream is the fat part of the milk. It contains approximately ten times more fat than homogenized milk. Coffee cream is a special cream prepared for use with coffee. There is at least 18 percent milk fat in this product. Whipping cream has popular use commercially. It contains at least 30 percent milk fat. Sour cream or cultured sour cream is a fluid or semifluid cream resulting from the souring of pasteurized cream which contains not less than 0.20 per cent acidity. Cream is soured by the addition of lactic acid bacteria. Many cooks sour small quantities with fresh lemon juice.

Half and Half

This is a less costly homogenized milk and cream product that is used mostly for coffee. It contains approximately 12 to 15 percent fat.

Milk Concentrations and Powders

These products are used extensively in the commercial areas of cooking. They last longer than fresh milk or cream and, because of this, have special uses. Some powders are always on reserve in establishments where fresh milk is used.

Evaporated Milk

Evaporated milk is fresh milk that has had some of the water removed through the process of evaporation. In so doing, the original volume is reduced. The concentrated milk is then homogenized. It contains 8 percent fat, $7\frac{1}{4}$ percent protein, $10\frac{1}{2}$ percent lactose, $1\frac{3}{4}$ percent mineral salts, and 72 percent water.

Condensed Milk

Condensed milk has gone through essentially the same process as evaporated milk, but cane sugar is added as a preservative. It contains 8 percent fat, $7\frac{3}{4}$ percent protein, $10\frac{1}{2}$ percent lactose, $1\frac{3}{4}$ percent mineral salt, 31 percent water, and 41 percent sugar.

Dried Whole Milk

This is a powdered milk made by the evaporation of almost all the water from whole milk.

Skim Milk Powder

This is powdered milk made by the evaporation of almost all the water from skim milk.

Cream Powder

Modern dehydrating equipment now produces a powdered cream made by the evaporation of almost all the water from cream.

Nondairy Cream

A fine-tasting item is now available under various labels for use with coffee as a cream. This product can also be whipped and used as garnishing or topping for desserts. Low in calories, it will keep under refrigeration as long as two weeks.

Ice Cream

A frozen product made from a pasteurized and homogenized cream, milk, and milk-solids mixture. Added to this is sugar, fruits, berries, nuts, flavoring, and sometimes stabilizers. In the French-type ice creams eggs are cooked with the other ingredients.

Care of Milk

The grading of the producers' milk is under the sanitation specifications of local health departments. Fresh milk must always be transported and stored under refrigeration. Milk should not be exposed to kitchen temperatures for any length of time. The amount required for immediate use should be poured from the container and the rest of the milk returned to the refrigerator as soon as possible. Unopened canned milk can be stored in a cool, dry place. Once it is opened it must be kept under refrigeration in either its original can or another container. Containers of dried skim milk must be kept tightly closed. Cans of dried whole milk must be kept tightly closed and must be refrigerated.

Butter

Butter is an important milk product. The term "butter" refers to the fat of cow's milk that is free of other fats and prepared in the churning process. Prior to churning the cream is ripened. This is done by adding lactic acid ferment. Butter's low melting point is an advantage over other edible fats in culinary preparations. In spite of its relatively high cost, its use in the cooking processes has added greatly to the reputation for haute cuisine in many establishments. A small portion of salt may be added to impart flavor and act as a preservative. A bit of color may be added to provide the light yellow tone. Sweet butter refers to top quality butter made from sweet cream with no salt added.

Standards of Quality

Figure 16-1 is the USDA grade mark used on butter, cheese, and nonfat dry milk. It is printed on the carton and on the wrappers of quarter-pound sticks of butter.

Butter that carries the U.S. Grade AA mark (Figure 16-1) is the best quality. It has a delicate, sweet flavor. There are second and third grades that are labeled U.S. Grade A and U.S. Grade B, respectively. Grade A is almost as good as the better grade and sells for less. Grade B does not have as good a flavor and is still less expensive. The rating is similar for cheddar cheese and Swiss cheese except that there is no AA grade. There is also a Grade C for cheddar and C and D grades for Swiss cheese. Grades for nonfat dry milk are U.S. Extra Grade and U.S. Standard Grade.

The quality approved mark (Figure 16-2) may be used on cottage cheese, processed cheese, and sour cream. It means that the product is of good quality and was manufactured in a clean plant under the supervision of a USDA grader. At present, only a few plants are using this mark on their products.

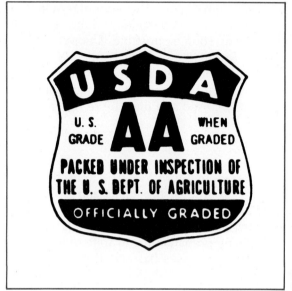

Figure 16-1.   A grade mark used on butter.

Figure 16-2.   A grade mark used on cottage cheese, process cheese, and sour cream.

What the Grades Mean

The higher grades of butter have a pleasing and desirably sweet flavor. They are made only from cream that has such flavor. Grade B butter is generally made from selected sour cream and therefore lacks the fine fresh flavor of the top grades.

The top grades of cheese indicate desirable and consistent flavor, body, and texture. This is true for sharp, mellow, and mild cheddars.

The U.S. grade shield on packages of nonfat dry milk is assurance of dependable quality and compliance with sanitary requirements. It also guarantees, in the case of instant nonfat dry milk, that the milk powder will dissolve quickly and completely.

CHEESE

How Cheese Is Made

The art of cheese making is aided by many new discoveries in scientific laboratory control and by the development of new methods and equipment. However, the fundamental principle has not changed since people first discovered how to make cheese. This is based upon the use of rennet, an enzyme, which causes the formation of curds in whole fluid milk.

In the past, cheese and the rennet for setting the curds was commonly made in the home. American cookbooks of the early 1800s provided recipes and instructions on how to produce rennet in the home. Through the years people have added the discoveries of science and their own "know how" to the art of making a large variety of cheeses.

Cheese is a milk product that is made from the milk of cows, sheep, or goats. Most of it, however, is made from cow's milk. The basic factor in producing good cheese in a factory is the clean, wholesome milk that is received from the farm. Cheese companies are continually working with dairy farmers who provide the milk for their factories to ensure that the milk is produced by healthy well-fed cows. They also want to make sure that the milk is carefully and properly cared for until it reaches the factory.

Basic Method for Making Cheese

Cow's milk, in its liquid form, contains about 13 percent food solids by weight. These food solids are butterfat or cream, casein and other muscle-building proteins, milk sugar, and minerals such as calcium and phosphorus. Milk also contains liberal amounts of several of the necessary vitamins, but these are not measured by weight. When milk is taken into the body, certain digestive juices in the stomach cause the solids in the milk to form into small curds.

Cheese is made from curds of milk set in a cheese vat holding about 10,000 pounds of whole milk. A starter or rennet or both are added. A starter is sterilized milk in which selected ripening bacteria have been carefully developed. This helps produce flavor in the finished cheese. Other bacteria may be added for different varieties of cheese.

Commercial rennet is extracted from the lining of the fourth stomach of a suckling lamb or calf. It is a coagulating enzyme secreted in the gastric juice.

Figure 16-3. Cutting liederkranz cheese.

Three ounces of rennet in 1,000 pounds of milk will cause the curds to form a spongy mass. The curds must then be cut into about ⅜-inch cubes by special wire cutters. The liquid that remains, the whey, is then drained off. As the whey is removed from the curds, they adhere together and can be handled in slabs. After the curds are well drained, they are cut into small cubes in a milling machine. They are then salted because salt helps drive any remaining whey out of the curds and contributes to good flavor.

The drier curds are now dipped into metal or wooden forms that are the desired shape of the finished cheese. While in these forms, the last of the whey drains from the cheese. The following morning the cheese can be removed from the forms and placed on shelves for the first step in ripening or curing.

Approximately eight hours elapse between the receipt of the milk at the cheese factory and the placing of the curds in the forms or hoops. During the various steps in production of the cheese, the manufacturer has been cleaning and sterilizing the equipment already used so that it will be clean and ready for its next use.

The present-day cheese factory is equipped with modern, usually electrically operated, machinery. This saves time and helps the cheese maker maintain a uniform quality. Science also provides information and methods that ensure a uniform product.

Uses Made of Whey

The butterfat and nearly all the proteins and the vitamins of the original milk remain in the curds. The lactose, or milk sugar portion of the milk, is in the whey. The whey that is drained from the curds is usually run through a mechanical cream separator to remove any remaining butterfat.

At some cheese factories, the dairy farmers take the whey home and feed it to their farm animals. If the cheese factory is located near enough to a plant where milk sugar, or lactose, is made, the whey may be taken there. The milk sugar will be extracted in the factory and converted into powdered lactose for human consumption. Powdered or condensed whey can also be used in making process cheese foods and cheese spreads.

In America we have the good fortune of having an abundant variety of cheeses. These were brought with the many peoples and cultures who settled this great land. American cheeses represent the best of many countries combined to form a great family of fine and best-loved cheese.

Cheddar is an English cheese that continues to be one of our favorites. It ranges in flavor from mild to sharp. From Switzerland we get the ever-popular Swiss cheese. It is now made in this country and is as delicious as that made in the Old World. From Italy we acquired the secrets of making Provolone, Romano, Parmesan, and mozzarella.

The cultures of people from foreign lands have added greatly to fine cheese making in America. These cultures made many contributions to the art and skill of producing good cheese.

Cheese can be made in a number of ways, depending on the type and the taste as well as the desired hardness and shape. Basically it is a process of fermentation. It is in the ripening phase that much of the character of the cheese is developed.

Varieties of Cheese

The many different cheeses available on the market are not customarily nor satisfactorily classified into groups. There are several hundred different names of cheese. They have many similarities as well as many distinct qualities. The varieties of cheese depend on factors that develop the texture and flavor of cheese. The texture of a cheese and distinctive flavor characteristics are due to:

1. the kind of milk used
2. the method used in curdling the milk and in cutting, cooking, and forming the curd
3. the type of bacteria or molds used in ripening
4. the amount of salt and seasoning added
5. the ripening conditions of temperature, humidity, and time
6. the butterfat content
7. the amount of moisture left in the cheese

Natural cheese is made directly from milk or, in some instances, whey. This is the opposite of processed cheese, which is made by mixing or combining one or more kinds of natural cheese. Natural cheese is made by separating most of the milk solids from the milk by curdling with rennet or bacterial culture or both. The curd is separated from the whey by heating, stirring, and pressing.

After cheese is formed into its shape, it is given a coating of wax or some other material. In some instances a wrapping is used. The cheese is then allowed to cure or age for varying periods, depending on the kind of cheese being made.

All natural cheese should be kept refrigerated. Ripened or cured cheeses should be stored under refrigeration and protected from mold contamination and drying out. It is wise to cover the cut surface of cheese with waxed paper. The mold that may develop on natural cheeses is not harmful. It can be easily scraped or cut from surface.

Fresh cheese is the natural coagulation of whole milk or, more often, coagulation by addition of rennet. It is eaten in this fresh form.

Process cheese refers to one cheese or a combination of similar cheeses that have been ground, emulsified, and melted. Sometimes special seasoning or foods are added. The resulting product is molded into desired forms. Process cheese develops a taste character different from the raw cheese used. It has no additional ripening change. Process cheese is packaged in large loaves or small packages. It has no rind. Process cheese may be either hard or soft in texture.

PASTEURIZED PROCESS CHEESE FOOD. Pasteurized process cheese food is prepared in much the same way as process cheese with the exception that it contains less cheese. Nonfat dry milk or whey solids and water are added. This cheese food has a lower milk fat content and more moisture than process cheese.

Pasteurized process cheese food may also contain fruits, meats, or vegetables and may also have a smoked flavor. This cheese is milder, has a softer texture, spreads more easily, and melts quicker than process cheese because of its higher moisture. Pasteurized process American cheese is the most popular variety. It is packaged in rolls, slices, links, and loaves.

PASTEURIZED PROCESS CHEESE SPREAD. This cheese product is made in much the same way as pasteurized process cheese food but generally contains a higher level of moisture and the milk fat content is usually lower. A stabilizer is used in the preparation of this product to prevent separation of ingredients. This kind of cheese is more spreadable than process cheese food. Cheese spread may contain pimentos, fruits, vegetables, or meats and may also have a smoked flavor.

Pasteurized process cheese spread has various flavors, depending largely upon the flavor of the cheese used in the mixture and the other food items added. These cheese items are packaged in jars and loaves.

COLD-PACK CHEESE. Cold-pack cheese, or club cheese, is a blend of fresh and aged natural cheese. Two cheeses of the same type or two or more varieties may be used. The cheese is mixed into a uniform product without heating. It may also have a smoked flavor. The principal varieties are cold-pack American cheese and cold-pack Swiss cheese.

The flavor of this cheese is the same as the natural cheese from which it was made. It is usually aged or sharp. The cheese is soft and spreads easily.

This cheese is packed in jars, rolls, or links and is especially good as an appetizer, snack, or dessert.

COLD-PACK CHEESE FOOD. Cold-pack cheese food is prepared in the same way as cold-pack cheese but with the addition of dairy ingredients that are used in process cheese food. It may also include sweetening agents such as sugar and corn syrup.

This cheese food may contain pimentos, fruits, vegetables, or meats, and may also have a smoked flavor. The flavor is similar to but slightly milder than the flavor of the cheese from which it was made.

Cold-pack cheese food is softer and spreads more easily than cold-pack cheese because of its higher moisture content and the other ingredients that are added. It is packaged in the same way as cold-pack cheese and used in the same fashion.

Classification of Cheeses

Cheeses can also be classified as very hard, firm, semisoft, and soft. They can, in addition, be classified as ripened or unripened as well as by the method used in ripening. Cheese can be ripened by bacteria, mold, surface organism, or a combination of these methods. The degree of hardness is determined by the amount of liquid that is left in the cheese. The harder the cheese, the less liquid there is remaining.

Examples of cheese listed according to hardness are:

1. Very Hard Cheese (grating)
   a. Ripened by bacteria: Parmesan, Romano, Sapsago
2. Firm Cheese
   a. Ripened by bacteria: Cheddar, Caciocavallo, Edam
   b. Unripened: mozzarella, Mysost
3. Semisoft, Ripened Varieties
   a. Ripened principally by bacteria: brick munster
   b. Ripened by bacteria and surface microorganisms: Port du Salut
4. Soft
   a. Ripened: Camembert, Bel Paese
   b. Unripened: cottage, cream, ricotta

5. Blue-Vein Mold Ripened—Curing is accomplished by the aid of bacteria, but more particularly by the use of a characteristic mold culture. The curd is innoculated with pure cultures of mold that grow throughout the interior of the cheese to produce the familiar appearance and characteristic flavor: blue, Gorgonzola, Roquefort

Ripened or Aged Cheese

The ripening of cheese can be defined in terms of the steps or changes the cheese goes through in developing its characteristic flavor, odor, body, texture, and color. In this process the raw and elastic product is changed into a smooth or crumbly finished product. Cheese may be ripened, or aged, by cultures of selected bacteria added to the milk before the curds are formed, by molds added after the curds are formed, or by both bacteria and molds acting together. Active enzymes can also aid the ripening process.

In molding soft cheese the larger pieces of curd are broken before the product is placed in the mold. With hard cheese, the small pieces of curd are pressed to remove excess liquid. It is in this phase that the process of fermentation begins. Aging requires special conditions of light, dampness, and coolness. Other varied processes are used in making the vast number of cheeses that are available today.

Ripening Classification of Cheeses

UNRIPENED. These are the soft, unripened varieties such as cottage cheese. These cheeses contain a high percentage of moisture and do not undergo any curing or ripening. They are consumed fresh soon after manufacture.

SOFT RIPENED. With soft ripened cheese, the curing process develops from the rind of the cheese toward the center. The molds, cultures of bacteria, or both that grow on the surface of the cheese assist in developing the characteristic flavor, body, and texture during the curing process. The curing process continues as long as the temperature is favorable.

SEMISOFT RIPENED. These cheeses ripen from the interior of the cheese as well as from the surface. With the aid of a characteristic bacteria, a mold culture, or both, the ripening process begins soon after the cheese is formed. Curing continues as long as the temperature is favorable.

FIRM RIPENED. With the aid of a bacterial culture, these cheeses ripen throughout the entire cheese. The ripening process continues as long as the temperature is favorable. The rate and degree of curing are also closely related to the moisture content. Since firm ripened cheeses are lower in moisture than the softer varieties, they usually require a longer curing time.

VERY HARD RIPENED. These cheeses are also cured with the aid of a bacterial culture and enzymes. The rate of curing, however, is much slower because there is very little moisture and a higher salt content.

BLUE-VEIN MOLD RIPENED. Curing is accomplished by the aid of bacteria but more particularly by the use of a characteristic mold culture that grows throughout the interior of the cheese and produces the familiar appearance and characteristic flavor.

The time and effort spent in curing and aging cheese naturally add to its cost just as they add to its flavor and eating enjoyment.

The problem of the cheese maker is to control the action of the helpful bacteria and molds and keep out the kinds that are not wanted. The science of cheese making has grown through the years so that uniform, flavorful, and dependable cheese is an almost certain result in an organization with good laboratory control.

Use of Cheese

Some of the many ways of using different kinds of cheeses are as follows:

1. Main Dish—Cheeses used in main dishes are the attention getters in the cheese family. These dishes include fondue, soufflé, Welsh rarebit, omelet, and pizza. The cheese is the dominating flavor. Cheese in the main dish can also be combined with other foods such as meat, potato or other vegetables, rice, macaroni, noodles, and spaghetti.
2. Salads and Salad Dressings—Cheeses can be the main part of a salad, such as cottage cheese, or a garnish to a salad, such as julienne strips of Swiss cheese on a salad bowl. Cheese can also be grated or cut in chunks and added to a salad dressing.
3. Appetizers—A wide selection of cheeses is available. Used alone or in combination with other foods, they can be made into dips or spreads.

4. Sandwiches—Cheese is a favorite item in a sandwich made with any number of breads to compliment the cheese. Cheese is also used widely in combination with meat, poultry, fish, and vegetables. Cheese can be used sliced in toasted or cold sandwiches or as an ingredient in sandwich spreads and sauces.

5. Garnish—Cheese can be cut in fancy shapes and used to decorate and embellish cold foods. It can also be grated and used as a garnish for soups, sauces, and hot dishes.

6. Desserts—When it is used as a dessert, cheese can be served by itself with plain or toasted crackers. Sometimes a sweet preserve may be added. Cheese can also be used in combination with the desserts, such as cheddar cheese on apple pie.

TIPS ON USES. When cooking foods with cheese, a moderate heat should be used so as not to develop an undesirable rubbery consistency. If moderately heated, the cheese will remain soft and light in appearance.

Process cheeses generally have the best keeping quality. Hard cheeses also have a good keeping quality. Cheese should be stored under refrigeration and covered with either the original covering or a wet cloth soaked in vinegar. If the refrigeration box is too moist a mold might start that should be cut off before it goes too far into the cheese.

Popular Cheeses

American cheese is pale to dark yellow and is used as an appetizer, sandwich filling, dessert, or as an ingredient with other food. It is also called cheddar cheese.

Brick cheese is brick shaped, semihard, contains holes, has a brown waxy surface, and is used as an appetizer and in desserts.

Blue cheese has a green, marble mold and is used in salads, desserts, and canapés.

Camembert is yellow, soft, creamy, wrapped in foil, and is used in desserts and canapés.

Cottage cheese is unripened, white, with curds, and used in salads, pastries, dips, and fillings.

Cream cheese is unripened, white to cream in color, smooth, and is used in canapés, salads, pastries, dips, and fillings.

Gruyère is pale yellow, has small holes, and is used in appetizers and desserts.

Parmesan is very hard, pale yellow, and crumbly. It is often grated and used in desserts and salads.

Romano is very hard, white to pale yellow, crumbly, is often grated, and is used in desserts and salads.

Roquefort is semihard, is made from sheep's milk, has a green marble mold, and is used in canapés, salads, and desserts.

Swiss cheese is white to pale yellow, has large holes, and is used as a dessert and in sandwiches.

Buying Cheese

The labels of natural cheese, pasteurized process cheese, and related products carry important descriptive information. The name of a natural cheese will appear as the variety, such as "Cheddar cheese," "Swiss cheese," or "blue cheese." Pasteurized process cheese labels will always include the words "pasteurized process" together with the name of the variety or varieties of cheese used, such as "pasteurized process American cheese" or "pasteurized process Swiss and American cheese."

Cheese food also contains ingredients in addition to cheese and is labeled "pasteurized process cheese food." Cheese spreads have a different composition from cheese foods and are labeled "pasteurized process cheese spread." The ingredients used in the preparation of these products are listed on the label together with the varieties of cheese used in the mixture. The milk fat and moisture content may also be listed on the label. Cold-pack cheese and cold-pack cheese food are labeled the same as cheese and cheese foods except that "club cheese" or "comminuted cheese" may be used as the name of this cheese.

Information on labels of certain types of natural cheese refer to the age or degree of curing. A Cheddar cheese may be labeled mild, medium, mellow, aged, or sharp. A pasteurized process cheese may be labeled to indicate a sharp flavor if a large proportion of sharp or aged cheese was used in its preparation.

Generally, process cheese has the best keeping quality. Very hard cheese and hard cheese have slightly less keeping quality.

Consumption of Cheese in the United States

Americans consumed a record quantity of cheese in 1968 (Table 16-1). Sales rose to an all-time high of 10.1 pounds per person. Few foods have experienced as rapid an expansion in consumer demand as has cheese

TABLE 16-1. CHEESE SALES PER PERSON IN THE UNITED STATES*

YEAR	POUNDS	INDEX (1957–59 = 100)
1950	7.6	103
1955	7.3	99
1957–59 average	7.4	100
1960	8.2	111
1961	8.4	114
1962	8.4	114
1963	8.5	115
1964	8.6	116
1965	9.1	123
1966	9.8	132
1967	9.6	130
1968	10.1	136

* This chart does not include consumption of cottage cheese.

during the last ten years. Since the 1957 to 1959 period, for example, per capita sales of cheese have increased by more than one-third. A number of factors are responsible for this long-term increase in market demand for cheese. First, the industry has widened consumer acceptance with innovative products and packages. In addition, industrywide educational programs have proved effective in informing consumers of the nutritive value of cheese.

Slightly less than 2 billion pounds of cheese were produced in the United States last year. American varieties, principally Cheddar, accounted for nearly two-thirds of the annual production. Cheese imports totaled less than 0.2 billion pounds.

There are many popular American varieties of cheese. Table 16-2 lists some of the more common types. The numbers of the cheeses refer to the numbers in Figure 16-4.

Imported Cheeses

The consumption of cheeses of all types is greater today than ever before. This is true for both the American-made and the imported varieties. Germany ranks first among European nations in poundage of cheese shipped to America. The nearest competitors are Denmark, Italy, Switzerland, the Netherlands, Austria, and France, in that order. Some of the popular cheeses of these countries are listed in Table 16-3. The amounts are expressed in millions of pounds.

TABLE 16-2. POPULAR AMERICAN-MADE CHEESES

TYPE	COLOR, TEXTURE, FLAVOR	USE
1. Cheddar	Semihard cheese ranging from nearly white to yellow in color. Mild to sharp in flavor depending upon aging. Firm to crumbly in texture.	Appetizers, sandwiches, salads, in cooked foods, desserts.
Cheddar-type 2. Colby 3. Monterey or Jack	Mild in flavor. Somewhat softer body than cheddar.	Generally used for sandwiches and appetizers.
4. Pasteurized Process Cheese 5. Cheese Foods 6. Cheese Spreads 7. Cold-Pack Cheese Food or Club Cheese	Blend of natural cheeses that have been shredded and mixed. Semisoft, smooth texture. Spreads easily, melts quickly	Appetizers, sandwiches, salads, in cooked foods, desserts.
8. Gouda and Edam	Red wax outer surface; yellow interior. Semisoft to firm. Nutlike sweet flavor.	Appetizers, salads, in cooked foods, desserts.
9. Camembert	Smooth creamy yellow with edible white crust. Soft, surface ripened. Mild to pungent flavor.	With crackers or fruits for appetizers or desserts.
10. Muenster	Creamy white; semisoft with small holes. Mild to mellow flavor.	Appetizers, sandwiches.
11. Brick	Creamy yellow; semisoft with small holes. Mild to sharp flavor.	Appetizers, sandwiches, salads, desserts.
12. Swiss	Light yellow, large holes. Firm. Nutlike sweet flavor.	Appetizers, sandwiches, salads, in cooked foods.
13. Limburger	Semisoft surface-ripened cheese. Characteristic strong flavor and aroma. Creamy white interior.	Appetizers, desserts.
14. Blue	Blue veined, crumbly. Semisoft to firm. Sharp salty flavor.	Appetizers, salads, salad dressings, in cooked foods, desserts
15. Gorgonzola	Blue-green veined. Semisoft to firm. Sharp, salty flavor. Less moisture than blue.	Appetizers, salads, salad dressing, in cooked foods, desserts.
16. Provolone	Light yellow, semihard, smooth and somewhat plastic. Mellow to sharp, smoky flavor.	Appetizers, sandwiches, in cooked foods, desserts.

TABLE 16-2. (Continued)

TYPE	COLOR, TEXTURE, FLAVOR	USE
17. Romano	Yellow white. Hard, granular, brittle. Sharp, piquant flavor.	Grated in soups, on breads, on spaghetti, in cooked foods.
18. Parmesan	Yellow or white. Hard, granular, sharp, piquant flavor.	Grated in soups, on breads, on spaghetti, in cooked foods.
19. Mozzarella and Scamorze	Unripened semisoft cheese. White stretchy cheese. When served hot it becomes chewy. Varying moisture content. Sometimes designated for pizza. Delicate, mild flavor.	Sliced, in cooked foods, on pizza, sandwiches.
20. Cottage cheese	Soft, mild, white to creamy-white unripened cheese. May be small, medium, or large curd. Creamed cottage cheese has added cream.	Appetizers, casseroles, main dishes, cheesecakes, sandwich fillings, salads.
21. Cream cheese	White unripened cheese. Soft and smooth. Mild, delicately flavored.	Appetizers, sandwiches, salads, in cooked foods, desserts.

TABLE 16-3. *POPULAR IMPORTED CHEESES*

COUNTRY	MILLION POUNDS	POPULAR CHEESES
Germany	25	Muenster, Dotter, Fruhstuck, and Hop
Denmark	24	Gislev, Mysost, and Runesten
Italy	18	Parmesan, Romano, Provolone, and Gorgonzola
Switzerland	17	Gruyere, Emmental (or Swiss) Sapsago
Netherland	15	Gouda, Edam and Kummel
Austria	11	Schloss, Shutsenkase and Styria
France	10	Roquefort, Camembert, and Brie

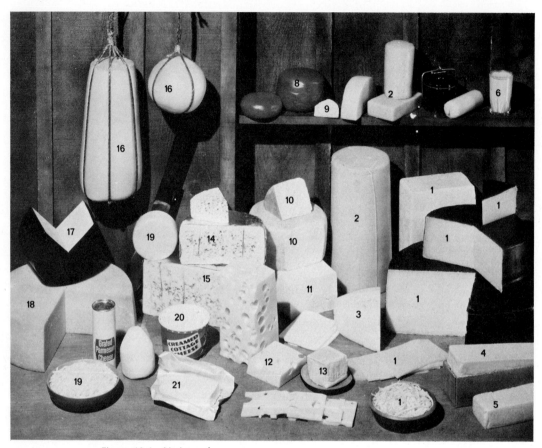

Figure 16-4.   Various cheeses.

chapter 17

eggs and egg cookery

Hen's eggs, like milk, are one of the most important food components in the daily meal. An egg is a highly nutritive food with a large number of uses, either as a main dish or in combination with other foods. The egg is a most versatile and complete food that finds its way into many recipes as an ingredient or as the principal food.

EGG USES

Clarifying Agent

The coagulating property of the eggs will absorb tiny particles. Eggs are used as clarifying agents in the making of a consommé.

Binding Agent

Eggs are used to bind several ingredients together, such as in a meat loaf.

Emulsifying Agent

Egg is used to keep oil evenly distributed throughout a mixture so that the oil will not rise to the top. Mayonnaise is an example.

Thickening Agent

Eggs act as thickening agents in the making of a pudding, custard, or fine sauce to be served with meat or fish.

Adhesive Agent

Eggs provide a base for coating fried food.

Main Food

At breakfast, brunch, or snack meals, eggs are served as a main dish.

Leavening Agent

Eggs act as leavening agents by bringing air through the egg whites and into the mixture, as in a soufflé.

Garnishing

Eggs are used in canapés, salads, and sandwiches.

EGG GRADES AND STORAGE

How are eggs graded? Eggs are graded by the condition of the inside of the egg as revealed by the candling process. A candled egg is one that has been inspected before an electric light so that the inside can be checked. The following points are considered in grading eggs by the candling process:

Depth of the air cell—the larger the cell the older the egg.
Visibility of the yolk—The yolk is dimly visible in a fresh egg. The firmness of the white keeps the yolk suspended. A blood clot indicates a developing embryo.
Cleanliness of the shell—The color of the shell has no bearing on quality.

Note: The size of egg has no bearing on the quality of the egg. Large, medium, or small eggs are to be found in all grades of eggs.

Two consumer grades of eggs are widely available at the retail level. Grade AA, or fresh fancy, and Grade A. These are especially good for frying or poaching, where appearance is important. Grade B eggs are more often used for mixing and baking.

What are the grades of eggs? United States Department of Agriculture has established quality standards for grades.

TABLE 17-1. GRADES OF EGGS

GRADES	AIR-CELL DEPTH	SHELL	WHITE	YOLK
Grade AA (fresh-fancy quality)	1/8" or less	clean, normal	clear, firm	Well centered, indistinct outline. No defects.
Grade A	1/4"	clean, normal	clear, fairly firm	Fairly centered, visible outline, almost no defects.
Grade B	3/8" or less (may move)	clean, may be abnormal	clear, weak	Off-center, defined outline, larger, some defects.

SIZE OF EGG

As established by USDA standards, egg sizes are based on minimum weights of eggs per dozen as follows:

Peewee—15 to 17 ounces
Small—18 to 20 ounces
Medium—21 to 23 ounces
Large—24 to 26 ounces
Extra large—27 to 29 ounces
Jumbo—30 ounces

In most areas well-graded eggs are available. These eggs may be graded according to state-established standards of measure that have been written into the state laws. These eggs carry a mark designed by the individual state that establishes this quality. Some states have adopted the standards for grade quality that have been developed by the United States Department of Agriculture. When these standards are used, they are called "federal-state" standards and they carry the mark designed by the United States Department of Agriculture, which shows both the size and the grade of the egg on the package.

Storage

A freshly laid egg starts to change from the moment it is laid. The warmer the temperature at which the egg is handled, the sooner the changes occur. Therefore the handling and care of fresh eggs is very important. If the locale is such that eggs are readily available, they should be purchased in moderate quantity and should always be kept under refrigeration. The temperature should be 44 degrees F or lower.

Color of the Yolk

Does the color of the yolk have any relationship to nutritive or taste value of the egg? No, it does not. The yolk varies from yellow to orange depending on what food the hen is eating and the time of year.

The term "fresh-fancy quality" is used only for eggs that have been produced under a special quality-control program designed to ensure freshness as well as high quality.

The top two grades (AA and A) are best for frying and poaching because they don't spread out very much in the pan and the yolk is firm and not easily broken.

Grade B eggs are just as good to eat, but the white is thinner and the yolk may be flatter than in eggs of the higher grades.

In most states, eggs that are marked with a grade and size—like "Grade A, Large" without the "U.S." in front of the name—are required to meet state laws. Many state grade standards are the same as the U.S. grades.

Smaller eggs sell for less than the bigger ones because eggs are really sold by weight, just as meat and other foods.

Figure 17-1 is the grade mark used on eggs. It is printed on the carton or on the tape used to seal the carton. It shows both the grade and the size of the eggs. The one shown here is U.S. Grade A. The size shown in this grade mark is large. Sometimes the size is printed separately on the carton and not printed in the grade mark.

TIPS ON EGGS

1. Variations in temperature while the eggs are being stored cause egg whites to become thin.
2. Cook eggs at low to moderate temperatures. High temperatures and overcooking toughen eggs.
3. Eggs are nutritious. They contain significant amounts of vitamin A, iron, protein, and riboflavin (vitamin B_2), as well as smaller amounts of many other nutrients.
4. The thick, white, cordlike material located on opposite sides of the

Figure 17-1. A grade mark used for eggs.

yolk is called the "chalaza" and is a normal part of the egg. The chalaza holds the yolk in place in the white.

5. Shell color is determined by the breed of the hen and does not affect the grade, nutritive value, flavor, or cooking performance of the egg.

6. Generally speaking, if there is less than a 7-cent price spread between one size and the next smaller size per dozen eggs in the same grade, you will get more for your money by buying the larger size.

Freezing of Egg

Freezing is a common method of preserving eggs. Frozen eggs are available in 30-pound tins as whole egg yolk and egg white. These eggs are sharp frozen at −10 degrees F and are used extensively in the bakery trade.

Dried Eggs

Drying is another important way of preserving eggs. Dried eggs retain their functional values in cooking, baking, frozen desserts, and confections. Store dried eggs under refrigeration.

Egg Cookery

Eggs are versatile. They can be used alone or in combination with many other foods. The following are common ways in which eggs are cooked.

POACHED EGGS. Eggs dropped in water and heated to just below the boiling point with salt and vinegar added. Cook to the firmness desired.

SIMMERING (Boiling). Whole eggs placed in water that is heated just below the boiling point. Cook to the firmness desired.

FRIED. Eggs cooked in a small amount of fat (Figure 17-2).

BASTED. Hot fat is spooned over the egg while it is frying.

OVER EASY. Fried eggs that are turned over on their top side and cooked lightly.

SHIRRED. Fresh eggs that are placed in a buttered shirred-egg dish, or ramekin, and cooked in the oven until firm. Sausage or other food items may be added.

Figure 17-2. A fairly typical American breakfast—bacon and fried eggs.

SCRAMBLED. Scrambled eggs are slightly beaten in a bowl to which a little milk has been added and then cooked in a pan with melted fat. The heat should be moderate so that the eggs do not cook too quickly.

OMELETTE. Whole eggs that are beaten together, placed in an iron pan with melted butter, and stirred briskly with a fork to heat them evenly. When it is cooked the omelette is rolled, beginning from the end opposite the handle, turned out on a serving platter, and placed in the oven for a few minutes to dry and puff up. Many omelettes, for example a Spanish omelette, contain meats, shellfish, cheese, or other food items.

DEEP FAT FRIED. Deep-fried eggs are used as garnish in specialty or nationality dishes.

FRIED POACHED EGG. These are drained and dried poached eggs that are floured, placed in a light cream sauce, breaded, and placed in fat that is hot enough to brown them. The finished eggs are then drained and served.

HARD-BOILED EGG. These are served cold and cut in slices, wedges, quarters, etc. They may be filled or covered with various food mixtures and served as an appetizer or entree.

Remember: Eggs are very easy to digest and important food for people of all ages.

Eggs should not be cooked over too hot a flame, and they should not be overcooked. The thick white attachment to the yolk is normal to all eggs.

Other Foods Served with Eggs

Eggs are easily digested and highly nutritive. For children as well as the elderly, eggs are often a prescribed item in the diet. There are many ways to cook and serve eggs, ranging from raw to baked.

Combined with other food items they make up some of the most attractive entrees on our menus. Cookbooks by the hundreds are available that list these recipes. Below are a few popular foods that are served with eggs:

chicken in an omelette
ham in an omelette or with scrambled eggs
shrimp in scrambled eggs
chicken livers in an omelette or scrambled eggs
jelly in an omelette
mushrooms in an omelette or scrambled eggs
herbs in scrambled eggs
truffle in scrambled eggs
crayfish tails in an omelette or scrambled eggs
anchovy in fried eggs
creole sauce in an omelette
artichoke bottoms in an omelette
minced onion and green pepper in an omelette
asparagus tips in an omelette
cheese in an omelette or scrambled eggs
baked potato shell with scrambled or poached eggs
bacon with fried, scrambled, and poached eggs
sausage with shirred, scrambled, and poached eggs

Egg Production

The peak season for the production of fresh eggs is from March to late May. An excess of eggs produced in this period but not processed by freezing or drying is held in cold storage to be used in low production periods. As long as the proper temperature, humidity, air circulation, and clean air are provided, no change will occur in eggs that are stored.

chapter 18

meat, poultry, game, and seafood

Meat dishes make up the larger part of restaurant menus or meals generally served to the public. Meat, of course, is the edible parts of, usually, domesticated animals. Game, poultry, and fish also are used.

MEAT

How and in what form meat is purchased varies from house to house, depending on the nature of the business being conducted. In some it is advisable to buy the prefabricated cut with which there is no trim or waste. This type of meat buying works well in a specialty-house operation where only one item, such as steak, is served.

For large institutions that have their own butcher shop or meat cutting department and that serve three meals a day, it may be more economical to buy the meat in the biggest piece possible. In this way a better price is obtained and all cuts and pieces are used in the various types of food that are prepared in the course of the day. In some locales it is not uncommon to buy the piece in the larger cuts in order to take advantage of price and then have the wholesaler break it at specified places. This makes the meat easier to handle in a smaller butcher shop or kitchen.

Handling of Meat

Meat is an expensive food that requires the utmost care in selection, fabrication, storage, and cooking.

In selecting a cut of meat for a dish, there are a number of important factors to be considered. This includes the taste and method of cooking to be used as well as the cost. Some meats are best when broiled. Others require a light saute in an open pan. Meat must be used so that the excellent qualities of each cut will be captured. If a dish requires tender meat cooked over a quick open fire, a less tender or chewier cut prepared this way will produce a tough dish at best. Through years of experience the culinary trade has created an endless array of dishes that utilize almost all cuts of meat. The principle to remember is that the various cuts must be used in the way established to get the benefit of their best qualities.

Fabricating or butchering meat into cuts that are served to guests requires a high degree of skill and precision. This cannot be done with a heavy hand, nor can it be done with speed as the foremost thought. Any extra tear, gouge, or misplaced cut reduces the dollar return that a cut of meat will yield. Great care should be taken in separating meat from bone. The bone is to be removed in such a way that the meat surrounding the bone is free from injury. This can be done by a skilled worker who knows how to handle a knife and understands the structure of meat. The skill of separating meat from bone is one that is acquired with much patience and practice. An expensive piece of meat, whether or not it is attached to a bone, is not achieving the result it could if it finds its way into a stock pot or stew. Furthermore, this pushes the cost of the stock or stew well above its proper ratio.

Storage

Storage is as important as correct handling and buying a good quality of meat. The best cut from a prime animal that has been properly aged will be ruined if it is handled carelessly or stored improperly. Many establishments do not have enough refrigeration space for the necessary aging of rib and loin cuts of beef. When such is the case, the wholesaler or jobber usually provides this service.

Meat that is being stored is cut either in sides or in quarters. If an animal is divided into two parts down the back, these are called sides. If the sides are then divided into two parts between the twelfth and thirteenth ribs, the four pieces are called the hindquarters and forequarters. The tail half is the hindquarter and the front half is the forequarter.

Two of the most important elements of meat storage are refrigeration and humidity. Meat should be kept at 32 to 36 degrees F. The moisture in the air, the relative humidity, should be between 75 and 85 percent. Care must be taken to keep the air in the refrigeration box moist enough to avoid shrinkage and loss of weight. However, the box cannot be kept too damp or the meat will become limp. This not only affects the taste of the meat, but encourages quicker growth of bacteria that will cause the meat to spoil sooner. Therefore, the temperature and moisture content of a box are most important to the cuts of all meat. The temperature must be constant at all times and the box must be large enough to handle the meat traffic of the house.

The fore- and hindquarters are used in different ways. The forequarter, except for the rib, is chiefly cooked in some form of moisture; ground or cut into small pieces and cooked by itself, as, for example, hamburger; or combined with other foods, such as in a meat loaf or stew. When meat is used in these ways, aging is not as necessary. The cooking will achieve the tenderness desired, and the taste of the meat is complimented by the savory tastes of the sauce and vegetables that may be part of the dish. Meat from the forequarter may be used within the week after it is received by an establishment.

The aging process is very important, however, for cuts of meat that are chiefly used in broiling, grilling, frying, and roasting. These cuts, except for the rib section of forequarters, come from the hindquarter. The aging process develops the much sought-after character in meat and enhances its juiciness, tenderness, and good taste. Properly aged meat is firm to the touch, deeper in color than fresh meat, and milder in aroma. Meat that has good age is easier to cut and bone than a piece of meat that has not been aged. The aging of meat involves the hanging in storage of "green" meat, which is meat that has been slaughtered only a few days before. Aging must be done under the proper conditions of refrigeration and humidity control. The meat is held for a period of at least three weeks, in some cases slightly more. Aging improves beef and lamb but has little effect on veal. Meat that is to be aged should be protected with a good thick covering of fat in order to prevent the meat from changing color or becoming too dry. Only the best grades are aged. The meat box, as well as the preparation area or meat room, must be kept clean and tidy at all times. Meat may absorb the food smell of items stored in the same room. For this reason, vegetables, cheese, etc., that have a characteristic odor are never stored in the same box with meat. A well-lighted and ventilated workroom that is kept clean and tidy produces a good meat product as well as a happy worker. It is in this area that the pennies saved in the shrewd purchase of quality merchandise can be pennies lost through careless or haphazard handling or storage. Remember: The best quality meat, which is demanded and used in hotels, restaurants, hospitals, clubs, etc., requires the best possible handling.

A meat box should be constructed in such a way that one part of it can be used for the large pieces that are to be cut. The other part is for the cut portions. These are placed on trays or on shelves in carts and covered with waxed or butcher's paper until they are taken to the place of usage.

The Menu

Meat plays an important part on the menu. Many of the other good qualities of food items are built around the meat items on the bill of fare. Appetizers, soups, vegetables, sauces, salads, breads, and desserts are on the menu essentially because they go with or compliment the entrée, which is usually the mainstay of the meal. Most often the meat is the first item of food decided upon by the dining guest. The suggestions made by service personnel and the discussion that occurs when orders are taken are mostly based on what goes well with the meat. When wine is part of a meal, the kind to be served is determined by the meat or other entrée.

Lined Up

"Lined up" is an expression used in the industry that essentially refers to how ready a worker is to serve the food in a short period of time. In a cafeteria or dinner menu format, this could mean simply the lining up of cooked food on the steam table. On an à la carte menu it would mean the lining up of raw materials so that they could be ready on a moment's notice for cooking as well as a reserve supply large enough to replenish the lined-up materials if the volume of business is heavy. In a fabricating room the daily menus are followed closely by the butchers so that they will have on hand the items that were sold or are being offered for sale to the public that day. To accomplish this, a fabricating room will have butchers working daily to get the meat needs cut and prepared for the next day's business. The number of individual cuts from each item will depend on the number of private functions and such things as the day of the week, the time of the year, and the weather. These are conditions that affect the eating-out habits of guests.

Butcher's Meat

"Butcher's meat" is an expression in the industry that refers to meat sold by butchers.

Beef

Beef is the name given to cattle that are one year of age or more. Cattle are developed primarily for the production of meat. Great care is exercised in their daily feeding routines. The cattle that are raised have the characteristic of rapid growth and develop heavy, well-stocked bodies.

Some of these cattle may be brought by the farmer directly to the market where they are purchased by the packer. This individual immediately puts the cattle through the processes of slaughtering and packaging. Some cattle are purchased by feeders who have a large area of feed pens. These feed pens may be located close to the packing house. The cattle are fed for a period of several months until a well-fleshed and stocked body is developed. The cattle are then taken back to the market where they are sold for packing purposes.

Corn-fed beef is cattle that has been fed on corn. This produces a select quality in the beef. It is characterized by the yellow cast in the fat covering and the slight corn taste to the meat.

Quality

Some of the things to look for in selecting beef are:

1. *Color*—Various cuts having a light to medium red color. The deep red coloring of the meat, which is caused by a blood agent, increases as the animal gets older.
2. *Firmness*—Meat should be firm to the touch and finely textured.
3. *Fat*—Fat should be slightly yellow to white, flaky in the higher grades, and firm to the touch.
4. *Bones*—These should be shiny with slight cast of pink.
5. *Marbling*—Tiny pieces of fat should be spread throughout the cut surface of meat.

The breed of cattle, how and what it was fed, the water it drank, and the part of the country in which it was produced are factors that affect quality. Remember that the parts of the body that an animal uses or moves the least are the most tender.

Classification of Beef Cuts

The most basic division of the steer after slaughtering is into two parts, each called a side. These sides are then cut in half between the twelfth and thirteenth ribs. Each of these pieces is called a quarter of beef,

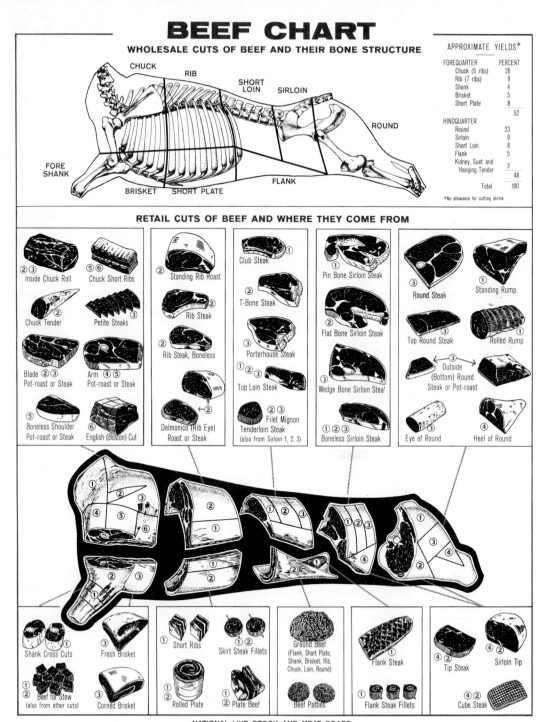

BEEF CHART

WHOLESALE CUTS OF BEEF AND THEIR BONE STRUCTURE

CHUCK
RIB
SHORT LOIN
SIRLOIN
ROUND
FORE SHANK
BRISKET
SHORT PLATE
FLANK

APPROXIMATE YIELDS*

FOREQUARTER	PERCENT
Chuck (5 ribs)	26
Rib (7 ribs)	9
Shank	4
Brisket	5
Short Plate	8
	52

HINDQUARTER	
Round	23
Sirloin	9
Short Loin	8
Flank	5
Kidney, Suet and Hanging Tender	3
	48
Total	100

*No allowance for cutting shrink

RETAIL CUTS OF BEEF AND WHERE THEY COME FROM

② ③ Inside Chuck Roll
⑤ ⑥ Chuck Short Ribs
② Standing Rib Roast
① Club Steak
① Pin Bone Sirloin Steak
③ Round Steak
① Standing Rump

② Chuck Tender
③ Petite Steaks
② Rib Steak
② T-Bone Steak
② Flat Bone Sirloin Steak
③ Top Round Steak
① Rolled Rump

Blade ② ③ Pot-roast or Steak
Arm ④ ⑤ Pot-roast or Steak
② Rib Steak, Boneless
③ Porterhouse Steak
③ Wedge Bone Sirloin Steak
③ Outside (Bottom) Round Steak or Pot-roast

⑤ Boneless Shoulder Pot-roast or Steak
⑥ English (Boston) Cut
Delmonico (Rib Eye) Roast or Steak ←②
① ② Top Loin Steak
② ③ Filet Mignon Tenderloin Steak (also from Sirloin 1, 2, 3)
① ② ③ Boneless Sirloin Steak
③ Eye of Round
④ Heel of Round

① Shank Cross Cuts
③ Fresh Brisket
① Short Ribs
① ② Skirt Steak Fillets
Ground Beef (Flank, Short Plate, Shank, Brisket, Rib, Chuck, Loin, Round)
Flank Steak
④ ② Tip Steak
④ ② Sirloin Tip

① ② Beef for Stew (also from other cuts)
③ Corned Brisket
① ② Rolled Plate
② Plate Beef
Beef Patties
① Flank Steak Fillets
④ ② Cube Steak

NATIONAL LIVE STOCK AND MEAT BOARD

Figure 18-1. Beef chart.

either the hind or the fore. The quarters break down into wholesale cuts. The most expensive and productive quarter in the sense of dollar yield is the hindquarter. It is also the one that requires the most exacting care in storage, handling, and fabrication.

The hindquarter produces the following cuts:

1. *short loin*—steaks—porterhouse, T-bone, club, filet mignon, tenderloin, bone-in or boneless sirloin*
2. *sirloin* (loin end)—roast and steaks—club, sirloin, filet mignon, tenderloin
3. *rump*—roast—rolled, standing
4. *round*—varied use—steaks, ground beef, roast, stew
5. *shank*—soups—cook in liquid
6. *flank*—varied use—steak, pot roast, braise

Popular Cuts of Beef

FROM THE HINDQUARTER. The full loin, which consists of the short loin and the loin end, without a doubt produces the best cuts of beef, including the ever-popular filet mignon, porterhouse, T-bone, sirloin, and club steak. The full loin includes the thirteenth rib and extends to the rump, which is a part of the round, and also includes the round bone and rump bone. Special cuts of beef that are routinely available in restaurants and hotels cannot always be found in a local supermarket. These cuts have proven to be the ones the dining-out public fancies. Therefore they are of popular usage in the industry. The round provides good-sized pieces of lean meat that are highly desirable for more economic servings of steak, roast, and braised dishes.

FROM THE FOREQUARTER. The prime rib of beef is, here and in England, perhaps the most popular cut of beef. If not, it takes second place only to steak. The prime rib includes the seven ribs from the fifth up to the twelfth. The very popular corned beef and boiled beef also come from the forequarter. Short ribs are another favorite dish from this cut.

THE FILLET. The fillet or tenderloin of beef is one of the most desirable cuts. From it we get the Chateaubriand, the famed filet mignon, and the small tournedos. The trim and small end of the tenderloin is generally used in such entrees as pepper steak or tenderloin tips.

---

* Variation in the use of the short loin: When the tenderloin is pulled and bones are removed, the short loin is called a boneless strip loin. This cut produces a variety of steaks with regional names such as New York cut, strip steak, strip sirloin, and New York sirloin.

The Federal Inspection of Meats

An establishment that slaughters meat that will be shipped into another state must have its meat inspected by federal inspectors. All the meat of the establishment is inspected prior to being slaughtered and at various times in the phases of butchering. The inspector's prime concern is to determine whether or not the meat being slaughtered is fit for human consumption and whether or not the physical facilities are sanitary. Meat that passes is stamped with a colored government stamp that is numbered with the packer's identification number and the abbreviations of the words "U.S. inspected and passed." The ink used to stamp the meat is made from vegetable coloring and has no affect on taste. It does not have to be removed prior to cooking. Federal meat inspectors are primarily concerned with those meats that are intended for interstate use. Packers who confine their trade to the state in which they are located are under state supervision. Some packing houses engage government graders to inspect their meat in accordance with the established federal method of grading. These meats must meet the local requirements that have been established and carry the inspection stamp of the city, county, or state, as the case may be.

The federal inspection of meats began shortly after the turn of the century. It is under the direction of the United States Department of Agriculture.

Inspection, Grade, and Brand Stamps

The inspection stamp is a federal stamp if the establishment engages in interstate business and a local stamp if business is local. This stamp only guarantees the health of the animal and sanitary conditions of the plant.

The grade stamp is the stamp that is used by the USDA. Grade standards that were developed early in the twentieth century serve as the basis for today's grading of meat. The official basis of grading beef began in several large cities in the year 1927. Later it was extended to include veal, mutton, and lamb. The grade stamp relates to the quality of the meat.

The brand stamp is a private name given to a specific quality of meat and used exclusively by the packer who originates its use. Examples of this are: star, certified, premium, etc.

THE USDA FEDERAL GRADES. The federal grades of meat for the different meats are shown in Table 18-1.

The top three grades are the ones encountered most often in the commercial trade. The meat grades used depend on the type of house, the clientele, and the price the customer can afford to pay. Canner

TABLE 18-1.   THE USDA FEDERAL GRADES OF MEAT

BEEF	VEAL	LAMB, YEARLING MUTTON, AND MUTTON
USDA Prime	USDA Prime	USDA Prime
USDA Choice	USDA Choice	USDA Choice
USDA Good	USDA Good	USDA Good
USDA Standard	USDA Standard	USDA Utility
USDA Commercial	USDA Utility	USDA Cull
USDA Utility	USDA Cull	
USDA Cutter		
USDA Canner		

and cutter grade meats are rarely seen in the commercial trades. This meat is used in canning or in the making of a specialty like sausage.

Young hogs do not have much variance in quality. Since much of the hog in the hanging state is not usable by the commercial trade, it is sold in smaller cuts. When an establishment orders pork, it specifies cut and weight. Pork is federally inspected and stamped for the health of the animal, but is not stamped with a grade of quality. U.S. grades of quality for pork, although not stamped on the meat, are No. 1, No. 2, No. 3, and cull.

An inspection stamp is required on meat, while the grade stamp is voluntary. The cost of grading the meat by federal inspectors is borne by the packer.

The grade of a piece of meat is determined by its conformation, finish, and quality. Conformation refers to the meat's build and shape and the proportion of meat to bone. Finish refers to the fat: the color, where it is located, and how it is distributed through the edible meat. Quality refers to the factors that relate to the eating quality of the meat, specifically its firmness, thickness, and the strength of its muscle fibers and connective tissues. The juices and the appearance of the marbling, caused by the distribution of fat through the meat, are also important indicators of quality.

The factors that are used in grading beef are also the basis of judging veal, pork, lamb, and mutton. The characteristics vary in the different kinds of meats. For example, pork fat is not as hard as lamb fat; beef has marbling but veal has very little, etc.

USDA Grades for Beef

The success of any meat dish begins with a suitable quality and cut of meat. The USDA grades for beef may be thought of as a guide to the best method to be used in cooking.

Beef that is federally graded is easy to recognize. Almost all cuts brought into the house will bear a series of the shield-shaped grade stamps that enclose the letters "USDA." This stands for U.S. Department of Agriculture. The name of the grade, prime, choice, or good, will also appear in the shield.

This shield-shaped grade stamp identifies quality. It should not be confused with the round federal meat-inspection stamp that bears the inscriptions "U.S. Insp'd & P'S'D." This stamp certifies wholesomeness.

Meat quality is so variable that it is nearly impossible to grade a small cut as "ready for the patron." The federal grader is very skilled in judging the whole carcass or the wholesale cuts. A roller stamp is used, and each piece is rolled from top to bottom.

In addition to the market price, the operator considers three things when purchasing beef: the grade, the cut, and the intended use.

Certain cuts of beef, such as tenderloin, T-bone, club, sirloin, and standing rib roasts, are fairly tender in all the trade grades. The flavorful tastes, for example of corn-fed beef, are more pronounced in the higher grades. These meats can be grilled, broiled, or roasted in the oven.

Other cuts of beef, like round, heel, shank, or flank, require different methods of cooking. They should be braised, stewed, or pot roasted.

The grades of beef, then, serve as guides that tell us how tender specific cuts of meat are and how flavorful and juicy the meat will be in cooking.

Prime beef is the best grade of meat and the most expensive. Prime cuts of beef are very tender, flavorful, and juicy.

Choice beef is of high quality and much used in the trade. The meat is tender, it has flavor, and it is quite juicy.

Good beef is not as flavorful or juicy as prime or choice. It is reasonably tender and does not have much fat in marbling or cover.

Standard-grade beef does not have much fat and the flavor is relatively mild. Although it lacks some flavor and juiciness, it is somewhat tender since it comes from younger animals.

Commercial grade beef is beef from older cattle. This grade is not very tender. It is seldom seen in the trade.

Other Grades of Beef

The other grades of beef—utility, cutter, and canner—are not used by the trade in their fresh form. Utility is usually produced from old cattle and not cooked in the form of fresh beef. Cutter and canner are chiefly used in processed meat products and not sold fresh.

Summary of Beef

1. Approximately 55 to 60 percent of the live weight of cattle is meat. The remainder consists of edible byproducts and waste.
2. The first wholesale cuts of beef, called sides, are the two halves made by splitting the carcass lengthwise down the backbone.
3. Each side is then separated by cutting across the side between the twelfth and thirteenth ribs. The front piece is called the forequarter and the back piece is called the hindquarter.
4. The following is a list of the approximate percentage of the weight of various cuts of beef to the dressed weight of the whole carcass in a typical choice grade.

TABLE 18-2.

HINDQUARTER	
Round, including the rump and shank	23%
Full loin, including short loin and sirloin or loin end	17
Flank	4
Kidney knob (suet)	4
	48%

FOREQUARTER	
Rib	9%
Plate, including the short plate and brisket	13
Shank	4
Square-cut chuck	26
	52%

This list shows that a slightly larger yield of meat can be obtained from the forequarter. The forequarter is a less costly wholesale cut to buy. The meat is used for specific purposes where the dollar return is smaller.

Veal

Veal is the name given to calves of cattle that are one year old or less. Calves that are approximately twelve weeks old and that were milk fed or suckling calves produce a whiter meat that is desirable in the trade. When a calf goes beyond this period it requires more bulk in its diet.

Since the calf is then fed grain feed, it will produce the darker meat that is on the market as veal or baby beef. The same guides that apply to beef grades largely apply to calf grades. However, veal will never be as juicy or flavorful as mature beef.

WHOLESALE CUTS OF VEAL. Wholesale cuts of veal are similar to wholesale cuts of beef. The calf is first split down the back. The two sides of veal are then divided in half between the twelfth and thirteenth ribs. This yields the fore- and hindquarters, as it does with beef.

The hindquarter of veal produces:

1. the round or leg
   round steak, roast, braise
2. the loin
   steaks, chops
3. the breast
   stew, roast, braise, bake

The forequarter of veal produces:

1. the rib
   crown, rib roast
2. the shoulder
   steaks, roasts, braise, fry
3. the breast
   roast, braise, bake, stew
4. the shank
   braise, stew

The lighter veal and calf carcasses may remain unsplit at the backbone. They are cut instead into a foresaddle and hindsaddle wholesale cut that is similar to the lamb wholesale cut. The foresaddle is separated from the hindsaddle by cutting across the back of the carcass between the twelfth and thirteenth ribs, as shown on the veal chart in Figure 18-2. When the animal is cut in this fashion, the wholesale cuts are double. They include both sides of the carcass.

Note: Veal bones are used in making the basic stock and sauces from which almost all good sauces for meats are derived.

A food operation buys these cuts of veal according to the type of business and clientele to which it caters. Large operations that are able to utilize all cuts buy the sides. Others may buy the quarter pieces

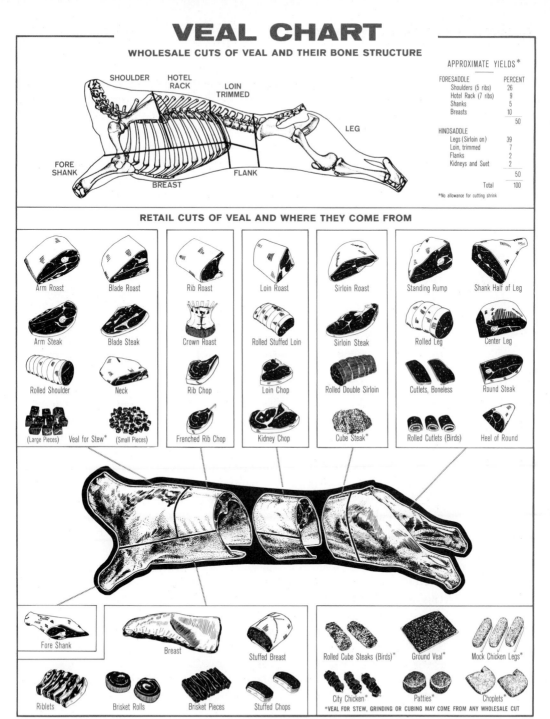

VEAL CHART

WHOLESALE CUTS OF VEAL AND THEIR BONE STRUCTURE

SHOULDER HOTEL RACK LOIN TRIMMED LEG

FORE SHANK BREAST FLANK

APPROXIMATE YIELDS*

FORESADDLE	PERCENT
Shoulders (5 ribs)	26
Hotel Rack (7 ribs)	9
Shanks	5
Breasts	10
	50
HINDSADDLE	
Legs (Sirloin on)	39
Loin, trimmed	7
Flanks	2
Kidneys and Suet	2
	50
Total	100

*No allowance for cutting shrink

RETAIL CUTS OF VEAL AND WHERE THEY COME FROM

Arm Roast Blade Roast Rib Roast Loin Roast Sirloin Roast Standing Rump Shank Half of Leg

Arm Steak Blade Steak Crown Roast Rolled Stuffed Loin Sirloin Steak Rolled Leg Center Leg

Rolled Shoulder Neck Rib Chop Loin Chop Rolled Double Sirloin Cutlets, Boneless Round Steak

(Large Pieces) Veal for Stew* (Small Pieces) Frenched Rib Chop Kidney Chop Cube Steak* Rolled Cutlets (Birds) Heel of Round

Fore Shank Breast Stuffed Breast Rolled Cube Steaks (Birds)* Ground Veal* Mock Chicken Legs*

Riblets Brisket Rolls Brisket Pieces Stuffed Chops City Chicken* Patties* Choplets*

*VEAL FOR STEW, GRINDING OR CUBING MAY COME FROM ANY WHOLESALE CUT

NATIONAL LIVE STOCK AND MEAT BOARD

Figure 18-2 Veal chart.

253

or wholesale cuts. Still smaller operations may buy only the individual cuts and only enough for one meal at a time.

Remember: It is cheaper to buy the larger pieces, but only if you have the type of operation that can utilize all cuts. It stands to reason that a hotel with a coffee shop that is open twenty-four hours a day, a dining room, a banquet department, and a specialty room use all types and cuts of meat. On the other hand it is wise buying for a steak house to buy only those cuts that produce steaks. The cost may be higher for this cut alone but the return is also greater.

Offal

If our industry were to follow the dictionary's explanation of the utilization of meat, we would rob our patrons of many tasty and nutritious dishes besides adversely affecting costs. The dictionary refers to "offal" as those parts of a butchered animal that are rejected as worthless. These parts consist of the heart, liver, tongue, brain, and sweetbreads, to mention but a few. There are seventeen in all. Almost all parts of domestic animals can be used in some way.

One of Europe's greatest modern-day chefs says, "Veal sweetbreads may be looked upon as one of the greatest delicacies in butchers' meats." Veal liver, besides serving as a base for countless tasty entrees, has long been prescribed by doctors in diets for anemia.

While calves heads are the best-known heads, pigs heads are also used as are the tongues and feet of both. Calves livers are the most popular livers, but beef, pork, and lamb livers are also used.

So offal is not rejected and useless as the dictionary tells us. It is not only called for in the daily demands of the food service industry, it is also most valuable. Offal of veal is particularly popular because of the tenderness and tastiness of the young calf.

HEAD. Head is used both hot and cold in entrees. One popular dish is calves head vinaigrette. Head is also used to make aspic.

TONGUE. Tongue is boiled and braised for use in entrees or cold sandwiches.

BRAINS. These are usually blanched (par boiled) then prepared as entrees with eggs, other foods, and sauces.

SWEETBREADS. These are usually soaked for several hours in cold water before being blanched, after which the skin is removed. From there they may simply be broiled, basted with butter, and served. There are more than two hundred recipes for more sophisticated appetites.

LIVER. Liver may be merely sliced and fried or sautéed, but there are hundreds of other recipes. These include liver dumplings, calves liver à la Suisse, and broiled or baked liver, to mention just a few.

KIDNEYS. Kidneys are made into famous breakfast dishes in Germany. They are mostly used in stews in this country. They are also used as part of mixed grills, to make some hot hors d'oeuvres, or just split and broiled.

FEET. Pigs feet are a great delicatessen item when made boneless, breaded, and fried. Featured in this way they were a famous specialty in one of New York's great hotels. They are also served plain, boiled, and cold. Calves feet form the basis for cold summer dishes. Our ancestors made jelly or aspic of calves feet for gifts to invalids.

HEARTS. Beef, veal, mutton, and lamb hearts are all used in the preparation of menu dishes and in many different methods of cooking.

Lamb and Mutton

The distinction between lamb and mutton is made according to the age of the animal. Up to one year old the animal is called a lamb. A sucking animal or one fed on milk is called a milk-fed lamb. The lamb may be either male or female. Older lamb stages are classified as yearling or mutton. Lamb is lighter in color than mutton. The flesh is red and covered with a white tallow fat. The best eating is lamb or yearling. Mutton is not as tender, has a stronger lamb flavor, and is a deeper red in color. The wether is the castrated male sheep. The female is called the ewe and the male is called ram. When graded, the word "lamb," "yearling," or "mutton" will appear along with the grade mark.

STORAGE. Lamb carcasses are refrigerated in one piece by the packer. The wholesale cuts are rendered as they are requested.
   Carcass cuts of lamb produce:

1. lamb hindsaddle—chops, roast, stew, braise
2. lamb foresaddle—chops, roast, stew, braise

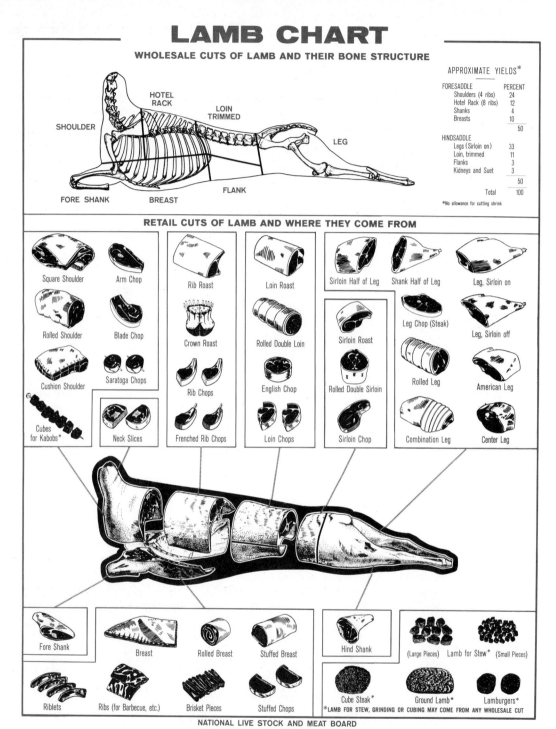

LAMB CHART

WHOLESALE CUTS OF LAMB AND THEIR BONE STRUCTURE

SHOULDER
HOTEL RACK
LOIN TRIMMED
LEG
FORE SHANK
BREAST
FLANK

APPROXIMATE YIELDS*

FORESADDLE	PERCENT
Shoulders (4 ribs)	24
Hotel Rack (8 ribs)	12
Shanks	4
Breasts	10
	50
HINDSADDLE	
Legs (Sirloin on)	33
Loin, trimmed	11
Flanks	3
Kidneys and Suet	3
	50
Total	100

*No allowance for cutting shrink

RETAIL CUTS OF LAMB AND WHERE THEY COME FROM

Square Shoulder
Arm Chop
Rib Roast
Loin Roast
Sirloin Half of Leg
Shank Half of Leg
Leg, Sirloin on

Rolled Shoulder
Blade Chop
Crown Roast
Rolled Double Loin
Sirloin Roast
Leg Chop (Steak)
Leg, Sirloin off

Cushion Shoulder
Saratoga Chops
Rib Chops
English Chop
Rolled Double Sirloin
Rolled Leg
American Leg

Cubes for Kabobs*
Neck Slices
Frenched Rib Chops
Loin Chops
Sirloin Chop
Combination Leg
Center Leg

Fore Shank
Breast
Rolled Breast
Stuffed Breast
Hind Shank
(Large Pieces) Lamb for Stew* (Small Pieces)

Riblets
Ribs (for Barbecue, etc.)
Brisket Pieces
Stuffed Chops
Cube Steak*
Ground Lamb*
Lamburgers*

*LAMB FOR STEW, GRINDING OR CUBING MAY COME FROM ANY WHOLESALE CUT

NATIONAL LIVE STOCK AND MEAT BOARD

Figure 18-3.   Lamb chart.

Summary of Lamb

1. Approximately 45 to 50 percent of the live weight of the lamb is meat. The remainder consists of byproduct and waste.
2. The lamb carcass is not split into sides like beef, pork, and veal. It is separated between the twelfth and thirteenth ribs. The front half becomes the foresaddle and the back becomes the hindsaddle. From these the other cuts are made that provide the hotel rack, leg, and so on.
3. The approximate percentage the weight of various cuts of lamb to the dressed weight of the whole carcass is as follows:

TABLE 18-3.

HINDSADDLE	
Leg	33%
Loin	15
	48%

FORESADDLE	
Hotel rack	14½%
Shoulder	24
Breast and shank	
minus the breast	13½
	52%

4. The tender flesh of lamb permits most parts of lamb to be quite good when roasted.
5. Lamb does not keep as long as some other meats.
6. A kid is a lamb that is five to ten weeks old. It may be a spring lamb or early spring lamb.
7. Hothouse lamb refers to baby lamb that has been produced indoors under artificial climate conditions. They are on the market in some areas from late winter to early spring.
8. Genuine spring lamb is a milk lamb that is usually three to four months old. It is on the market in the early spring.
9. Spring lamb is an older lamb but is less than a year old. It is grass and grain fed and is on the market in late summer and through the winter.
10. Yearling lamb is lamb one to two years old. It is no longer lamb but is not mutton.

11. Mutton is the carcass of male or female sheep that was over two years of age. There is not too much mutton on the midwestern market. Most sheep are marketed as lambs. Mutton is a deeper red in color and the flesh is firmer. This makes it a chewier piece of meat. The fat is white and brittle.

Pork

In a few restaurants, religion prohibits the use of pork. Generally it is used fresh, smoked, and pickled. There are many popular pork dishes in almost every method of cooking used for other meat. Fresh pork must be fully cooked because the animal is a carrier of trichinae, parasites that may cause discomfort and even illness if they are not destroyed by complete and proper cooking.

STORAGE. About 70 percent of the live weight of hogs is meat. The balance is byproduct and waste. The dressed carcass of pork is split down the back similarly to beef. However, from that point the wholesale cuts vary somewhat.

Since pork is all marketed from young hogs there is not too much variance in the quality of the hog. As a result pork is usually graded in quality by No. 1, No. 2, No. 3, and cull. Pork is different from other meats in the sense that it is uncommon to sell pork in a large cut, such as a side. The catering trade will more often buy pork by weight-size. That is, by calling the cut by name and then mentioning the weight desired. Hogs slaughtered at various stages of growth may be uniform and consistent in quality but vary in size.

TYPES OF HAM

Regular—A ham that is smoked but not skinned or cooked.
Skinned—A larger ham that is skinned and has had the excess fat taken off.
Tenderized—An uncooked ham that has been smoked and heated short of cooking.
Precooked—A cooked ham ready to eat.
Sugar cured—This kind of ham is given a sweet salt cure in addition to the smoking.

A 240-pound porker produces about 10 pounds of center-cut pork chops.

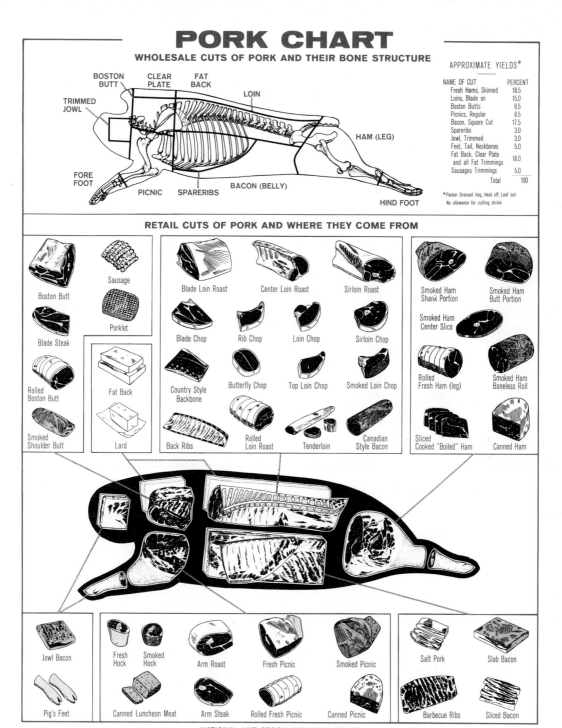

Figure 18-4. Pork chart.

THE CARCASS CUTS OF PORK AND METHODS OF PREPARATION

Ham (smoked or fresh)—The ham is fried, broiled, or boiled. Boiled ham is sometimes also baked.

Loin chops—These are fried, roasted, broiled, or braised.

Spareribs—These are boiled, braised, barbecued, or baked.

Sides—Sides are used to make bacon.

Fatback—This is rendered for lard and used raw for larding other meats.

Butts—Whole butts are boiled, braised, or roasted. Sliced butts are fried as pork steak.

Picnic—The picnic is boiled, fried, or broiled, the same as smoked or fresh ham.

Bacon—Bacon is fried, grilled, or boiled.

The approximate percentage of the weight of the various cuts to the dressed weight of the entire carcass is as follows:

ham	18½%
pork loin	15
fatback	6
spareribs and side	17
Boston butt	6
picnic with hock and foot	10
jowl	2
lard and miscellaneous	25½
	100%

Summary of Pork

1. Pork is the meat of hogs that are usually less than one year of age.
2. There are more than seventy-five products that are the result of processing a hog.
3. Aging is not a factor in the use of pork as it is in beef. Pork is used after approximately two weeks of hanging.
4. A pig is called a boar when it is a male; a sow when it is a female; and a hog when it is a castrated male or a spayed female.

Preservation of Meat

Meat is a highly perishable item that requires special attention in handling and in keeping. There are various ways of storing and preserving meat for future use.

Refrigeration is used to keep meat for a short period of time. The meat is exposed to air in cold storage.

Freezing makes meat last for a long period of time, but the use of frozen meat is not popular in some establishments. Frozen meat has to be used soon after it is taken from a freezer. Once thawed, frozen meat has less keeping quality than fresh or aged meat. Meat should be thawed out slowly so that the liquid is absorbed by the meat.

Cured meat is meat that has been preserved by drying, smoking, or pickling. Dried meat has had its water extracted and has been conditioned with warm air. Smoking meat is one of the oldest ways of preserving meat. The smoking removes the water from the meat and gives the meat a characteristic flavor and color. It also kills bacteria that could be in the meat. Pickling meat is another old method of preserving meat. Pickled meat has been treated with salt, brine, sugar, and other chemicals. The sugar, salt, and spices dissolve in a juice that penetrates the meat.

Canned meat is often meat that has been cooked. A certain amount of canned meat is always good to have on hand to protect against an unpredicted rush or busy periods when a food is to be prepared quickly. These items should be stored in a cool and dry area. Canned meats and their juices or gravies will change if subjected to warm storage.

Crovac meat is a process of preserving a cut of meat by protecting it from exposure to air. This is done by covering the piece of meat with clear plastic and sealing the ends so that an airtight container is formed. Very light plastic is drawn tightly to the meat by submerging it in a hot-water bath. This process arrests the growth of molds, yeasts, and bacteria that are present and, at the same time, keeps other microorganism from developing.

Sausage

Sausage is a special product that is made from raw muscle, fat, and various offal such as tongue and liver. This meat, combined with the appropriate spices and sometimes with other liquids, is housed in a skin. The skin is usually the cleaned intestines of sheep, cattle, or pigs, but it may be made from a synthetic cellophane material. Sausage is mostly a pork product, although beef is also used.

Sausage is classified in the following way:

1. Uncooked—This includes fresh, link, and patty.
2. Cooked—Cooked sausage may be smoked or plain. Examples are frankfurter, bologna, some liverwursts, etc.
3. Uncooked (smoked)—This includes Polish sausage, some liverwursts, etc.

4. Hard sausage—This includes salami and pastrami, both of which have excellent keeping qualities.

Frankfurters are made with a combination of ground beef, pork, fat, and seasoning. Some may be smoked. There are a host of sausages by other names.

Glandular or Variety Meats

These additional edible parts of beef, veal, lamb, and pork offer much variety to the menus of the catering trades. They are used by themselves or combined with other meats to produce exquisite dishes.

Under the heading of "Offal" we explained the designation and use of most of these parts of our meat animals. We did not mention ox-tails, a common term for the tails of these animals. Nor did we mention tripe.

Oxtails are used in a famous soup. They are also braised with veg-etable accompaniment to become a very popular entree.

Tripe, the lining of a steer's stomach, is parboiled and then some-times breaded before frying. Tripe is also a component of the famous pepper pot soup, but its real worldwide fame comes from Caen, France. In this French method it is cooked after soaking the two-inch squares with ox feet, vegetables, seasoning, and a small amount of brandy or cider liqueur. This is called "tripe a la mode de Caen."

Variety meats from beef, veal, lamb, and pork include the fol-lowing:

Heart—Hearts vary in size. They are cooked in moist heat.

Kidney—Kidneys vary in size and in color from off-white to dark. Kidneys from larger animals can be cooked in liquid. Smaller kidneys are sliced or split for either broiling or frying.

Liver—Young liver is sliced, broiled, and fried. The older beef liver is cut into larger pieces, braised, and then ground. It is used in liver loaf or paste.

Tongue—Tongue is available fresh, pickled, canned, or smoked. A fresh tongue is cooked in water until tender. After cooking the skin is removed and excess is trimmed.

Oxtail—This is the name given to the tails of all cattle. It is very good in casseroles and soup dishes.

Pig's tail—These tails are sold whole. They are used in casserole dishes.

Pig's foot—The foot is sold fresh and pickled. This part is not widely used in the trade.

Brains—Brains are sold fresh. They must be washed and their connective tissue must be removed. They can be parboiled for a casserole dish or pan fried.

Sweetbreads—This is sold fresh. It is the white thymus gland. Sweetbreads must be soaked in cold water to remove blood and connective tissue. It can be parboiled and used with another dish or it can be broiled. It can also be breaded and pan fried.

Tripe—Tripe is sold slightly precooked. It is used in soup or casserole dishes chiefly. Tripe is available fresh, pickled, and canned.

The Cooking of Meat

The most important knowledge the chef possesses in cooking meat is what cut of meat to use for each dish.

BOILED MEAT DISHES. Fresh or smoked meat can be boiled. Most boiling is done with beef, pork, or mutton. Meat should be added to the boiling water. This seals in the juices that provide the added flavors. Boiled meat is usually served with a sharp sauce to compliment the taste of the meat. Mustard and horseradish go well with it. Some boiled meat dishes that are prepared are corned beef and cabbage, New England dinner, fresh brisket of beef, short ribs of beef, pig shanks, spareribs, sweetbreads, brains, fresh ham, and beef tongue.

ROAST MEAT DISHES. Roast meats range from rare, with its redness in color, to well done, where the blood coloring has mostly disappeared. The doneness of meat can be determined with a meat thermometer. The bulb end should be inserted in the thickest part of the meat. When the temperature of the interior of the meat reaches the prescribed level, the meat is done. Doneness can also be determined by cooking meat a specific number of minutes per pound. This is not as accurate as a thermometer because of the difference in the shape, fat, and thickness of meat. Knowing how done meat is by touch requires much practice. It develops with experience. The uncooked piece of meat is soft and springy to the touch and becomes more firm as it cooks.

Prime ribs of beef, pork loin, shoulder of beef, round of beef, leg of veal, whole stuffed leg of lamb, crown rib roast of lamb, and fresh ham are the usual roasts.

To avoid shrinkage, a roast should be cooked at a low temperature. A high temperature extracts more liquid from the meat. Meat continues to cook for a short period of time after it is removed from the oven.

BRAISED MEAT. To cook by braising means to cook with a combination of dry and moist heat. The meat is browned by dry heat in the oven or on top of the stove. A small amount of water or broth is then added and the pan is covered for additional cooking. This type of cooking best prepares the less tender cuts of meat. Pot roasting is one method of braising. Some braised dishes include beef tenderloin, tips, lamb (leg or shoulder), veal round or shank, and various other beef cuts such as rump and short ribs.

STEWS. Meat stews are made from small pieces of meat and vegetables. The ingredients produce their own essence while cooking. Most stews thicken while cooking, but they may have thickening added. The best-known stews are Irish stew, which is made with lamb; American stew, which is made with beef; and veal and kidney stew.

There are also several foreign dishes that fall in the stew category. Hungarian goulash can be made from beef alone or beef combined with pork. In other European cooking the so-called stewed dishes appear as ragouts, navarins, etc. Fricasse can also be called a stew. Most fricasses are made from poultry.

BROILED AND GRILLED MEAT. As a general rule the more tender cuts of meat are cooked over charcoal fires, gas fires, or electrical broilers or grills. These meats are cut thinner and are usually cooked to order as the customer waits in the dining room. Steaks, chops, tenderloin, and some specialty cuts are most often broiled or grilled. These include ham steak, club steak, lamb chops, sirloin steak, pork tenderloin, and Chateaubriand. Chicken, seafood, and other food combinations are also cooked this way.

Pan frying is the same as sautéing and is the most approved method of cooking the more tender meats. A small amount of fat in the pan is used to first frizzle the item. The fat, whatever kind is used, must be very hot. After the frizzling, the cooking proceeds at a lower temperature. Poultry that is sautéed may be finished in oven.

Sauteing, or pan frying, is not to be confused with deep fat frying. Deep frying employs an entirely different principle and medium. Deep fat frying is generally used for foods that, by their nature or by their preparation, can be cooked quickly by immersion in deep fat. The frying kettles are thermostatically controlled so that the fat is maintained at the temperature that is required by the food being cooked.

The first deep-fried food that comes to mind is French fries. Many establishments also use deep fat frying for croquettes, chicken, small fish and fish filets, oysters, scallops, and fritters. In fact, almost all items that are breaded are fried in deep fat.

Inspection Marks

In addition to grading foods for quality, the USDA also inspects some foods for wholesomeness. Listed below are marks that are used on foods that have passed USDA inspection. These marks must not be confused with the grade marks mentioned previously. They are round or shield-shaped. All meat and poultry sold across state lines must be federally inspected and carry the round inspection mark. Grading is not required. The inspection mark assures wholesomeness. The grade mark tells the quality.

The inspection mark on fresh and cured meat says that it has been inspected and passed. It is more often seen on the larger cuts of meat: rounds, sides, hams, etc. This mark certifies that the meat was produced from healthy animals and that the plant is clean and operated in a sanitary way under the constant supervision of a USDA inspector.

An inspection mark is also used on processed meat products, canned, frozen, dried, or packaged. It means that the product is clean and wholesome. It also certifies that the label has been approved by the USDA.

An inspection mark is used on poultry and poultry products, whether they are fresh, frozen, canned, or dried. It means, as it does with meats, that the product is clean, wholesome, and fit to eat. Assurance of this is given by the label. As with meat, inspected poultry may also be graded for quality. Grade A is the best grade.

An inspection mark is used on fruit and vegetable products including jam and jelly. It is not required by law. It, too, gives assurance of a good clean product that was produced under the supervision of a government inspector. Labels with this mark must be approved by the USDA.

A shield is used to mark the U.S. Department of the Interior (USDI) inspection service that is available on a voluntary basis. It is used on seafood. Firms under continuous inspection are permitted to display this emblem.

POULTRY

Poultry is the term appplied to domestic birds raised for breeding, production of eggs, and the all-around production of fowl. This includes chicken, duck, goose, turkey, pigeon, and guinea fowl. Although poultry is not sold this way, for purposes of classification poultry can be distinguished by the difference in the color of the meat. The types of

TABLE 18-4. TYPES OF POULTRY

TYPE OF BIRD	MARKET NAME	WEIGHT	AGE	SEX
Chicken (light meat)	Broiler or Fryer (Tender-meated with soft, pliable, smooth-textured skin and flexible breast cartilage)	1–2½ lbs.	9–12 weeks	M or F
	Roaster (Same as above other than a less flexible breast bone cartilage)	3 lbs. plus	3–5 months	M or F
	Capon*—(Tender-meated with soft, pliable, smooth-textured skin)	4 lbs. plus	8 months or less	None
	Hens or Fowl—(Meat is less tender than that of a roaster; nonflexible bone tip)	4–6 lbs. plus	10 months or more	F
	Cock—(Mature male chicken with coarse skin, toughened and darkened meat, and hardened breastbone tip)	4–6 lbs. plus	12 months or more	M
Turkey (light meat)	Old Toms/Old Hens—(Tender-meated with soft, pliable, smooth-textured skin)	8 lbs. plus	5–7 months	M/F
	Fryer or Roaster—(Young, immature, tender-meated, soft, pliable, smooth-textured skin	8–12 lbs.	16 weeks or under	M or F
	Old Toms/Old Hens—(Course skin and toughened flesh)	12 lbs. plus	15 months or more	M/F
	Yearling—(Fully matured, tender-meated, smooth-textured skin)	12 lbs. plus	15 months or more	M or F
Duck (dark meat)	Broiler or Fryer Duckling**—(Tender-meated, soft bill, and soft-windpipe)	4–6 lbs.	8 weeks or under	M or F
	Roaster—(Tender-meated; bill is not completely hardened; and windpipe is easily dented)	4–6 lbs.	16 weeks or under	M or F
	Mature or Old Duck—(Toughened flesh, hardened bill and windpipe)	4–6 lbs.	15 months or more	M or F

* A capon is a male chicken that is castrated when young.
** "Long Island Duckling" is a young duck produced in a Long Island duck farm and specially fattened for tender meat.

TABLE 18-4.   (Continued)

TYPE OF BIRD	MARKET NAME	WEIGHT	AGE	SEX
Geese (dark meat)	Young Goose—(Tender-meated and has a windpipe that is easily dented)	6½–11 lbs.	7 months or more	M or F
	Mature or Old Goose—(Toughened flesh and hardened windpipe)	6½–11 lbs.	15 months or more	M or F
Guineas (dark meat)	Young Guinea (Keets)—(Tender-meated and has a flexible breastbone cartilage)	1¼–3 lbs.	8 months or less	M or F
	Mature or Old Guinea—(Toughened flesh and a hardened breastbone)	1¼–3 lbs.	12 months or more	M or F
Pigeons (dark meat)	Squab—(Extra tender meat)	12–16 oz.	3–4 weeks	M or F
	Pigeon—(Coarse skin and toughened flesh)	Over 1 lb.	Over 4 weeks	M or F

poultry that are more frequently used in the catering trade are shown in Table 18-4.

The poultry that is available for commercial use is most often poultry that is New York dressed and drawn. A New York dressed bird is one that has had its feathers removed. A drawn bird is one that has had the liver, heart, and neck removed. These parts are washed, put in small bags, and placed in the cavity of the bird.

The dressed and drawn birds may be frozen but today most frozen poultry is in the ready to cook form. Some are whole birds and some are cut in pieces.

Canned poultry is available in different forms. Both parts and entire birds are available. The poultry item may be completely cooked and simply require heating, or it may be precooked. In the latter case it needs to be finally cooked in a different form.

Inspection

As in the case of meat, all poultry that is shipped from one state to another must be inspected for the health of the bird and sanitary conditions of the plant and workers. Poultry that has been inspected for wholesomeness bears a federal label that indicates this.

The USDA inspection and grade marks may appear on a paper wing tag, on the giblet wrap, on an insert, or they may be printed on the overwrap or transparent wrapper.

The official inspection mark is in the form of a circle. The inspection mark means:

1. that each bird has been individually examined by a USDA inspector to make sure that it is wholesome and safe for eating
2. that the poultry product was processed in a sanitary manner in an approved plant that has proper facilities
3. that the poultry product is not adulterated
4. that the poultry product is truthfully and informatively labeled

The words "Inspected for Wholesomeness by the U.S. Department of Agriculture" are a certification of wholesomeness by a trained government inspector. Such inspection is required by law for all poultry and poultry products that move in interstate or foreign commerce. There are no levels of wholesomeness. The poultry is either wholesome or condemned as unfit for human consumption. The inspection mark refers only to wholesomeness of the product. It does not refer to the quality of the product.

The grade mark refers to the various qualities of the product. Before poultry can be graded, it must first have been inspected for wholesomeness.

To be assured of always serving wholesome poultry that is of the desired quality, look for both the official USDA inspection and the grade mark.

Labels on USDA inspected poultry products will show:

1. the inspection mark
2. the common or usual name of the product
3. the net weight or other appropriate measure
4. the name and address of the packer or distributor
5. the plant number of the official establishment and, on further-processed products, a statement of ingredients listed in order of decreasing proportions

Poultry that has passed the federal inspection by the Department of Agriculture is then placed in grade qualities. The best grade poultry is marked "U.S. Grade A." The lesser grades are U.S. Grade B and U.S. Grade C. The following factors are taken into consideration in grading poultry:

1. the shape of poultry and the amount of pin feathers
2. the color of the skin and the fat distribution

3. the thickness of the flesh on the bone
4. any damage or tears to the skin

The class of the bird appears on the label. It is a guide to its tenderness and to the appropriate cooking method. Class is indicated by the words "young," "mature," or "old," and by such terms as "broiler," "roaster," and "stewing hen."

The Poultry Products Inspection Act has been in effect in recent years.

Some states also participate in the grading of poultry. The identifying stamp designates "federal-state." In other states the stamp mentions only U.S. Grade.

Inspection is mandatory when poultry is sent to other states. Grading is not mandatory.

The official grade mark is in the form of a shield. It tells the grade or quality of the product; that is, whether it is U.S.Grade A, B, or C. It also tells that the quality of each bird has been determined by a trained government grader.

The grade mark is used only on poultry that has first been inspected for wholesomeness.

In grading poultry some of the qualities that are sought are the same as in grading other meat products. They are:

1. a full-fleshed and meaty body
2. a good finish on the surface of the bird
3. an attractive appearance in distribution of fat and meat

Some tips on the handling of poultry are as follows:

1. Poultry furnishes many essential nutrients, especially high-quality protein, the B vitamins, and the minerals phosphorus and iron.
2. Poultry is perishable. Use care and cleanliness in preparing, cooking, cooling, and serving it.
3. Frozen poultry should be kept solidly frozen until it is time to thaw it. Cook poultry promptly after thawing.
4. When cooking poultry, cook it completely. Never partially cook it, then store and finish the cooking at a later date.
5. Leftover cooked poultry, broth, stuffing, and gravy should be separated, covered, and refrigerated. Use it within one to two days. Freeze it for longer storage.
6. Most kinds of ready-to-cook poultry are available as parts and in

whole, halved, and quartered forms. Some are also available as boneless roasts and rolls.

Cooking of Poultry

The edible portion of poultry is approximately 55 percent of the live weight. This runs close to the ratio of beef and pork.

ROASTING. In roasting poultry the skin of the bird should be protected so that the skin is not overly dried in cooking. This can be done by using a covered roast pan or by covering the bird with a moistened cloth or with aluminum.

BROILING. Young tender birds are used for broiling purposes. A young bird is split in half down the back. The bird is brushed with an oil and placed directly over or under a flame. Seasoning is applied as the bird is cooking.

FRYING. A young tender bird will fry in twenty to twenty-five minutes. A cast-iron pan is best suited for frying poultry and a steady heat is desired. The chicken is placed in the pan with the fat side down. When cooking the first half of chicken the pan can be covered.

DEEP FAT FRYING. Many places do most of their fried chicken cooking in deep fat fryers. The chicken can be started and finished in deep fat or it can be started in deep fat and finished in roasting pans in the oven.

GAME

This is the term that refers, in the catering trade, to the meat of wild animals that are feathered or furred. As a rule not much of this meat finds its way into commercial kitchens although many game items are available from purveyor outlets. On occasion patrons will bring in game to be cooked for their guests. Certain phases of the catering trade cook more game than others. For example, a private club will do more of this than a commercial restaurant.

FISH

In the culinary trades fish refers to all forms of edible meats that come from the water.

SCALE FISH (Vertebrate). Scale fish are covered with scales. The salt-water scale fish include cod, halibut, haddock, and sole. The freshwater fish are catfish, mountain trout, salmon, etc.

SHELLFISH (Invertebrate). Shellfish are covered with some type of shell. The mollusks, such as scallops, clams, and oysters, have hard shells. The crustaceans are covered with a brittle shell and have meatlike bodies. These include lobster, crab, and shrimp.

COMMERCIAL CUTS. Fish can be obtained in several different forms: fresh, frozen, canned, salted, smoked, and dried. They are also available as whole fish, as a steak, and as a fillet.

GRADING OF FISH. Some fish products are inspected and graded by the U.S. Department of Interior according to standards that have been developed. This is a voluntary program for the seller. The freshness is judged largely on appearance, color, elasticity of the flesh, smell, and whether or not the fish sinks to the bottom when it is placed in water. Most fish items are graded U.S. Grade A or U.S. Grade B.

Inspected seafoods display the official USDI grade or inspection shield on their labels. Only those firms that process fishery products under continuous inspection are permitted to use these emblems.

HOW TO USE FISH

As an appetizer—The shellfish and crustaceans are popular appetizers. Oysters and clams are served on the half shell. Shrimp is cooked and served in cocktails and supremes. Lobster and crabmeat are also served in supremes. Sometimes combinations of them make up an appetizer. They also find favor cooked as the starter or first course.

As a soup—Seafood soups are popular. They may be clear, chowdered, or creamed.

As a course—In many banquets or elaborate menus a separate course of fish is provided and almost always precedes the entree of meat.

As a main dish—Fresh, frozen, canned, or dried fish can be prepared in a large number of ways. Some dishes use the whole fish. Others use the steak or fillet.

METHODS OF COOKING

Broil—The fish is placed in a pan approximately 3 inches from the heat and brushed with butter.

Pan Fry—Floured fish is placed in shallow pan with melted fat and browned.

Bake—Whole fish, thick steaks, and fillets can be baked.

Poach—The fish is placed in a tightly closed pan with a small amount of water.

Boil—The fish is placed in pan with simmering water. The water must not be heated to a boil.

Deep Fat Fry—Small thin pieces of fish are usually floured and cooked entirely submerged in fat.

STORAGE OF FISH

Fresh Fish—Fresh fish is stored whole or in the round. It must be kept refrigerated in a fish box and covered with cracked ice. The water from the cracked ice should be poured off the fish quite frequently. Many establishments buy fresh fish fillets. Icing these may result in loss of flavor. Keeping them wrapped at or near 32 degrees F will suffice although fresh fillets should be used on the day they are cut.

Frozen Fish—Frozen fish must be kept frozen. Once the fish is thawed it must be cooked immediately. Some fish can be cooked before the fish is completely thawed.

Smoked Fish—Smoked fish must be kept refrigerated. Salted fish must be kept in a cool dry place.

Canned Fish—Canned fish can be kept in a cool dry storage area. It should be used once it is opened.

Fish vary considerably in size, appearance, color, texture, and flavor. Although fish differ from one to the other, they have one thing in common. They are all easy to prepare.

In cooking fish great care is placed on not overcooking the meat. Fish vary in fat content and this factor permits some fish to be more suitable for baking or broiling. Others may be better for poaching, steaming, or boiling. However, a lean fish such as a cod, halibut, or haddock can be broiled or baked if it is basted with melted fat or served with a sauce covering.

A properly cooked fish permits the flesh to be removed from the bones easily. At the same time it is moist and tender to the bite.

NUTRITIVE VALUE OF FISH.

Fish are an excellent source of nutritive value. Fish provide protein, minerals, vitamins, and fats—in fact all the nutrients but carbohydrates. The kinds and amounts of nutrients vary in content depending on the fish product. Fish foods contain:

Proteins that build and repair body tissue

Minerals that are needed for the performance of certain body functions and for the maintenance of teeth and bones; the iodine content in fish is greater than beef

Vitamins that are required for good health and growth

Fats that are needed by the body to provide heat and energy; the fat content in fish varies in the species of fish

VARIETY OF FISH. Fish offers an interesting variety of foods to meal planners. In general more use could be made of fish in planning and preparing foods. The average diner confines his culinary appreciation of fish to the handful of old reliables with which she or he is familiar. There are more than 150 varieties available throughout the year in the United States.

Some of the more common types of fish available are:

Whole or round—This is fish that is marketed in the form that it came out of the water. The fish has to be eviscerated and scaled. The head, tails, and fins may be removed depending on size of fish and its intended use.

Drawn—A drawn fish is one that is marketed with the entrails removed. For preparation the fish has to be scaled and the head, tail, and fins may be removed, depending on the size and contemplated use.

Dressed—This is a fish that is scaled and has had the entrails removed. Most often the head, tail, and fins are also removed.

Steaks—Steaks are usually made from larger fish. These are crosscut slices of dressed fish. The steaks are usually cut into portion sizes and have only a small cross section of the backbone in each portion.

Filet—A filet is a side of fish cut away from the backbone. This cut is usually free of bone and ready for cooking. It may have scaled skin left on fish or may be skinless.

Butterfly—This is two pieces of filet that are held together in the center by uncut flesh and skin. It may be slightly pressed.

Stick—Fish sticks are uniform pieces of fish that are cut lengthwise or crosswise from filets and breaded. They can be purchased cooked or uncooked. Fried fish sticks must contain not less than 60 percent fish.

Chunk—This is a cross section of a large dressed fish. A cross section of the backbone is the only bone.

Portion—Portions are cut from frozen blocks of fish, coated with a batter, breaded, packaged, and frozen. They may be cooked or uncooked. They are heavier servings than fish sticks. Raw breaded fish portions must contain not less than 75 percent fish. Fried fish portions must contain not less than 65 percent fish.

Breaded—This is a small dressed fish or portion-cut fish that has been dipped in egg and rolled in bread crumbs or flour.

FRESH FISH. Points to remember in buying fish in the round:

eyes: clear, bright, full, bulging
scales: tight to the skin, shiny, bright
gills: reddish-pink, no slime or odor
flesh: solid and elastic, does not pull away from bones
smell: fresh, not objectionable

QUANTITIES TO PURCHASE. A general guide for serving fish:

1. 5 to 8 ounces per person of edible flesh
2. 8 ounces per person for dressed fish
3. 16 ounces per person for whole fish

Shellfish

Oysters, clams, and scallops are shellfish. There are few menus that do not carry them. Freshness is indicated when the shells are tightly closed. They are also sold opened in bulk, in gallons or less, and in their juice.

OYSTERS. Fresh oysters are sold alive in the shell. Shucked oysters are sold in bulk in their own juice. The count of oyster, in the bulk, varies depending on size from extra large to small. Oysters are one of the most popular shellfish. They start many menus raw on the half shell and are also served stewed, fried, and baked.

CLAMS. The littleneck and cherrystone clams are served raw on the half shell. The cherrystone is also served in entrees such as baked casino. The larger quahog clam is minced and used for clam chowder. It is also steamed or baked at shore dinners or clambakes. All three have thick round shells. The same waters produce soft clams, which are slightly longer and have thinner shells. They are used by some for chowder. Around Boston they are very popular fried. Razor and pismo clams are popular where they are found. They are seldom shipped.

SCALLOPS. A scallop is a shellfish similar to the oyster. The scallop shell is thin, round, and fluted. The meat is usually fried. The small bay scallop is the finest. Sea scallops are larger and the flesh is not quite as delicate.

CRABS. The soft shell occurs when crabs molt. During the molting period, which is from early spring to early fall, the hard shell is shed and the crab is called a soft-shell crab. Crabs are served in many ways. They are very popular items during their season. Crab meat is picked from hard crabs and is found on menus as starters, cocktails, and entrees.

LOBSTERS. The demand for lobster is second only to steak. A fresh live lobster has movement when tapped or picked up. The tail in particular springs to the underside of the body when the lobster is placed on its back. The meat of the smaller lobster is generally more tender than the meat of the larger lobster.

MUSSELS. Mussels are a plentiful shellfish similar to clams. They are used a great deal in Europe. They are not used much in this country except when canned.

SHRIMP. Fresh shrimp are sold as is or with shell removed. Shrimps are sized according to how many come to the pound. Fifteen to twenty means there are between fifteen and twenty shrimps to a pound. Fresh frozen shrimp are sold with the head removed and are light gray in appearance. When shrimp is cooked it turns a light pink in color.

A prawn is a crustacean similar to a shrimp. In our market that name is generally given to larger-sized shrimps. These get as big as 6 to 8 inches in length.

Frozen Fish

Freezing has made good quality fish products available throughout the year. Almost all varieties of fish are available to the trade in those areas close to the sea as well as in parts of the country more distant. Fish products that are sold in frozen form are usually packed during seasons of abundance and held in cold storage until they are ready for distribution. In this way the consumer is given the opportunity to select different species of fish throughout the year. High quality frozen fish that have been properly processed, packaged, and held at 0 degrees F or below will remain in good condition for relatively long periods of time. Frozen fish can be purchased by the pound in any of the market forms:

whole, dressed, steaks, filets, chunks, portions, and sticks. Frozen fish of good quality have the following characteristics:

flesh: solidly frozen. The flesh should have no discoloration or freezer burns. Most deterioration in quality is prevented when fish are properly held in the frozen state. Frozen fish that have been thawed and refrozen are poorer in quality.

odor: little or none. A strong fish odor means poor quality.

wrapping: most filets, steaks, chunks, portions, and sticks are wrapped individually or packaged in various weights. The wrapping should be of moisture–vapor-proof material. There should be little or no air space between the fish and the wrapping.

When whole or round fish is thawing prior to being cooked and there is no fish box, the fish should be wrapped in additional covering prior to being stored in the refrigerator. This covering prevents fish odors from entering other foods.

Frozen fish that is packaged will keep as long as it remains in the frozen state. Frozen fish should be used immediately upon thawing. It should not be refrozen once it has been permitted to thaw. Frozen fish can be thawed in a refrigerator under 40 degrees F or by submerging it in cold running water.

Canned Fish

A large selection of canned fish and specialty items is available on the market today. The more abundant varieties of canned fish used in the trade are:

1. Tuna. Several species of fish are marketed as tuna, all of which are equally desirable. On the Pacific Coast the catch includes albacore, bluefin, skip jack, and yellowfin. The same fish are caught in the Atlantic with the addition of blackfin and a little tuna. Albacore has lighter meat than the other species and is the only tuna permitted to be labeled "white meat" tuna. The other species are labeled "light meat" tuna.

    Canned tuna is available in three different styles of pack. The pack does not indicate a difference in quality but refers to the size of the pieces in the can. All types of tuna are packed with all the skin and bones removed and seasoned with salt. Tuna fish is also available packed in olive oil.

    a. Fancy or solid is the most expensive pack. There are three or four large pieces to the can and they are packed in oil. It is ideal to use as a cold plate item.

b. Chunk tuna is packed in oil in chunk-sized pieces. It is used in salads and main entrée dishes. This is the medium-priced pack.

c. Flaked or grated tuna is cut into smaller pieces than the chunk style. This pack is also in oil. These small pieces of tuna are very good for fillings, canapé pastes, and as combination main-dish entrées. Tuna can be purchased in cans that have from 3 to 13 ounces.

2. Salmon. There are five distinct species of Pacific Coast salmon. They are usually sold by name since that indicates the differences in the type of meat. These differences are a matter of color, texture, and flavor. The more expensive varieties have a higher oil content and are a deeper red. The more expensive salmons are: red or sockeye salmon; Chinook or king salmon; medium red, coho, or silver salmon; pink salmon; and chum or keta salmon. Canned salmon is available in cans that contain from 3 to 16 ounces.

3. Mackerel. Mackerel is available in 15-ounce cans.

4. Maine sardines. These are available in cans that contain 3 to 4 ounces.

Cooking Fish

Fish is cooked to develop its flavor, to soften the small amount of connective tissue present, and to make the protein easier to digest. When fish is cooked at too high a temperature for a long period of time, it becomes tough and dry. Such cooking destroys the fine flavor of fish.

When is fish cooked? Uncooked fish has a watery, translucent look. In the cooking process the watery juices become milky in color and make the flesh nonshiny and firm to the touch. When fish is completely cooked, the flesh will easily separate into flakes and come away from the bones.

For the large part, fish tends to break up easily. It must be handled very gently and as little as possible during cooking and while being served.

Miscellaneous Information on Fish and Shellfish

Anchovies are very tiny fish. The average one measures approximately 3½ inches. They are prepared as filets and come packed in olive oil in flat cans. They are also available rolled and stuffed with capers and other foods.

Antipasto is an Italian fish relish packed in olive oil. It contains a selection of seafoods and vegetables.

Caviar is fish eggs that are specially prepared as an hors d'oeuvre food. It comes in small tins or jars. Black caviar is caviar prepared from sturgeon. Red caviar is prepared from salmon. The black caviar is more expensive and generally more appreciated in the trade.

The eggs of all fish are called the "roe." The roe of fish other than sturgeon or salmon are used as an hors d'oeuvre, but they are not as popular as caviar.

Sardines are a small canned fish that are similar to herring. Sardines are canned in flat units and are packed in cottonseed oil or olive oil. They are also packed in various vegetable and herb marinates.

Kippered herring is split herring that has had all the bones removed. It is pickled and sealed in vinegar with onions and other spices and seasoning.

Roll mops are herring filets that have had all the bones removed. These filets are rolled up with a piece of cucumber or onion and held together by two small wooden skewers. The roll mops are sprinkled with spices and herbs. They come in a container that is filled with vinegar brine.

Lox is a red to pink smoke-cured salmon.

Dried fish should be stored in a dry, airy place. Before use it must be soaked and bathed in a series of fresh- and lye-water baths.

Stockfish is the term given to a variety of dried fish. This fish has been dried and cured without the addition of any preservatives.

Lutefish is the name given to stockfish that has been soaked in a lye-water and a fresh-water bath before it is ready for preparation.

chapter 19

fats, oils, shortenings, and salad dressings

ANIMAL FATS

Fats in animals are found in the milk of the female animal and in tissue deposits of males and females. Fats are stored in the body and serve as depositories of energy for periods of food scarcity.

Animal fat varies according to the food the animal feeds upon and the part of the country in which the animal lives. Fat and oil imply the same thing. One is in liquid form and the other is in solid form.

Lard

Lard is the melted fat rendered from the fat tissues of the hog. Lard is pure white in color and firm to the touch at room temperature. The flavor and smell of lard depend upon the part of the body it is taken from and the feed that the animal ate. Leaf lard is lard that comes from the inner fat of the abdomen of the hog. The best grade of lard is kettle-rendered leaf lard which is rendered under slow heat in an open-top kettle. Prime steam lard is lard rendered from trimmings and all fatty parts of the pig. This is done with live steam in a closed tank.

Suet

Suet is the fatty tissues of cattle. The fat is dried, cut into small pieces, and either placed in a pan that goes into the oven or melted in an open kettle or pot on top of a stove over a slow fire. Because of the strong odor that accompanies the process of rendering suet, it is usually done in the off-cooking hours. The quality oil produced is good for frying purposes. If an operation uses much beef, suet is cost free.

Vegetable Fats and Oils

Vegetable fats and olive, corn, coconut, and sesame oils have always been used in cooking. Today they are also the basis of many compounded shortenings and frying mediums.

Coconut oil is obtained from the flesh of coconuts. It is snow white in color and has no characteristic flavor. It is used extensively in the making of shortenings.

Shortening is a hydrogenated fat. This is a vegetable oil that has been treated with hydrogen to change it from its liquid state to a semisolid creamed fat. These fats have no flavor or odor because of the high refining processes they have been given. These shortenings keep well without refrigeration and hold up very favorably during frying. They have very high smoking points. Hydrogenated fats blend easily with the other foods used in baking. Products are also available that combine hydrogenated vegetable oils with lard. They are marketed under many trade names.

Corn oil is extracted from the germ portion of the kernel of Indian corn. Refined corn oil has no flavor or odor. Corn oil can stand a very high degree of heat before reaching its smoking point.

Cottonseed oil is extracted under pressure from the seed of the cotton plant. It is golden straw in color. The finished product has no taste or odor.

Soybean oil is extracted from soybeans. It is very light in color with no particular odor or flavor.

Peanut oil is an oil made by crushing peanuts and cooking them to extract their oil. Processing refinements produce a tasteless oil with a high smoking point.

Virgin peanut oil is derived from an uncooked first pressing. It is high in color and needs no refining. It has somewhat of a peanut flavor.

Olive oil is made from ripe olives that are crushed and pressed. Olive oil labeled "virgin" is oil extracted from a cold first pressing. Following this pressing there may be subsequent pressings in which steam or hot water is added to soften the pulp for the extraction of more oil. These later pressings produce a heavier and darker oil than the extract from the first pressing. A virgin olive oil is light in body and a slightly greenish golden-yellow color. Its flavor and aroma are distinctive.

Margarine is made from refined vegetable oil, meat fat, or a mixture of both churned with cultured pasteurized skim milk to the consistency of butter. Vitamins and a harmless food coloring may be added. The taste may vary in flavor depending on milk culture and oil used.

Oleo makes reference to the early period of making margarine when the oil used was made from beef fat and laws required its being called oleo margarine. Today, as we mention, most margarines are made with vegetable oils. The public acceptance of margarine is very good. This is largely due to the fact that a much better product is on the market.

SALAD DRESSING

Salad dressings are included in this section of main raw materials because of their wide range of uses. They play an important role in the dressing up of a salad, sandwich, or appetizer. Excellent salad dressings are available on the commercial market but many operations make their own and build a reputation for salad dressings as well as for other dishes.

All salads require a dressing to add to the finished dish by complimenting the ingredients used. The salad may consist of vegetables, fruits, various seafoods, and an endless variety of meats. All of these foods require a factor to set off their tastes.

A good dressing does several things in addition to providing food values:

1. It adds to the eye appeal of the dish. Vision is perhaps the most critical of the senses. If food passes the test of looking good, it may get to the other senses that ultimately lead to the palate. Conversely, if a dish does not pass the eye test it may never reach the palate.
2. Salad dressing is a stimulant to the appetite. The combination of spices, herbs, vinegars, and oils creates flavors that open the taste buds.
3. It is a healthy lubricant to the body. The oil aids in the digestion of bulk greens and other foods.

Types of Dressings

There are three fundamental dressings that become the basis for making a large number of others. The three distinct types are:

FRENCH DRESSING. In France and on the Continent, French dressing is called " oil dressing." It is made from oil, vinegar, salt, and pepper. In the United States, French dressing usually has oil for its base. It may be clear or reddish in color and thick or thin. There are so many different formulas used that they could not be listed here.

MAYONNAISE. Oil is mixed with egg yolks beaten with seasoning such as cayenne, vinegar or lemon juice, and salt.

SALAD DRESSING. This is the name given to mayonnaise-type dressings that are usually cooked. Most resemble mayonnaise in that they have an agreeable flavor and serve the same menu purpose.

These dressings are made in either the cold meat department, pantry, or the salad preparation area depending on the size and type of the operation. Cooked salad dressings are used extensively in institutional-type operations and in less expensive eating establishments where a lower cost is necessary. The cooked-base dressings are made from varied combinations of egg yolk, milk, flour, sugar, butter, vinegar, and seasonings. The cooked-base dressing may vary in taste from mild to strong. It also has a number of uses. Generally these are the same as mayonnaise. The cooked-base dressings are not as costly as mayonnaise. They are important to operations that maintain limited budgets.

Mayonnaise has many uses. Many of the more substantial salads, such as those that may be the principal course if not the entire meal, are put together with mayonnaise. Of these a few examples are chicken salad, lobster salad, shrimp salad, and crabmeat salad. Mayonnaise dressings and French dressings are used by themselves or as a base for other dressings in quality operations.

To the basic dressings described above one can add, individually or combined in mixtures, some tasteful foods such as roquefort or blue cheese, tarragon, sardines, anchovies, curry powder, paprika, tomato puree, chili sauce, tabasco sauce, sour cream, fresh onion, green pepper, chives, and hard-boiled egg. These are but a few of the combinations common to the trade.

TYPES OF VINEGARS

1. Cider—Made from the fermented juice of apples.
2. Distilled—White in color. Distilled vinegar is made by fermenting diluted alcohol.
3. Tarragon—Vinegar that has been flavored with the aromatic leaf of the tarragon herb.
4. Wine—May be light or dark in color depending on the type of grape that is fermented.
5. Malt—Golden brown in color. Malt vinegar is made by fermenting barley malt.

Salad Dressing Uses

ON GREENS. Very little should be left in the bottom of the bowl when salad dressing is used on greens. It should provide an even coating. Remember, vinegar is a miser and oil is a spendthrift.

SEAFOODS. Dressing is used to loosely bind the seafood together. It is given uniform coating.

MEATS. As with seafoods, the dressing loosely binds and gives body to the substance of the salad.

FRUITS. Dressing is used to enhance the appearance and contrast or compliment the sweetness or tartness of the fruit as desired.

chapter 20

grains and grain products

A grain is the seed of a type of grass that is used for human consumption.

FLOUR

Flour is the finely ground and sifted meal of wheat or other plants. Meal is the coarsely ground and unsifted seed. Flour is made from wheat, corn, rice, rye, buckwheat, and oats. The gluten content of wheat makes it best to use in making bread. This common use has made flour popularly understood as meaning wheat flour. However, flour can be milled from any of the grains. If it is not made from wheat it is referred to as rye flour, barley flour, etc.

WHEAT

Almost all the bread that is eaten all over the world is made from wheat flour or wheat combined with other flours. Wheat is grown in most parts of the world but a large production of wheat comes from the United States.

There are many varieties of wheat but they can generally be classified in one of two categories:

1. A hard wheat contains more gluten than starch.
2. A soft wheat contains more starch than gluten.

Gluten is the protein substance remaining after starch is removed. It is tough and sticky. This permits the doughs to cohere and expand.

284

THREE PARTS TO ALL GRAINS

There are three separate and distinct parts to the kernels of all grains. They are:

1. the bran, or outside covering
2. the germ, which is on one end just under covering
3. the endosperm, which makes up the large part of kernel

In the milling process the three parts may be separated and then re-blended. If only the endosperm is used, the product is a white flour that may be enriched by the addition of nutrients. The product that has all parts of the kernel blended is a whole-grain product, such as whole wheat. From a nutritive standpoint it is superior to a nonenriched flour.

Durum wheat is a variety used in making of pasta (an Italian word for semolina products): spaghetti, macaroni, etc. Special dies make different shapes of pasta including spirals, bows, and shells, all in large and small varieties.

In the United States, pasta foods include all types of macaroni, spaghetti, and noodles. They were once made in small batches and extruded in hand presses. Modern manufacture is continuous. There is a constant flow of product from storage bins to final weighing and packaging. Quality and cleanliness are jealously guarded. Most steps in manufacturing are automatic and done in sealed compartments of different machines. It is quite possible to enjoy pasta food that has never been touched by hand—from the seed in the field to the ripened durum wheat, the semolina, and the finished product—until you open the package.

How Semolina and Durum Flour Become Macaroni

Durum semolina, granular or flour, clean and golden, comes from the mill to the macaroni plant in special trucks, cars, or sacks. Modern plants keep supplies in huge bins to feed to the machines twenty-four hours a day. Samples are regularly tested for quality. The system is almost completely automatic from beginning to end.

One machine produces as much as 1,500 pounds an hour. Water is carefully added to make a stiff dough. Most macaroni foods are enriched with iron and B vitamins, thiamine, niacin, and riboflavin. These are added either at the mill or to the dough. Enriched egg noodles also contain 5.5 percent egg solids as a specified ingredient.

Under pressure, the dough is forced through dies. The die for long goods like spaghetti consists simply of a metal plate drilled with holes. As the spaghetti extrudes, a rack moves against the soft strands and neatly folds them. Knives cut the product to desired length. Pins in the openings of a macaroni die force the dough to flow around them to make a tube. A revolving knife cuts it off at the right length. Alphabets are forced through openings and cut short to make letters. Noodle dough is rolled flat, cut to desired width and length, and then dried.

Long goods on racks move slowly into a dryer or a series of dryers where moisture is removed under carefully controlled conditions.

Some plants keep finished products in similar storage units before they are finally packaged. Short goods, like elbow macaroni, go through other dryers on endless belts and screens.

Spaghetti, macaroni, and other long goods are cut to an exact length before weighing and packaging. They move forward on conveyor belts that are part of a continuous process.

Popular Pasta Shapes

There are more than 300 different macaroni foods. Shown in Figure 20-1 are the most popular and readily available kinds of macaroni shapes:

1. noodle bows
2. long spaghetti
3. elbow spaghetti
4. medium noodles
5. alphabets
6. shell macaroni
7. spaghettini
8. fine noodles
9. elbow macaroni
10. broad noodles
11. small macaroni shells
12. jumbo macaroni shells

Some unusual Pasta Shapes are shown in Figure 20-2:

1. yellow and green egg cappelletti
2. mafalade
3. rigatoni
4. attuppatelli lisci
5. fusilli senza buco
6. shells
7. mostacciolini
8. margherite (flat macaroni)
9. tiny egg novelties
10. green noodles
11. fusilli bucati
12. cavatelle
13. tufoli
14. cresta di gallo (rooster's crest)
15. lasagna
16. rosetta
17. long zitoni
18. rotini
19. manicotti

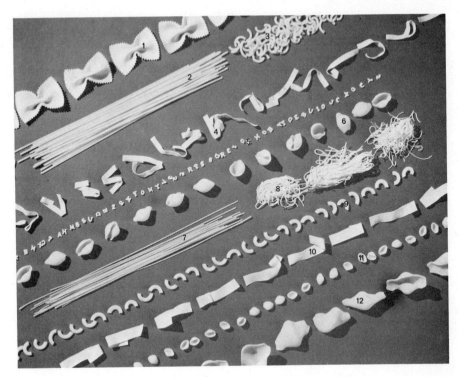

Figure 20-1. Some popular macaroni shapes.

Hard wheat is preferred in the making of bread. A flour that contains a high gluten factor is also referred to as a strong flour. A strong flour will absorb more liquid and consequently will give a bigger yield.

A soft wheat flour is weaker and very good for making sweets and pastry items. Flour is at its best for baking purposes when it has been stored for several months after being milled. To avoid the necessity of this aging process and put it on the market sooner, flour is also bleached. This approved chemical treatment has no effect on the taste or nutritive values of the flour. Aging also gives a whiter color to the flour.

An enriched flour is one that has had synthetic vitamins added to it. The natural vitamins are lost in the normal milling process. An enriched flour that is off-white in color is one that has been milled in a special process where none of the natural nutritive values are lost.

An all-purpose flour is one that can be used for a number of purposes. It is composed of a mixture of different soft wheats, hard wheats, or both types of wheat.

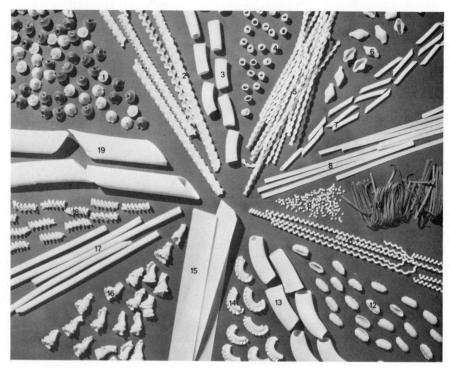

Figure 20-2.   Some unusual macaroni shapes.

BARLEY

Barley dishes, although of somewhat limited use in the trade, are very nutritious. Barley finds more of a market in distilling and brewing, but its grains are used in our trade in casseroles, soups, bread flours, and with green vegetables. For best baking results, barley flour is often mixed with wheat flour.

BUCKWHEAT

A coarse meal of buckwheat is very popular for making fowl dressings and soup garnishes. Buckwheat flour is mixed with wheat flour for best taste results when making batters.

Buckwheat flour, sometimes mixed with other flours, was formerly one of our breakfast standbys. Buckwheat pancakes are still popular. In restaurants with a continental flair, the service of caviar, particularly fresh caviar, is generally accompanied by blinis. These are small pancakes of buckwheat flour.

CORN

Corn meal is the coarsely ground kernel of corn. Corn flour is the finely milled grain similar to wheat flour.

RYE

Rye flour is used in making various dark breads, such as pumpernickel.

RICE

Rice is one of the most versatile of grain foods. It can be the foundation of any meal and be used with great success in any part of the meal—appetizer, main course, or dessert. Rice is quick and easy to prepare. The bland taste of rice makes it ideal as an accompaniment to more flavorful dishes. It enriches the spicy flavors of food. Rice is easily digestible and contains an insignificant amount of fat.

There are several thousand varieties of rice but they can be generally classified in three main groups:

1. Short- and medium-grained rice—This type of rice has a short plump grain that remains moist and tender when cooked. The pieces tend to stick together. This rice can be used as part of a main course or dessert dish.
2. Long-grained rice—This rice is several times longer than it is wide. When this rice is cooked the grains separate and the rice is fluffy in appearance. This type of rice is used by itself to accompany a main course or other dish, such as salads or curries. As rice comes in from the field, it is put through a drying process to reduce its moisture content. During the drying procedure the rice is given a coarse cleaning that removes any foreign particles.
3. Brown rice—This rice has had its husks removed from the grain. Brown rice is the whole unpolished grain with only the outer hull and a small amount of bran removed. This rice is sold with no treatment other than grading. It has a nutlike flavor and a chewy texture.

White rice has an additional layer of bran removed. The rice is white in color. Whole grains of rice are more costly.

Enriched rice has had additional vitamins added to the grains.

Parboiled rice has been subjected to steam and pressure in the milling process.

Precooked rice has been cooked after milling and then dehydrated. It requires only a short period of time for preparation, mostly that of restoring the moisture.

Figure 20-3. A rice field in Texas.

Rice flour is made from broken fragments of unglazed rice. It is not commonly used in the commercial trades.

Whole-kernel rice is brown in color.

Polished rice has had the bran and germ removed and a polish put on the kernel by a machine process.

WILD RICE

Wild rice is sometimes called Indian rice. It is grown in shallow water. It is the seed of a water grass that grows tall in shallow water. The grains are thin and resemble rice. It is cooked in the same fashion as conventional rice and used mostly as a dressing with game. Wild rice is not produced in large quantities. It is very expensive.

STARCH

The most popular starch is a corn product. It is used to thicken stocks, soups, and sauces. It provides a high gloss to the completed liquid.

TAPIOCA

Tapioca is a solid starch found in the roots of some tropical plants.

chapter 21

additional foods–spices and herbs

SUGAR

In our industry the sugar that is used is made from sugar cane or beets. Our tables provide this in tablet, granulated, or powdered form. Our kitchens use all three in addition to brown sugar. Some corn sugar and glucose, in various forms best suited to the preparation of certain foods, are also used. Most restaurants now offer sugar substitutes as well for those whose diets prohibit sugar.

Sugar is available in the following forms:

1. Granulated sugar is sugar that is ground to various degrees.
2. Powdered sugar is made by grinding granulated sugar and sifting it through a fine cloth. Also called extra fine powdered sugar, it pours and dissolves easily making it ideal for drinks.
3. Confectioner's powdered sugar is very fine sugar used especially for pastries and candies. Some confectioner's sugar has a 39 percent starch content to prevent caking.*
4. Brown sugar is a refined sugar mixed with a refiner's syrup. It is a soft sugar that has a molasses flavor.
5. Solid sugar is made by pressing damp sugar into molds such as cubes and tablets.
6. Maple sugar is made by boiling maple sap until almost all the water has evaporated.

* When starch is added it is mentioned on the label.

BEVERAGES

Coffee, tea, chocolate, and cocoa comprise the four principal drinks prepared for serving with meals in our restaurants.

Coffee

Coffee is made from the coffee bean, which is the seed of the coffee tree. Coffee grows in hot climates. Brazil, today, is the most important coffee-producing country in South America and the world. The home of the coffee tree is the mountain regions of Abyssinia. From there the use of coffee spread through the Middle East. Now coffee is grown in many varieties in almost all hot climates. The best qualities come from the higher altitudes. Central and South America's coffee beans are rated among the best in the world. The green coffee bean keeps for a long time. It is shipped in this form. Coffee is roasted to varying degrees of brown but never overly browned. Coffee should be used soon after it is roasted because it does not keep its aroma or flavor long afterward. After roasting, coffee is ground and packaged in airtight containers.

COFFEE BLENDS.   All coffees have flavors of their own and most coffees are blended to produce a desired characteristic in taste. Different combinations of coffee are used until the preferred taste is achieved. Coffee is ground to various sizes to meet the needs of the equipment used in brewing. A fine grind should be used for drip brewing, a medium for the percolator, and a coarse grind for the conventional method.

ROASTING COFFEE.   The coffee bean is green in color after it is picked and processed. Coffee is roasted to give it the brown coloring and the well-known coffee smell and taste.

INSTANT COFFEE is made from concentrated liquid coffee that has had the water evaporated from it.

DECAFFEINATED COFFEE has had more than 95 percent of the caffein removed. This coffee tastes slightly different and is more expensive because of the additional process required.

LIQUID COFFEE is a concentrated coffee in a liquid form. It is reduced to this form by evaporating nine-tenths of its original volume.

Tea

Tea is probably the beverage used most, all over the world, since its leaves were first brought from Asia where it grows as an evergreen bush. Tea is served hot or cold in most eating establishments. In England, which really established it as a beverage, tea is also used as an ice cream flavor. Many of our old-time family doctors used to recommend hot tea as a quick stimulant. Today the largest use is for iced tea. Like coffee, it is now available in a powdered instant form.

KINDS OF TEA. Tea varies due to the age of the leaves at picking time, differences in the soil where it is grown, and different methods of drying, fermenting, etc.

GREEN TEA is produced not by fermenting the leaves but by drying them with heat while they are still green. Black tea is that in which the leaves are fermented and then dried by heat, thus turning the leaf black.

The finest tea comes from the bush that is grown at a higher altitude.

JASMINE TEA is a black tea that is scented with flowers of the jasmine plant.

Cocoa

Cocoa, from which chocolate is derived, is made from the seeds of the cacao tree. As it evolves into chocolate in the manufacturing process it becomes probably the favorite flavor of most Americans. Our restaurants serve it as a beverage and an adjunct to many desserts. It is used to flavor so many dishes and products of our kitchens that we cannot list them all in these pages.

The cacao tree is a tropical plant that bears the podlike cocoa fruit with its cluster of seeds. Cocoa is the name given to the dried bean as well as to the roasted and ground bean. After the fruit is harvested, it is split open and the seeds are removed. The seeds may be dried in the sun or placed in piles to ferment for a period of several days in order to obtain a finer flavor. After this the beans are spread and permitted to dry in the sun. The cocoa fruit that houses the cocoa bean is available all year around.

The quality of the cocoa depends on how the fruit was harvested and the care given to it in the drying process prior to its going to the factory. The treatment in the factory involves the various phases of cleaning, roasting, and milling. The process of developing cocoa powder also involves pressing out approximately 50 percent of the cocoa butter. The cocoa butter is used in other edible and nonedible materials. In the making of chocolate, sugar, milk, nuts, and other specialties are combined and added to the cocoa powder. This mixture is heated, rolled, and grated before it is cooled and dispensed into molds. The molds are placed under refrigeration.

Cocoa was discovered in the early sixteenth century by Cortez, the Spanish explorer. History tells us of the Aztec Indians of Mexico whose emperor, Montezuma, was reported to have introduced this wonderful new drink to the conquerors. They in turn took it back to their homeland. From there its use spread throughout the royal courts of Europe. For some time its manufacture was a guarded secret and its use was enjoyed by the few who could afford the price. With the commercial use of chocolate in eighteenth-century England came the need for production in quantity. Then its use became more widespread and desired throughout the European countries.

SPICES AND HERBS

Spices and herbs are legion. Without them our food and drinks would, indeed, be tasteless. While some food articles provide their own distinctive flavor when cooked, it is a rare item, whether it be vegetable, fish, poultry, meat, or game, that does not have its table appeal enhanced or its eating pleasure increased by the use of spices and herbs in its cooking.

The use of some spices and herbs to aid and enhance the natural flavors of food as well as to provide medical remedies was known to the early Greeks and Romans. Pages of history record how spices accompanied people through their searches and travels. The names of cities, people, and events that were exposed to us when we first began learning history were associated with man's curiosity for an improved taste of food. This was to be found chiefly through the use of spices and herbs.

The Bible mentions trade in spices and the acceptance of spice as a valued gift. China, Java, Greece, Arabia, Rome, Egypt, Portugal, and England all contributed to the romantic history of spice. Emperors, kings, queens, and adventurers such as Marco Polo, Columbus, and Magellan, all touch on the story of spice. In those times spices were used as gifts, as a medium of exchange, as medicine, and as a compliment to food. The desire for spice led these travelers to seek new routes, passages, and waterways to the Orient. Spices were in great demand then, as they are today.

Today America is the spice-buying center of the world. Spices are not only consumed in the home. Our modern methods of food manufacturing and distribution have opened new areas of use in manufactured products of all types. The term "spice" refers in the trade to both spices and herbs. Spices are the various parts of aromatic plants. Herbs are the leaves or flowers of other aromatic plants. Figure 21-1 shows some popular herbs and spices.

Seasoning

Seasoning in our industry is generally accomplished by the intelligent use of spices and herbs. Salt, sugar, vinegar, and some wines are also used.

OTHER FOOD PRODUCTS

The following are used to enhance the flavor of food.

Vinegar is an acid seasoning that imparts flavor and also preserves food. There are various types of vinegars on the market.

Wine vinegar is a pleasant-flavored vinegar that may be red or white and is made from wine. It is very popular in a luxury trade house. An herb vinegar such as tarragon vinegar is named after the herb used to season it.

Cider vinegar is made by fermenting the juice of apples. Widely used, it is light to dark in color. Malt vinegar, made by fermenting the malt of cereal, is another popular vinegar. It is golden brown in color.

Distilled vinegar is made by fermenting diluted distilled alcohol. The acid strength of the vinegar is determined by the acid content. Strength may be expressed in percentage or by grain. A 40-grain vinegar is the same as a 4 percent acid content. The higher the figure, the stronger the vinegar.

FLAVOR EXTRACTS

Flavoring extracts find use mostly in bakery, pastry, and ice cream departments. Many products in these departments will also use natural foods such as berries and fruits to produce the desired flavor.

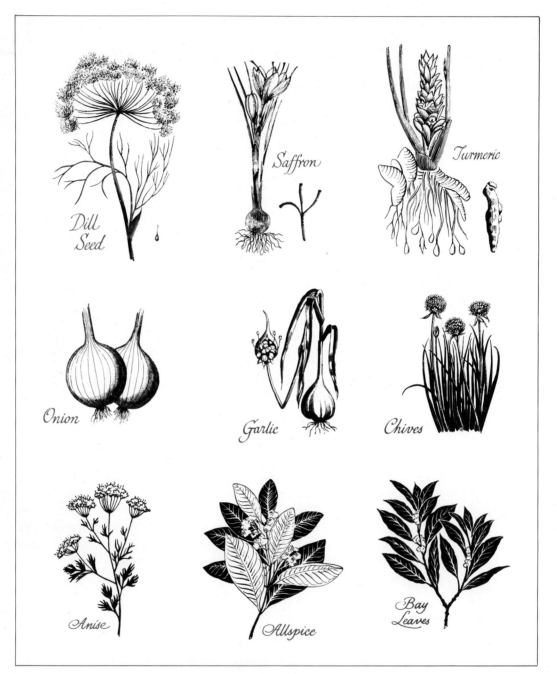

Figure 21-1. Various spices and herbs.

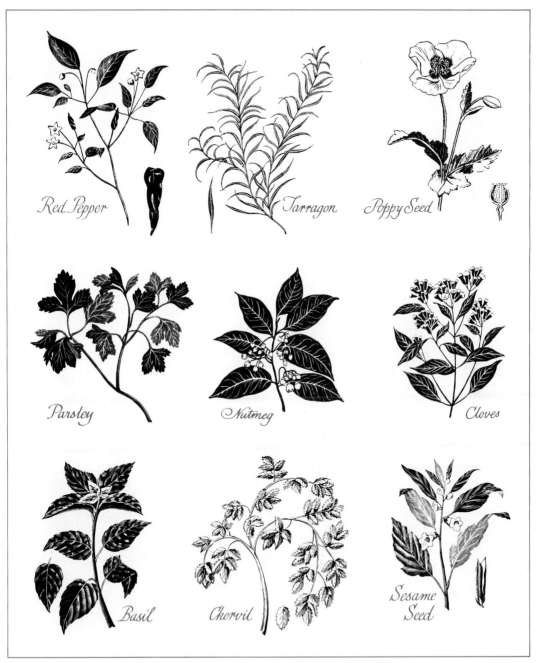

Figure 22-1. (Continued).

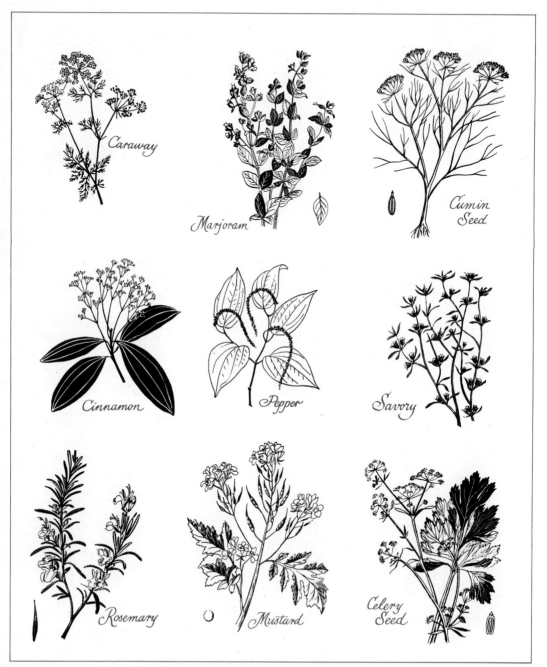

Figure 22-1. (Continued).

Figure 22-1. (Continued).

MEAT
EXTRACTS

Meat extracts are another flavoring medium used in the kitchen. Originally it was made by reducing stock to its essence. The generic term or name for the much-reduced brown stock is glacé de viand. At the present time many establishments are using essences produced commercially, both here and abroad, under various trade names. The products are marketed nationwide by the purveyors of convenience foods.

In the same category as meat extracts and also used for flavoring are bouillon cubes and concentrates, both chicken and beef. These are offered in liquid or granule forms.

PASTRY FOODS
AND AIDS

Yeast is a living plant that is grown in containers of warm malt mash and other organic materials. The yeast cake comes in a compressed form. When it is added to the dough, it begins to grow and multiply. It is in this process that the leavening of dough begins. When yeast grows, a gas is formed that permits the dough to rise.

Yeast is available in a fresh form and also in a powdered form. The fresh yeast acts faster than the dried form.

Baking powder, also a leavening agent, is produced by artificial, chemical methods. All baking powders have baking soda as a base to which an acid agent is added. To absorb any moisture in the air, flour or starch is also mixed in. This ensures the product's strength until it is used because baking soda discharges its leavening qualities in moisture.

Baking powder varies according to the amount of acid used. The amount of acid determines whether it is a slow- or fast-acting powder.

According to the fastness of action desired, baking powders can be listed in the following order:

1. cream of tartar
2. phosphate
3. double acting or combination
4. sodium aluminum sulphate

For best results baking powder should be as fresh as possible.

PASTES

Almond and macaroon pastes are both used in pastry departments.

BUT-R-OMA

This is a new powdered butter-flavor substance. It is available in 200-pound drums and in 10-pound tins.

CANNED FRUIT

A large selection of fruit, peel, and mixtures are used in bakery departments. These are available whole, in pieces, or crushed to meet the varied demands of the bakery trade.

CHEESE—DEHYDRATED

This baker's cheese is available in 100-pound drums or sold by the individual pound. It is used in cheesecake and pastry.

CHOCOLATE

Baker's chocolate is available in sweet or unsweetened form. Milk chocolate contains milk solids and sugar. Cocoa is made from chocolate mass with an approximate 50 percent of the butterfat content removed.

COCONUT

The grated white flesh inner lining of a coconut. Coconut meat is available in dry or moist pack. The different ways coconut is sold have to do with the way the meat is cut. It may be cut in long shreds, shorter shreds, or chips. All are sweetened. The very small pieces of coconut are called macaroon coconuts.

STABILIZER

An egg-white stabilizer added to egg whites provides extra stiffness. It is added when the egg white is near its peak. Flavor can be added as desired.

FONDANT

Fondant is a base for icings. It is sold by the pound and is available in 60- and 120-pound pails and 50-gallon steel drums. Fondant is made of sugar, water, glucose, or cream of tartar. Most pastry chefs make their own as needed.

HONEY

Honey is available in a 5-gallon pail (60 pounds) and sold by the pound. It comes in various-sized containers.

MALLOWHIP

A marshmallow powder used in making marshmallow fillings. Available in various-sized containers, it is whipped with boiling water, powdered sugar, and a small amount of pure vanilla.

MEROWHIP

A meringue powder used in making meringue. It is sold by the pound and available in 5- or 10-pound tins. Meringue powder and granulated sugar are dry mixed and added to warm water.

MINCEMEAT

Mincemeat is available in glass jugs, #10 tins, kegs, and barrels. Very high-grade ingredients produce a high-grade mincemeat. Mincemeat may be the meatless English variety or the United States variety where meat is always included.

NUT MEATS

The kernels or meats of nuts such as almonds, brazils, walnuts, cashews, peanuts, pecans, etc., are used in many ways in our culinary practice. They are all sold by the pound and are available in various-sized containers or tins.

SEEDS

Anise, caraway, cardamon, poppy, and sesame seed are all sold by the pound and available in 10-, 25-, or 100-pound sacks All find uses in baking.

WHIPPING-CREAM STABILIZER

This is a product that, blended with powdered sugar, adds stiffness to partially whipped cream. There are now vegetable substitutes for whipped cream on the market that are used as dessert toppings. These have longer keeping quality, which is a favorable cost factor.

GELATIN

Gelatin finds many uses in cookery. Of these perhaps the best known to the restaurant patron are gelatin desserts. However, the most spectacular work of our cooks and chefs, which compares with the world's finest artistes, are cold meat department display pieces for buffets, hors d'oeuvres, and cold entrees. These could scarcely be made without gelatins.

Gelatin was originally produced in the home. Today practically all the gelatin used in cooking is produced commercially. It comes in sheets, powder, or granules.

COLORING FOOD

Foods themselves provide many colors. When these colors do not fade out or get destroyed in cooking, they are most certainly desirable because they are very pleasing to our second stomach: the eye. Unfortunately cooking fades some colors, but they can be replaced by those made artificially or others made naturally in the kitchen. For example, green can be obtained from spinach, red from the coral of lobsters and beets, and yellow from saffron or egg yolk.

chapter 22

stocks,
sauces,
and soups

The importance of the use of stock as a prime ingredient in cookery has not changed over the years. Modern technology has made it possible for operations of all sizes to have a variety of concentrates or convenience-type foods at hand for instant use. This means that an operation buying prefabricated meats and no longer doing its own meat cutting, no longer has the bones or trimmings with which to prepare its own stock. Nor does it have the skilled labor to prepare the stocks and maintain the desired consistency of quality. If these are the operational practices of an establishment, a large variety of outstanding convenience items are available to provide the house with stocks that taste homemade. However, those operations that do break down and fabricate their own meats have the abundant supply of bones and trimmings necessary for the preparation of fine stocks. Such places still prepare their own stocks in abundant quality and quantity.

The old method was to have stock pots cooking around the clock. A large variety of scrap vegetables, bones, and trimmings were added in the course of the day. This practice has now been given up. It has been recognized that continuous cooking is not necessary to extract the nutritive values, the color, or the taste of the ingredients. The leaves, stalks, and bulb parts of vegetables as well as other foods that are not needed in other departments are still used to make stock. The cooking time, however, has changed. A good stock can be available for use after only four to five hours.

STOCKS

The term "stock" refers to the extracted liquids used in the preparation of soups, sauces, and other items on our menus. In a busy, well-managed operation a good stock is as important as any of the basic ingredients.

A busy kitchen of moderate size may have a stock pot on top of the stove much of the time. A larger operation may have one or several steam jacket kettles brewing several stocks at the same time. The ingredients necessary to provide a rich stock are available in many kitchens and in most instances require no added expense.

Types of Stock

White stock is made from the meat of veal bones together with the carcasses of fowl and vegetables. It is used as the base for consommes, sauces, and other foods.

Fish stock is made with the bones and trimming of fish. Onion, parsley, thyme, and sliced lemon are added. Water and white wine are the liquids.

Brown stock is made with beef, veal, scalded pork rind, and blanched ham. It cooks for approximately six hours. Bones are browned in the oven prior to the addition of water. This gives color and flavor to the stock.

Chicken stock is made from poultry and other fowl.

When making light stocks, where the bones and meats are placed directly into the water, parboil the bones until scum rises to the top of the pot. Discard this water and start afresh with the addition of aromatic vegetables such as carrots, onions, and celery. The stock must not be permitted to boil hard or it will produce an unclear product. It should simmer steadily for a period of from four to five hours or slightly longer.

Vegetables and seasonings are added to all stocks for additional flavor. To extract the flavor from food items all stocks should be begun in cold water. Overcooking or cooking on too hot a flame will produce a heavy unclear stock.

Remember: Salt should not be added to the stock. This will be done when it is combined with other foods. If the stock is good, the work that follows will be easy. If, on the other hand, it is bad or only fair, it is fruitless to try to produce an excellent dish. The stock is the secret to the preparation of a good soup or sauce.

Importance of Good Stock

The use of stocks in a kitchen is basic to the principles of good cookery. Stocks are the foundation of almost all good soups and sauces. Stocks play an important part in the preparation of almost all dishes. Stocks are basic to some foods and complimentary to others. If a stock is weak or poorly prepared, it will add little to any food. If the stock is good, it will produce a good dish.

SAUCES

A sauce may be a complimentary food to an expertly prepared dish. It may also be the main ingredient in a combination of foods that imparts flavor, taste, and appearance to the food as well as nutrition to the body.

A sauce enhances the palatability of a dish by providing contrast in flavor and texture. A sauce must have a velvety texture and it must flow smoothly. A sauce will not cover up a poorly prepared dish. A sauce is not supposed to dominate the flavor of the food with which it is served but rather add to and compliment its flavors. It is for the preparation of these sauces that the classic French cooking gained renown.

Learning how to make sauce is important for a student because it teaches the art of combining different foods to achieve a specific taste. A sauce adds the important light touch to a given food.

In the culinary world there are many sauces made in different ways. Each is recommended to be served as a compliment to a particular dish.

Types of Sauces

The many varieties of sauces may be divided into two main categories: hot sauces and cold sauces.

Hot Sauces

These sauces include the basic warm sauces from which other sauces are made. They are also called the leading or mother sauces. Sauces that are made from these are called the small sauces. The basic sauces are prepared in large quantities. Then, by skillfully blending liquids, spices, juices, etc., the professional cook very quickly prepares the desired quantities of a large variety of smaller sauces.

1. Basic brown sauce (Espagnole) — A combination of brown roux (see page 308) with brown stock. It is used in almost all types of dishes.
2. Basic cream or milk sauce (Béchamel) — Scalded milk added to a lightly cooked roux. It is used in vegetable, fish, meat, cream, or macaroni dishes.
3. Basic white or light sauce (Velouté) — White stock added to a pale roux. It may be made from chicken, fish, vegetable, or meat stock.
4. Basic tomato sauce — A combination of tomato, white stock, seasoning, and roux. This is a versatile sauce. It can be used as an accompaniment to food dishes or combined to make other preparations.
5. Drawn butter sauces — Butter simply melted to be used on vegetables, fish, or other items that are served without sauce.
6. Butter sauce — Butter-based sauces such as hollandaise and béarnaise. These sauces are widely used in various egg, fish, and vegetable entrees.

These are the leading sauces. From them can be made an almost endless variety of others. They can be incorporated in a dish or used to compliment a meat, fowl, fish, or vegetable dish.

These compound sauces reflect the artistry and skill of a saucier, who is a sauce cook or master chef. These people have the ability to consistently prepare a classic sauce or to create a special sauce on request to satisfy the most critical palate. A wide selection of sauces have come to us from the various schools of cooking. They have not changed in makeup through the years.

The French school is the most notable. Many of the sauces we know today were named after persons who first prepared or created them in the kitchens of royalty or nobility. An example would be Béchamel sauce, sauce Robert, or Escoffier sauce.

Cold Sauces

These sauces, which are served cold, may or may not require cooking. They are served with every part of the meal. They may be tart or sweet, thick or thin. Cold sauces include sharp sauces, such as a cocktail sauce served with cold seafood, cold sweet-and-sour sauces, and savory butter that is served with a hot entree. A variety of sweet sauces are made from fruit juices, the pulp of fruit, cream, and combination of egg yolks and sugar. These sauces may be mixed cold or cooked quickly over flame or double boiler. Flavorings of wines, brandy, and spices impart flavor.

The Roux

The roux (pronounced roo) is the thickening agent in the basic sauces. The three types of roux are:

1. white roux for white or light sauces
2. pale roux for cream or milk sauces
3. brown roux for brown sauces

Roux is made by mixing flour and fat in a saucepan over steady heat while stirring constantly. The fat used may be shortening, oil, butter, meat drippings, etc. The difference between the three kinds of roux is a matter of cooking or browning the combination of fat and flour to the desired degree. White roux is the mixture of fat and flour cooked over steady heat. With pale roux the same mixture is cooked until the color has begun to change. Brown roux is the same as above but is permitted to cook until it has reached a light brown color.

POINTS ON MAKING ROUX. To avoid ending up with an uncooked starchy flavor, the roux must be cooked before it is added to a liquid. If the roux is cool, the liquid should be hot. If the roux is warm the liquid should be cool. This will produce a smooth sauce. The sauce must be stirred with a whip while it is cooking and brought to a boil. To avoid sticking on the bottom of the pan, the roux or sauce should not be overcooked. Prolonged cooking can make the consistency too thick. Diluting may slightly alter the taste.

The Hot-Cold Sauces

The chaud-froid (show-fwa) sauce is a hot-cold sauce. A chaud-froid sauce may be a cream or white sauce to which aspic has been added. Aspic sets when cooled. In addition to the aspic, various food colors may be added to the sauce for special decorative effects. The sauce is warm when spooned over the meat item it is to cover. The meat item should be cool. It is returned to the refrigerator for a short time to set before subsequent layers of sauce are added. As the sauce cools it becomes firm and has a high gloss or sheen on the surface. This type of sauce is used extensively in the decoration of food.

Aspics

The aspic referred to above can be made by cooking veal bones, calves' feet, etc., until their natural gelatinous components prevail. When clarified, this product is added to the sauce that is appropriate to the dish being prepared. Gelatin is sometimes also added to a natural product to provide the proper consistency in coating a food.

The Dessert Sauce

This may be either hot or cold. It may be the fruit or the pulp of the fruit with added syrup, wine, and liquors or a dairy product or custard-type sauce with wines and fruit preserves added to it.

Meat Glaze

Meat glaze is a reduced concentration of brown stock. It is used to fortify other sauces and to lightly coat dishes as they are served. The coating enhances the flavor of the food and gives sparkle to the plate.

SOUPS

Once again, a good stock will produce a good soup. For a soup to be tasty, well colored, and nutritious, it must have the support of a good stock. Soup plays an important role in the two heavy meals of the day.

Soup is to a meal what a heading is to a paragraph. It must be in harmony with the entire meal and must be selected wisely so that it will open the appetite and compliment the foods that are to follow.

Types

Soups can be classified into two main groups: clear and thick.

Clear Soups

Clear soups consist of the liquid that is derived from the cooking of fish, meat, fowl, and vegetables. Typical clear soups are broth, bouillon, and consommé.

Thick Soups

Thick soups are thickened by the addition of thickening agents. These soups are also made from meats, fish, and poultry that make their own essence or stock. Vegetables are sometimes added. Examples of thick soups are English beef soup, lobster bisque, and clam chowder. Any of these thick soups may start from the stock in establishments still using stock pots.

Cold Soup

Cold soups are very popular during the hot months. These soups may be clear, thick, or jellied. Some favorite cold soups are found on the bill of fare of first-class houses throughout the year. These soups are exceptionally popular for luncheon or supper dining. They are served in bouillon cups that are placed in ice supremes.

THICKENING AGENTS

Flour, rice flour, cornstarch, arrowroot, egg yolk, and cream are the basic thickeners for soups, sauces, entrees, and desserts. Vegetables such as potatoes, beans, and lentils and cereals like rice have the same properties and are also used.

Cornstarch

Cornstarch is used as a thickening agent in various sauces that accompany or are part of entrees or dessert dishes. It gives the sauce a good appearance by providing a glossy, clear finish. The cornstarch is added to cool water to make a thin smooth paste. This is added to the liquid that is to be thickened. The liquid is then brought to a boil and removed from the fire. Many prefer cornstarch to roux.

A Whitewash

A whitewash is a combination of liquid and uncooked flour. This not too common mixture is used to thicken a sauce in a very short period of time.

part VII

convenience foods

chapter 23

convenience foods

A dictionary definition of "convenience" is anything handy or labor saving. "Labor saving" is the salvation of many a restaurant—whether it is an off-the-street type, a hotel, an institution, a motor hotel, or a club.

One veteran of the food service industry once mentioned that he saw the beginning of convenience foods thirty-five years ago when a contemporary of his, operating a nightclub, startled others by producing two items. One was chop suey and the other was chicken à la king. The items were frozen and served to patrons after reheating. This veteran said "Everyone in our business that heard of it was skeptical. Some predicted ptomaine. But this was the start!"

It is doubtful that convenience foods, the most important change in the restaurant industry since gas replaced coal, could have survived had it not been for the far-reaching and revolutionary changes that also were taking place in two related industries: refrigeration and packaging.

It was inevitable that convenience food would also appear for home use. However, there was and is one factor that compelled bringing these foods to restaurants and the public feeding industry. That is the shortage of chefs, cooks, and other trained culinary workers.

This shortage is principally due to two factors:

1. restricted immigration
2. lack of culinary schools in this country

Leaders of other aspects of the food industry further contribute to the shortage of master chefs. They engage in executive capacities those willing and capable of heading commissary operations. Under the supervision of these master chefs, almost all the national advertisers, among them Swift, Armour, Kraft, and General Foods, are producing menu components. Rolls, breads, pastries, desserts, and hors d'oeuvres as well as entrees are available. Some are fully prepared and some are partially prepared.

The use of convenience foods has changed many small operations from losing to profit-making enterprises. It has even helped the larger ones get along in spite of the shortage of trained culinary workers. This shortage has been growing more acute year by year.

Final approval of the unrestricted use of convenience foods in our restaurants came editorially in the chef magazine of New York City, the mouthpiece of the National Chef's Association. They naturally qualified their approval by saying that such food should only be "used under the direction of a capable chef." This was their stance in spite of the fact the supply of qualified chefs is so limited. A recent buyers' guide in the same magazine listed some 300 firms supplying products to the restaurant trade. Perhaps half of these offer convenience foods.

It is not the purpose of this book to suggest which convenience foods will help an operator. Each establishment has its own requirements. However, a careful study of all convenience items now offered may make apparent opportunities for savings in production costs as well as additions to and possibly improvements on the present menu.

Not all restaurants should completely supplant their own production with convenience food. Those establishments with fine kitchen crews that are able to secure replacements for workers who leave will continue to operate as they have. But even these few will find some items of convenience food useful and others indispensable.

Hotels and some restaurants have in the past been slow to give up the old ways and the old traditions. Today things are different. Speeches and articles written by many leaders in the industry confirm this. One report said, "A lady well-known for the excellence of her table, and herself of quite some cooking ability, recently returned from a cruise on one of the well-known (non-American) cruise ships. She related having had a most excellent apple pie for dessert one evening. It was, she said, 'the best I have ever eaten.' On asking the steward if the ship's pastry cook had prepared it, she was told, 'Oh no, all the pies we serve are Mrs. _____' and mentioned the name of one United States firm whose products are available to all restaurants."

To repeat, convenience foods are not a cure-all for any problems an establishment might have. The degree to which they are incorporated into an operation depends on a number of factors. The most important are:

1. the skilled help employed
2. the type of operation
3. the operational practices of the establishment

This much is certain. Convenience foods are here and they are here to stay. The next decade promises more growth than there has been in any previous period in the history of the food service industry. As the pace of society quickens and the projected growth becomes a reality, we can expect an even greater role for convenience foods.

Convenience foods vary in the degree of readiness. Some require no more than heating prior to serving. Others have to be blended in with a cooking food. Still others need to be reconstituted prior to cooking. Some require no cooking prior to use. There are convenience foods that can be used just as they are. Others are only ingredients that have to be added to other foods in the preparation of a main dish. Still others consist of a mixture of ingredients that are ready for use with the addition of a liquid.

Convenience foods are not really new to our industry, but they are still in their infancy as a product category. Among the newer convenience foods being used by the military are instant applesauce, instant orange juice, instant sweet potatoes, bakery mixes, and freeze-dried cottage cheese. Dehydrated foods include onions, pie apples, cheddar cheese, green pepper, and soups. None are altogether new. All are victories in our battle against perishability, a real enemy to our industry. The future will bring more products in these areas. Tomorrow more distributors will be warehousing new items.

Let us take the freeze-drying process as an example. It is just a few years old and already an estimated 18 billion dollar industry. Food processing people are working to achieve color, flavor, aroma, and texture in new products that will match, almost identically, whatever they replace. A long-range effect is bound to be felt in the area of food service preparation.

In the near future textured soy proteins, which simulate beef, chicken, ham, and bacon, will become important to food service. These soy foods, such as soy cutlets, will first appear on luncheon menus and in the fast food industry. The almost instant methods of microwave and convection cooking will make changes all the more radical.

"These trends mean challenge, change, and, more important, opportunity. Opportunity to grow. Opportunity to gain a bigger stake in the American way of life. Opportunity to go further than you ever dreamed in a business that offers wall to wall opportunity to the ambitious, creative, hard-working individual. It's there for the taking."*

Convenience foods run the gamut from bases for soups, sauces, gravies, and breading materials for employees to use in primary cooking

---

* Notes from speech: Richard W. Brown, past vice president of the National Restaurant Association.

processes to vegetables ready for finish. Complete entrées that only have to be heated are available. Roasts of beef, turkey, and veal and some of the more exotic dishes such as beef tenderloin Wellington, coq au vin, breast of chicken Rossini, coquille St. Jacques, quiche Lorraine, and seafood Newburg are also available. The list is endless and growing day by day.

The use of convenience foods will make it possible for an operation to be laid out so that the entire menu, from appetizer to dessert, can be prepared in fine establishments referred to as commissaries. Naturally such a food service operation will require less kitchen space and preparation equipment. Also, probably most important, it will need a food-conscious operator. An operator, to be successful, is most often a person who has had previous restaurant training.

The Future

To achieve the full potentialities of convenience foods requires strong and open lines of communications between equipment manufacturers, food processors, and package suppliers. The full value of a new development by one of these industries is possible only when the other two segments give their enthusiastic support and provide modifications as needed. It is then that the manufacturers, suppliers, and dining patrons realize the benefits of the new forward thrust that has been made.

As a result, a piece of equipment does not have limited use because of lack of special containers to use with it. An example is the microwave oven. It is self-defeating to package food in a large semirigid foil container requiring an extended period of time to reheat. Also, the quality of the food itself must not change in appearance, flavor, or texture as a result of the method used in reheating.

Progress has been made chronologically with convenience food by segments of the industry working individually. Progress that lies ahead may come infinitely faster if talent and professional know-how are focused, by the related segments of the industry, on the desire to make or serve a better product. To achieve this it is vital that there be strong communication and understanding between the operator, the food processor, the equipment manufacturer, and the packager.

chapter 24

automatic food service

The vending machine is an important and growing segment in the business of feeding people away from home. It is a new approach that is found today in various installations. A vending machine may be an elaborate and decorative machine for a high-rise building lunchroom or a simple unit that dispenses a small selection of refrigerated fruit in a bowling alley.

FIRST VENDORS

The history of vending goes back to 100 B.C., when Hero of Alexandria invented a dispenser for holy water. When a five-drachma coin was dropped into the opening of an urn it tripped a valve that released a spurt of water. Vending next appeared in England in the eighteenth century. An honor box for tobacco was used in taverns and other public places. After opening it with a coin, the customer could help himself. In 1884 in America a vendor for drinking water marked the beginning of the industry in this country. Thereafter, as the age of mechanical invention flowered in this country, vendors were produced in many different shapes and sizes. Candy, chewing gum, peanuts, and cigarettes were vended in railway depots, subway stations, and other locations. Such products as postcards, perfume, and even collar buttons were offered for sale in coin-operated devices.

There was no big growth till the thirties. By the thirties, vending was well established as a method of selling items that did not require refrigeration, such as candy, chewing gum, peanuts, and cigarettes. The next development was equipment to sell bottles of cold soft drinks. At first tubs of iced water were fitted out with coin-operated tops that pulled the bottles through the water. In Kansas City, Missouri, a firm produced a then revolutionary top that rotated the opening of the machine to the bottle. This firm subsequently produced a line of upright, refrigerated vendors before diversifying into other products in the forties.

FOOD VENDORS AFTER WORLD WAR II

Food vendors manufactured overseas as well as some experimental U.S. models were available in the fifties. Vendors for hot canned food were produced in the U.S. in the same decade. It was not until 1960, however, that a line of vendors for hot, cold, and frozen foods was marketed by the same Kansas City manufacturer that had invented the rotating top. The introduction of Visi-Vend food vendors broke the barrier to automatic food service. Soon hundreds of automatic installations were making food available around the clock in industrial plants, offices, universities, hospitals, and other locations. Today rising wages and problems in recruiting and training workers are contributing to the popularity of automatic food service. The future for the industry appears bright.

Coffee Vendor

Vendors for coffee were first produced during the period immediately following World War II. Acceptance of coin-operated coffee makers has shown a dramatic increase. Today, vendors are available that brew coffee in many different forms ranging from regular grind to freeze dried.

This rapid growth has brought vending machines into a large variety of installations. Today food dispensing machines are found in athletic stadiums, bowling alleys, banks, convention halls, military posts, motor hotels, office buildings, drugstores, department stores, all types of factories, federal buildings, hotels, schools, railroad stations, and many other businesses, both large and small.

The flexibility of the coin-operated machine permits a variety of combinations to satisfy the specific needs of an installation. No two installations have to have exactly the same equipment. The needs of the companies installing the machines also vary.

There are three categories into which these services can be classified:

1. Single Purpose—Units that dispense only one item are placed in various locations. The item may be candy, milk, a soft drink, etc. This is the simpler kind of installation. Such units are located in schools, businesses, and areas where large numbers gather.
2. Snack or Light Lunch—This installation has more of a varied selection. It may be the only source of food at the location, or it may be used in conjunction with a cafeteria by offering snack foods during the nonserving hours.
3. Complete Automatic Food Service—This installation takes the place of a short-order or cafeteria service. It is arranged in a very decorative way and serviced by a supervisory staff that provides personal touches. An excellent variety of food items are available in this arrangement. Hot and cold foods are dispensed. Some installations are complete with a service section where chilled foods can be heated by the patron in a matter of minutes in a microwave oven. A large selection of condiments and seasonings to compliment the individual taste is also available.

The food that is dispensed may be brought into the facilities or prepared in kitchens on the site. Between the single purpose installation and the complete machine installation are many combinations that can be tailor-made to fit the particular needs of an establishment. Some locations have added a short-order counter to take away the machine feeling.

The vending machine service can be provided by a conventional food service contractor who supplies the machines and the food that is to be dispensed. It can also be furnished by a vending firm that supplies only the equipment and the service. The food comes from the institution's kitchens. A firm may also choose to buy or lease vending equipment. In that case the establishment will either have a vending service staff in the organization or contract a vending firm to provide stock and servicing.

Advantages of Owning Machines

1. Higher net income from sales.
2. Quality control of products. Machine maintenance is also best assured when the machine is controlled by the house staff.
3. Closer to the needs of the organization which is in a better position to handle special needs.
4. Control of price structure.

Advantages of Renting Machines

1. A return with no investment.
2. Turnover of machines provides newer units as they become available.
3. Experienced personnel are available to handle the units. Vending machines require highly skilled personnel.

An estimated 1,500 vending service firms presently operate their own food preparation commissaries. Statistics show that in many instances these commissaries began with the sole purpose of preparing food for the vending machines. Once in operation, however, greater productive capacities led the vending operators to take in the additional food outlets of cafeterias and counter services in large office firms and factories.

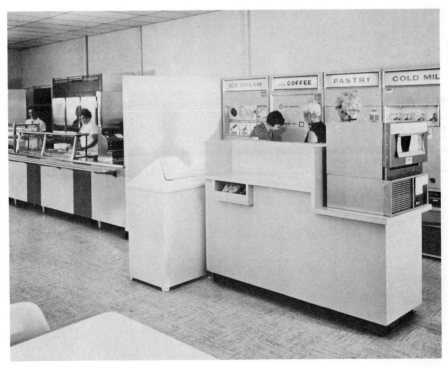

Figure 24-1.   Vending machines.

Other vending operators have branched into the rapidly growing field of mobile catering. The mobile-catering truck presents another approach to the small volume installation. It permits an added selection of foods at specific times of the day that could not be handled in any other way. The use of mobile trucks permits an operator to cater to special functions and also provides an opportunity to service temporary gatherings on work sites. One fourth of all vending firms already operate their own food production facilities. Vending service companies number over 6,000.

Keeping pace with the projected growth of the food service industry, vending firms expect a bigger growth in the next decade as well as more diversification of services and products.

Vending machine sales are growing at the rate of 7 to 10 percent a year. The total number of vending machine sales has risen from 600 million in 1946 to nearly 8 billion yearly. According to yearly surveys conducted to measure the gross dollar volume of business in all categories of food service operations, vending service firms rank among the largest.

Vending machines and convenience foods promise to play an even stronger role in the task of offering larger numbers of meals to people away from home. As refinements in technology are incorporated into the task of providing a finished product to the patrons, a more consistent and better quality-controlled product will be more readily attainable in a dispensing unit than would be available in a service operation during its off-hour periods. For example, a cup of coffee dispensed from a machine would be freshly brewed, as opposed to a cup of coffee that was brewed in a diner two hours prior to reaching the patron.

part VIII

the house,
its employees,
and the public

chapter 25

the house rules, personal qualities, and public relations

THE HOUSE RULES

House rules are the fundamental tenets according to which the individuals who work in an establishment must conduct themselves. These rules provide operational direction to all employees and serve as a code of conduct for those whose work keeps them continually under public scrutiny. House rules may be unappreciated or misunderstood, but seldom completely ignored. Unfortunately, these uncomplicated ground rules of performance are often taken for granted by employees who are unaware of their importance.

As mentioned earlier in the book, guests are watching every act and all movements. The employees are onstage and in large part the house rules are the script. These rules are invaluable for providing guidelines of personal deportment. They also establish the mode of operation that is desired by the house and therefore permits the employee to rate his or her performance against a norm that is expected of everyone.

House rules begin by establishing a set of rules or guidelines for performance. They eventually develop into a set of habits and ultimately lead to a state of mind.

House rules may be of a general nature to cover all employees or they may also be specific, dealing with job groupings. For example, a hostess, counter person, bartender, or waitress may be alerted to behavior mistakes to watch out for. The storeroom person, butcher, baker, fry cook, etc., would not be exposed in the same way to this general and direct contact with the public. For these people specific guidelines are made known through work manuals. It is not uncommon to have several different manuals in one organization to cover various jobs such as waitress, bartender, or fry cook. These manuals define the duties to be performed by the employee.

The manuals are usually referred to as the waitress' manual, bartender's manual, or cook's manual.

The work manual may, in addition, cover information that is important to all employees, such as:

1. holiday work schedules
2. vacation policy
3. insurance information or details
4. service instructions
5. educational programs

An employee is better prepared to render a good job when she or he knows exactly what is expected and what he or she in turn can expect from the house.

Aid to Management

By providing employees with definitions and guides, a work manual is also an aid to management.

1. It furnishes information and directions for work that is to be performed according to a preestablished method.
2. It establishes operating practices and procedures that have been tried and proven successful.
3. It establishes guidelines that are constantly applicable to all employees.
4. It provides employees with immediate guidance in handling a situation.
5. It permits more flexibility and understanding in working with large numbers of employees.

Understanding House Rules and Controls

House rules and work manuals are tools that permit better understanding of controls. Controls in the food industry are those operating practices and procedures followed in order to achieve the maximum return in dollar sales on each food item used in the operation. When a busboy helps himself to a serving of ice cream; when ten eggs are used in a batter in place of four; when food is given away we have classic examples of poor controls.

Operators should be alert and sensitive to the types and extent of controls necessary. A good system of controls produces the desired results. Management should recognize that controls are not rigid. As a living thing they are subject to change. Every establishment develops those required and best suited for its own operation.

Books have been written on how to talk with other people, how to win friends, and how to create a positive image in the many day to day contacts with all kinds of people. In our industry this takes on special meaning. The complete understanding of how to deal with people means money in the pocket of the employee in the form of wages, gratuities, and additional revenue for the house.

The dining public always seeks out an operation where good food is complimented with graciously provided service. Establishments spend a great deal of time and money planning and developing a setting. The planning not only concerns the physical surroundings. It also encompasses:

1. the type food to be served
2. how it is to be served
3. the elegance of the surroundings
4. the uniforms to be worn
5. the caliber of employees

Nothing is to be left to chance. Nothing is unimportant. In the planning phases, experience from the past is coupled with the environment of the present. These are then focused into the development of a new and better establishment. The selling of food is not all that is considered. The customer satisfaction that employees and facilities must deliver is also of importance.

The following factors are considered in varying degrees when developing facilities for a guest's enjoyment:

1. glamour
2. adventure
3. comfort
4. excitement
5. showmanship

The deliberate, careful, and graceful blending of these factors, in addition to serving good food, is what brings patrons back time and time again. It is this living, illusive quality within the industry that is the essence and high point of the restaurant business.

The most important ingredient in this careful and deliberate design is the individual on the working level. If a job is performed well, a rapport will exist between the house and the patron. If there is a flaw at this level, the work of many others striving to reach a point of excellence will be in vain.

Because of the importance of details, exactness is carried over into the performance of all personnel. This is true particularly for the front of the house personnel who, as we have said before, are onstage. Just like the actor, they are under the scrutinizing eye of the public who unconsciously observe every move that is made.

The nature of the work done requires that the employee understand the relationship that exists among the house, the employees, and the patron. This is truer for the food service industry than the typical business of equal size in personnel, physical plant, and dollar volume in sales. To help workers understand this as well as to define the mode of operation, most food service establishments have prepared an outline to serve as a guide for personnel. The points mentioned in the guide may vary from house to house, but they generally include those listed below.

ATTITUDE AND CONVERSATION. Always try to keep yourselves in good spirits. Do not bring your troubles to work with you. Do not, if possible, discuss your troubles with other employees. If you need help with your personal problems, see your department head and discuss it with her or him. Also, do not degrade your fellow employee or be a needless gossip. If you feel that one or more of the employees is hurting the house, discuss it with your department head, not others. Respect your fellow employees in all parts of the house. Remember: It is easier to get along than to argue.

DIGNITY. Perform your work with dignity. Whatever the job, regardless of how menial it is or how exalted, it should be done in a dignified and friendly way. Your dress, speech, and attitude are reflected in your work. Your work is more than a living. It is partially your creation and something of which to be proud.

PROFESSIONAL ATTITUDE. Front of the house employees should always stand erect at their station when they are not busy. They must never engage in idle conversation with other personnel or lean on a wall or pillar. They must not carry on a long conversation with a customer. Beyond a cheery greeting, they must not start a conversation with a customer. Also, they must never repeat conversations overheard while providing service.

PERSONAL QUALITIES

Good grooming is essential to employees in the food service industry. The following grooming, health, and personal attitude tips should be regarded as essential to any successful food service career.

1. Fingernails and hands—Your hands always show. Nails must be kept clean and short. Cuticles must be pushed back. Women should use only clear polish on their fingernails.
2. Complexion—A healthy complexion is to large part a matter of rest and diet. Poor eating habits and the lack of proper rest detract greatly from your state of health. How you feel is largely reflected in your complexion.
3. Feet—In our industry much of the time at work is spent on your feet. The feet, for comfort at work, need continual care. Toenails should be kept trim and feet should be washed quite frequently. A good quality shoe that fits properly is also important.
4. Hair—Hair should be clean, soft, and shining. Hair should be brushed regularly and kept attractively trimmed. Men's hair should be neat and above the forehead. Women's hair should be kept close to the head. When providing service a hairnet is to be worn. Hair is not to be touched or adjusted in public.
5. Teeth—A clean mouth and bright teeth are extremely important to personal grooming. Teeth should be brushed regularly. Dental work must be taken care of promptly to ensure the well-being and appearance of the individual.
6. Diet—A program of well-balanced meals is the source of many good personal qualities of the outward appearances. A person who is eating well shows it in his or her looks, actions, and disposition.
7. Posture—Erect posture is important for all front of the house personnel. Standing correctly with a good bearing is very impressive to the dining patron. It is an important part of the illusive qualities the house wishes to create. The feeling that is conveyed to the public is that personnel who are erect and neat in their personal manners will reflect these qualities in all they do.
8. Uniforms and cleanliness—Uniforms of various colors and design are customarily worn by production and service personnel. They

are frequently changed. Uniforms are to be worn in the proper fashion as established by the house. No modifications are acceptable. Personnel are to be in complete uniform prior to reporting to work station.

9. Courtesy—A professional attitude should prevail at all times in personal contacts with guests and coworkers.

10. Speech and conversation—Much of what is done in the front of the house is selling—selling of the house, of food, and of beverages. The ability to communicate with the patron in a soft yet clear voice is essential. It is of paramount importance that personnel remember their choice of words. The tone of voice used must be in line with all other qualities that are working toward the image the house is creating.

PUBLIC RELATIONS

Good public relations are important to food service operations. They are practiced in various ways. A goal to be pursued by personnel and management daily is to have the public hold a positive image of their operation.

A small food operation may rely solely on the food and service provided daily by employees for creating good public relations. To fortify this image, occasional participation in civic and community projects is desirable. These activities aid in making known the positive qualities of an establishment.

Some noteworthy remarks on the subject of public relations were made a few years ago by the late Mr. Harry J. Fawcett, past president of the American Club Managers' Association. His words, stressing the educational needs of our industry, are applicable and meaningful to all types of food operations.

In my early days in our industry I worked under a man who had graduated from that great institution in New York City, the Waldorf Astoria Hotel, to open, also in New York City, what was then the finest hotel in the world, the St. Regis Hotel.

It seemed to me, as I absorbed hotel know-how from George A. Gazley, that he, and the other great hotel men of that day and age whom it was my good fortune to know and grow up with, had the two qualities Donald A. Adams wrote of at that time in the trade publications:

'The two qualities one must have in order to give real service are sincerity and integrity; and, as Mr. Adams pointed out, these are qualities which cannot be bought or measured with money. It was also my observation that the men I refer to practiced these qualities daily in the pursuit of their managerial tasks.'

In watching these professional people I saw, too, more than this. As each contact or request was made of these people, I would see a chain reaction arise in them, as if to say, 'What can I do for this person to win his friendship, to serve him better, to make of him a permanent and pleased patron?' Usually the thing they did, sometimes a very trivial service, too, achieved just that—made a permanent and pleased customer by the way it was done, with the readily apparent desire to be of service.

Come to think of it, most of the hotel greats of that day and age had this faculty.

Making money for your employer is, of course, paramount. But in doing this there is an old adage that should never be forgotten: in order to receive you must first give.

Your first thought for every day should be about service to the patron. In the last analysis they are the ones who pay your wages, so service to your customers comes first.

When this is the primary thought it follows that you will give service to your employer, too.

Along the way, each day, do not fail to think also of your fellow employees. There is always an opportunity to also be of service to them. When you help them with counsel, advice, and example, you cannot fail to help yourself.

If the customer, employer, and fellow employee are foremost in your mind, you will soon realize the truth in that old adage. For, by serving these three you will gain their goodwill and in doing this, you are also doing yourself a favor. This is the best way to promote your professional interest and your future.

glossary

Age To store at a certain temperature so as to (a) bring out the flavor of wine, (b) to tenderize meat, and (c) to ripen cheese.

A la, à la *French,* in the style of.

A la carte *French,* according to the menu; having a separate price for each menu item.

A la king In cream sauce with green pepper, pimento, mushrooms, and sherry.

A la mode *French,* in the style or fashion. 1. Served with ice cream as *pie à la mode.* 2. Served with a rich, brown sauce as *beef à la mode.*

A la Newburg In an egg yolk cream sauce made with sherry.

Al dente *Italian,* "to the teeth," medium cooked.

Amandine *French,* garnished or cooked with almonds.

Anglaise *French,* English style.

Antipasto An assortment of hot or cold hors d'oeuvres, as salami, anchovies, peppers, etc.

Apéritif A drink served before a meal to stimulate the appetite, as a cocktail.

Appetizer A food or drink served before a meal; a first course; an hors d'oeuvre.

Arroz *Spanish,* rice.

Aspic A gelatin dish usually prepared in a mold and filled with meat, fish, or vegetables.

Asti Spumante Italian champagne.

Au beurre *French,* with butter.

Au gratin *French,* baked with bread crumbs and cheese.

Au jus *French,* served with its own natural gravy.

Baba A light bread-like cake soaked with rum.

Bain Marie A hot-water bath container for keeping foods warm.

Baking powder A mixture of bicarbonate of soda and tartar used as a leavening agent.

Baking soda Sodium bicarbonate used in baking. It causes dough or batter to rise.

Baste To pour or brush drippings over meat, poultry, or fish to prevent drying while cooking.

Batter A mixture that is beaten together, as for cakes. A batter is loose enough to pour.

Béarnaise A sauce made from eggs, butter, and herbs.

Beat To mix rapidly so as to blend.

Béchamel A basic white cream sauce.

Bercy A sauce made with shallots, fish stock, and white wine.

Beurre *French,* butter.

Bigarade A sauce made with orange peel and juice.

Bill of fare Menu.

Bisque A creamy soup made with shellfish.

Blanch	To cook briefly in boiling water, either to aid in removing the skin, as of a tomato, or to prepare for later cooking.
Blend	To mix thoroughly.
Boeuf	*French,* beef.
Bombe	A fancy mold used for freezing ice cream or the resulting ice cream dish.
Bone	To remove the bones from.
Bordelaise	A strong brown sauce made of red wine and herbs.
Bordure	A decorative border, as of potatoes, used for platters.
Bortsch	A Polish or Russian beet soup.
Bouillabaisse	*French,* a thick fish soup.
Bouillon	A clear meat broth.
Bouquet	Aroma, as of a wine.
Bouquetière	A fancy vegetable garnish.
Braise	To sear in fat and cook with a small amount of liquid in a covered pan.
Brandy	An after-dinner drink distilled from wine or fruit.
Bread	To coat with an egg and/or milk mixture and dip in bread crumbs before frying.
Brine	A mixture of salt and water used as a pickling liquid.
Brioche	A soft breakfast roll, popular in France.
Brochettes	Skewers on which meat is cooked.
Broth	A liquid in which meat, bones, fish, or vegetables have been cooked.
Brown	To broil or fry food until the outside color darkens.
Brut	*French,* very dry, said of champagne or other wines.
Buffet	A meal at which people serve themselves from large dishes.
Café	*French,* coffee.
Canapé	An appetizer served on a small piece of bread.
Cannoli	A cone-shaped pastry with cream filling.
Caper	A small bud dried and pickled and used in sauces and relishes.
Capon	A young castrated male fowl.
Caramel	Sugar melted slowly until it darkens.
Carte du jour	*French,* menu of the day.
Casserole	A deep metal or earthenware pot in which food is baked and often served.
Caviar	The eggs of various fish served as an appetizer.
Chablis	A dry light white wine.
Chafing dish	A dish, usually set in a holder, for keeping foods warm, or for light cooking, as of desserts.
Chasseur	Hunter style.
Chaud	Warm.
Chaud-froid	Sauce prepared hot but served with cold dishes, such as aspics.

Chef's salad A tossed green salad mixed with cut meat and cheese and other garnishes.

Chowder A thick soup or stew, usually made with milk.

Chutney An Indian condiment made of fruits and spices and served with curry dishes.

Clarify To make a liquid clear, as to skim the milk solids off melted butter.

Coddle To cook in water just below the boiling point.

Compote A dish made of stewed fruits.

Condiment A relish, sauce, or spice eaten along with other foods.

Consommé A clear soup stock.

Cordial A liqueur.

Coupe St. Jacques A dessert of ices with diced fresh fruits.

Court bouillon A stock made of water, vegetables, spices, and wine and used in cooking fish or shellfish.

Cream To work one or more foods until a creamy texture is obtained.

Creole Tomato sauce with sweet pepper, shallots, and Madeira wine.

Crepe *French,* a thin light pancake.

Crimp To flute.

Crisp To make food crisp, as by toasting or letting (vegetables) stand in cold water.

Crouton Small toasted bread cubes used to garnish soups and salads.

Cuisine A style of cooking: *French cuisine, Russian cuisine.*

Cube To cut into small square pieces.

Culinary Relating to the kitchen or cookery.

Curd The semisolid part of milk that has been soured with an acid or enzyme. The curd is used in making cheese.

Cure To preserve a food, as by drying, salting, pickling, etc.

Curry An Indian dish seasoned with *curry powder,* a condiment made of various spices.

Custard A pudding-like mixture of milk and eggs.

Decant To pour (wine) from one bottle to another to separate a liquid from its sediment.

Deep-fry To fry foods in a deep layer of hot fat.

Deglaze To loosen the pan drippings from a pan by adding in a liquid.

Demi-tasse A small cup for strong coffee.

Dice To cut into small cubes.

Dough An uncooked mixture to be baked as into bread.

Drawn butter Butter that has been clarified.

Dredge To cover by sprinkling lightly with a dry ingredient, such as flour.

Dress To clean and otherwise prepare for cooking, as game or fowl.

Duchess A bordure of browned mashed potatoes baked in fancy shapes.

Dust To sprinkle lightly with sugar or flour.

Du jour *French,* of the day.

Entree, entrée	The main course at a meal.
Escargot	*French,* a snail.
Espagnole	A basic stock sauce. Also, Spanish style.
Espresso	A finely roasted after-dinner coffee.
Filet, fillet	The boneless flesh of meat or fish. Also, to bone meat or fish.
Flambé	*French,* served in a flaming liquor, such as brandy.
Flatware	Tableware utensils—knives, forks, and spoons.
Flute	To make small indentations in (the edge of a pie crust).
Foie Gras	*French,* fat liver. A special goose liver used in making pâté.
Fold	To combine ingredients gently into a batter so as to avoid loss of air.
Fondue	A dish that is cooked at the table. The diners spear the food and dip it into a hot mixture.
Frappé	Chilled or iced.
Freeze	To make solid by keeping at a low temperature.
Freeze-dry	To remove the liquid from (coffee, vegetables, etc.) so as to store without refrigeration.
French fry	To cook by immersing in hot fat at temperatures from 300 to 375 degrees F.
Fricasse	A stew of poultry, veal, or lamb.
Fry	To cook in fat usually over direct heat.
Galantine	An aspic filled with boned stuffed meat.
Garnish	An edible ornament served with other foods.
Gin	A liquor distilled from grain and flavored with juniper berries.
Glacé	*French,* glazed or iced.
Glaze	To coat food with a sugar-and-liquid combination so as to provide with a glossy covering.
Goulash	A Hungarian stew made from veal or beef.
Gravy	A sauce, usually thickened, made from the drippings of meat or fowl.
Grill	To cook on a surface over direct heat.
Gumbo	A thick Southern soup made with okra and often containing shrimp, oysters, chicken, or ham.
Hang	To age meat by suspending it from a hook.
Hard sauce	A dessert sauce consisting mainly of butter and sugar.
Head cheese	A jellied loaf made from the meat of a calf's or hog's head.
Hollandaise	A rich creamy sauce made of butter, eggs, lemon juice, and seasonings.
Hors d'oeuvre	An appetizer.
Horseradish	An herb whose ground root is grated, mixed with vinegar, and used as a condiment with boiled meat or fish.
Hull	To remove the outer covering of (fruits or vegetables).

Husk To remove the outer covering of (an ear of corn).

Jardinière Diced garden vegetables.
Julienne To cut into long, narrow strips.
Jus *French,* juice, especially drippings from meat.

Kabob Pieces of meat, poultry, vegetables, etc., placed on a skewer for cooking.
Knead To work (dough) with a rolling and pressing motion of the hands.
Kosher Conforming to Jewish ritual law, especially, indicates meat that comes only from certain animals killed in a certain way.
Kugelhopf A molded yeast cake.

Lard To insert small strips of fat into uncooked lean meat.
Lasagna An Italian pasta cut in the shape of wide ribbons.
Leaven To cause to expand by adding yeast, baking soda, etc.
Leek A small onionlike plant used as a seasoning.
Legume A vegetable, such as beans and lentils, having a seed pod.
Linguini Long thin flat noodles.
Liqueur A sweet alcoholic beverage, usually served as an after-dinner drink.
Liquor Any alcoholic beverage, especially one made of distilled spirits.
Lyonnaise A sauce made with onions and often used in cooking potatoes.

Macaroni Pasta cut in various shapes, especially tubular pasta.
Maître d'hôtel A headwaiter or catering manager.
Manicotti A dish made of a square of noodle dough which is rolled up and filled usually with cheese.
Marbling The pattern of fat in a piece of meat.
Marinade A liquid in which meat, fish, or game may be marinated.
Marinate To soak food in a liquid prior to cooking to improve its flavor, increase its tenderness, etc.
Marrow The fatty substance found in the interior of bones.
Marzipan An almond paste either made into a confection or used in decorating or filling cakes and candies.
Melba sauce A raspberry sauce served with ice cream, custard, etc.
Melt To liquefy with heat.
Menu The list of dishes and prices in a restaurant.
Meringue Egg whites beaten with sugar.
Mince To cut into very fine pieces.
Minestrone An Italian vegetable soup usually containing pasta.
Mix To unite two or more ingredients by stirring, beating, etc. Also, a commercially prepared mixture of dry ingredients: *soup mix, cake mix.*
Mold A container used to form or shape foods such as aspics.

Mousse	Any of various dishes prepared in a mold. There are basically two types; one, a meat, fish, or poultry preparation and the other, a dessert with a whipped cream or egg white base.
Mozzarella	A mild Italian cheese.
Mulligatawny	An Indian soup flavored with curry.
Napoleon	A rectangular pastry made of puff paste filled with whipped cream or custard.
Nesselrode	Made with candied fruits, as pie or custard.
Nougat	A candy made of nuts and fruits in a sugar paste.
O'Brien	Cooked in a small amount of fat with chopped onion and pimento.
Oeuf	*French,* egg.
Omelet, omelette	Fried beaten eggs which are rolled or folded and often filled with cheese, meat, etc.
Pan-broil	To cook in a heavy frying pan over direct heat.
Pan-fry	To cook in a pan with little fat over direct heat.
Papillote	Cooked in oiled paper.
Parboil	To cook partially by boiling before final cooking.
Pare	To remove the outside covering with a knife.
Parfait	Varied layers of ice cream, toppings, etc., served in a tall glass.
Parisienne	Parisian style.
Parmesan	A sharp dry Italian cheese that is used grated.
Pasta	Paste or dough, cut and dried into various shapes of macaroni and spaghetti.
Pastry bag	A cone-shaped cloth used with various tips for decorating pastry.
Pâté	A dish made of ground liver and other ingredients.
Pepperoni	A spicy sausage containing chili peppers.
Petit, petite	*French,* small.
Pickle	To preserve in brine that is seasoned with spices and/or vinegar.
Pilaf, pilaff	A rice dish served with meat, vegetables, and spices.
Poach	To cook in a gently simmering liquid.
Polonaise	Polish style.
Poulette	A sauce with a chicken stock base.
Preheat	To heat equipment to a desired temperature before use.
Preserve	To prepare (food) for storage by pickling, drying, smoking, etc.
Puff paste	A light dough that is rolled with butter or shortening and baked into a light, flaky pastry.
Purée	To put cooked food through a sieve.
Quiche	A pastry shell filled with various custard-like mixtures.
Quick bread	A bread, muffin, biscuit, etc., raised with baking powder.
Ragout	A dish of stewed meat.
Render	To melt animal fat by heating it at a low temperature.

Roast	To cook (meat) in an oven.
Roe	The eggs of fish, especially the eggs of female fish called caviar.
Roquefort	A French cheese used widely in salad dressings.
Sabayon	A sweet sauce made of wine, cream, sugar, and egg.
Saccharin	A white compound used as a noncaloric sweetening.
Saint-Germaine	A soup made of fresh green peas.
Sake	A Japanese alcoholic drink made from fermented rice.
Salami	Any of various smoked dried sausages.
Sauce	A liquid accompanying a solid food.
Sauté	To cook quickly on a hot fire with little fat.
Scald	To heat a liquid to a point just below boiling.
Scaloppine	Italian boneless veal cutlet.
Schnitzel	A veal cutlet served in various ways.
Score	To make shallow slits in two directions on the surface of meat.
Sear	To brown the surface of meat quickly with intense heat.
Season	To add some ingredient, such as herbs, spices, salt, etc., to enhance the flavor of food.
Set	To become firm, as by cooling.
Sherry	A dry or sweet wine fortified with brandy.
Shortbread	A rich crisp cookie with a high amount of butter or shortening.
Shortening	An edible fat used in cooking and baking.
Shred	To cut into fine slivers.
Shuck	To remove the shell or husk from clams, corn, etc.
Sieve	A wire-mesh utensil for straining or sifting.
Sifter	A finely meshed utensil for sifting flour or other dry ingredients.
Simmer	To cook in a liquid just below the boiling point.
Skewer	A long metal pin on which cubes of meat, fish, chicken, etc., can be barbecued or broiled.
Skim	To remove matter from (a soup, sauce, etc.).
Smoke	To cure (fish, meat, etc.) by exposing to smoke.
Smother	To cook under a covering of other food.
Sommelier	A person in charge of the service of wines; a wine steward.
Soufflé	A baked dish made of beaten egg whites folded into a food batter producing a light puffed-up dish.
Spit	A rod on which meat is turned while cooking.
Steam	To cook by exposing to steam.
Stemware	Glassware with a base and a stem.
Stew	To cook (meat) in a small amount of liquid usually with a variety of ingredients.
Stir-fry	A Chinese method of frying foods very quickly over intense heat.
Stock	The liquid in which meat, seafood, or vegetables has been cooked.
Sweetbreads	The thymus gland of calves and lamb, considered a delicacy.
Tabasco	The tradename for a hot peppery sauce used as a seasoning.

Table d'hôte	Meals served at a fixed price for the complete meal.
Tart	A small pie-like pastry. Also, sharp, bitter.
Tempura	A Japanese dish of meat, fish, vegetables, etc., coated with batter and fried.
Tequila	A popular Mexican alcoholic beverage.
Toast	To brown by applying heat to the surface.
Torte	A many-tiered cake similar to layer cake.
Tournedos	Small steaks cut from the end of a beef tenderloin.
Truffle	An edible fungus found in European countries. Because they are found in limited quantities, they are quite expensive.
Truss	To bind a roast or bird for roasting.
Velouté	A basic white sauce made from stock and vegetables.
Vermouth	An apéritif used in cocktails.
Vichyssoise	Cold cream of potato soup.
Vinaigrette	A sauce served in salads and cold dishes, made of oil, vinegar, and various spices and herbs.
Vodka	A Russian alcoholic liquor.
Whey	A clear liquid separated from the curd of curdled milk.
Wild rice	The brown seed of a tall grass that grows in shallow waters.
Wine	The fermented juice of the grape.
Wok	A Chinese cooking pan with handles and a round bottom.
Wurst	*German*, sausage.
Yeast	A substance containing fungi that is used as a leavening agent in bread, cakes, etc.
Yogurt	Thick curdled milk treated with bacteria.

index

NOTE: Illustrations are indicated by the page number in italics.